star... ...generation
of ... ... We were
all ...

MINDING OUR OWN BUSINESS

books by Charlotte Paul

MINDING OUR OWN BUSINESS

GOLD MOUNTAIN

HEAR MY HEART SPEAK

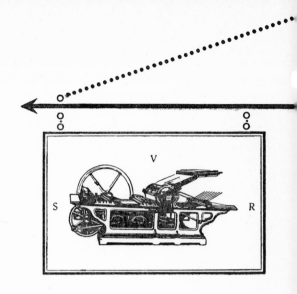

Minding
our own business

C H A R L O T T E   P A U L

Random House   *New York*

FIRST PRINTING

This book is dedicated to the first *Valley Record* subscriber who exclaimed, when told this book was to be published, "Good Heavens, are you figuring on moving away?"

MINDING OUR OWN BUSINESS

1

The little newspaper office in Snoqualmie, Washington, on a rainy afternoon five years ago was the scene of such earnest endeavor as to remain forever among my memories of moments that weren't funny at the time. The fact that it was rainy is hardly worth mentioning. The valley in which the town of Snoqualmie lies receives an annual drenching of fifty-five to sixty inches. Rain makes the trees grow big and keeps the pastures green, and is therefore an economic blessing. My disloyal objection to it on that particular afternoon was based on the fact that most of it was coming through the roof.

There were seven of us in the shop: our editor, a middle-aged woman who had begun her career in journalism only

3

five weeks before and was now frowning over a news item one of our country correspondents had scrawled in pencil on the back of an envelope; the printer, a man of seventy whom the years had given skill and ill humor in equally large quantities; our pressman, an eighteen-year-old boy whose heart was in Boy Scout work. The latter was running the big newspaper press, feeding huge sheets of newsprint by hand at the rate of 1,750 an hour and simultaneously reading the Scoutmaster's manual he had propped up on the feed board. Then there were our two sons, Hi and Johnny, five and four years old, respectively. They were at the shop because there was no one at home to take care of them. Last and least, Ed and I, the new owners, editors and publishers, keepers of the mortgage and the public trust. Between the two of us, we had four college degrees and a quarter of a century of experience on big-city newspapers. And between us we didn't know half as much about a country weekly as our teen-age pressman or our crotchety printer. To every man a job commensurate with his ability. So Ed was wrapping packages on the job-printing table, and I was running from one hole in the ceiling to the next, emptying the coffee cans into which the rain was spilling. Rain poured in sheets down the inside wall of our backshop, coursing like a waterfall over the one new piece of equipment our dwindling capital had so far afforded—a $550 type case. Rain had found all the old holes in the thirty-two-year-old frame building and seemed to be concentrating on drilling some new ones. If rain is a blessing, that was the day our cup ranneth over.

I poured the twenty-seventh can of rain down the sink about the time Ed looked up from tying his twenty-seventh bundle.

"You're getting good at that," he said. "In a couple of weeks I'll start you out making paragraph marks." He patted one of his packages. "That's what I like about being a publisher," he said wryly. "Every package is a challenge."

"Look at that broken window!" I moaned. "Just nailing up some cardboard won't keep this rain out. I wish someone would put in a new pane."

"I wish 'they' would, too," said Ed, going on to his twenty-eighth bundle. "We need the cardboard."

The front-office door opened, admitting a man known as a good customer. He was carrying two big boxes of printing we had delivered to him only the day before. "I asked for stamped envelopes," he complained. "These are plain."

Ed looked woefully from the good customer to the bad job. Here were two thousand envelopes, useless to anyone but the man whose name we had printed on them. No magic would turn them into stamped envelopes, nor make up for our loss if we had to throw them away. Inspiration struck. "Could you use them if we put stamps on them?"

"Sure. But I've got to have them by tonight."

"We'll stamp them right away," was the publisher's majestic reply.

But five out of seven of us were busy. Our eyes fell on the two unemployed, two little pre-school freshets to feed the *Snoqualmie Valley Record's* labor pool. Their heads were bent over a pair of coloring books. Ed cleared his throat. In a voice too cheerful and too loud, he said, "Well, boys, I've got a job for you. . . ."

We set them up in business, side by side at the old roll-top desk. Each little boy received one thousand envelopes, one thousand three-cent stamps, and a tall glass of drinking water. Hi, having had a month of kindergarten, had the edge on his little brother intellectually, but Johnny had spirit. No coloring book had ever held their interest so completely. An hour later we heard Johnny whisper, "Hi, do you like newspaper work?"

Five-year-old Hi nodded emphatically. "Except for the taste," he whispered back.

A new generation of publishers had been launched on a sea of ink.

Ed and I looked at each other. I had a silly lump in my throat. "Did you imagine it would be like this when we decided to go into business for ourselves?"

Ed grinned. "I never realized, until now, that 'ourselves' would mean all four of us, not just you and me."

It was true. Whatever we had got ourselves into, we were all in it together. We had heard for twenty years that it was too late to go back to the days when a man and his family could buy a small business and make a go of it. Taxes are too high, they had pointed out. Between the labor shortage and high wages to the labor you do find, you can't make a living in small business any more. They added that the big outfits squeeze you out—what chance for the little guy, with the big companies getting bigger and the small ones getting smaller? Besides, people aren't made the way they used to be. There used to be a place for daring and independence, but the world has changed. . . . We hadn't listened. We had gone back, in a sense, to the farm, where everyone who sat down at the dinner table had some part in providing the food he raised to his mouth. Or to the little shoe store on the corner, where the kids help out afternoons and Saturdays and Mama nurses the new baby in the back room between waiting on customers. Our small business was a weekly newspaper, and it appeared that all four of us had bought it and all four of us would have to accept responsibility for keeping it going. For us there would never be indifference to "Daddy's job" or casual acceptance of Daddy's pay check, as if whatever struggles he may have gone through to obtain it were his own affair. I and my children would know where our food and clothing came from because we would be earning it together. Together. That is the word that brought laughter through tears for five of the hardest and best years of our lives. No way in the world sixty inches of rain and a leaky roof could spoil *that*.

Smiling to myself, I sprinted toward an overflowing coffee

can, humming, poured some more good Snoqualmie Valley rain water down the drain.

ii

Why would two people with good jobs, congenial friends, and a home without a mortgage, suddenly abandon all these and at an age when security is the better part of valor, move 2,200 miles and go into business for themselves? On the first of August, 1949, we were comfortably situated on our small farm outside of Chicago, and expected to be there for the rest of our lives. By the first of September we were in the state of Washington, signing contracts which we knew would force us to mortgage everything but the cat—an oversight, she being the most productive member of the family.

We went from corn to trees; from freezing winters and long sizzling summers to ten months of rain; from a home we owned and loved to a house we rented, and hated; from a good-size monthly pay check someone else signed to daily risks and the weekly responsibility of signing a fistful of pay checks ourselves. No decision we had made in seven years of marriage had been half so big, unless it was the decision to get married in the first place. And yet we made it in two days.

Ed and I are never impulsive, except in handling those matters in which everything is at stake. Our courtship was like nothing so much as an eclipse of the sun; it didn't last long but the total blackout of reason was breathtaking. At the time Ed was the news editor at the *Chicago Daily Times,* and I was the assistant foreign news editor at the other side of the city room. When we were married, one beautiful autumn afternoon, we knew very little about each other. Among the issues we had not considered vital enough to discuss beforehand were religion, politics, music, and whether we believed in large families. Even on the way to the minister's house we didn't have time to check over these points. We were too busy reading letters from my mother and father, both of which arrived special delivery air mail that morning, both stating they did not approve of the marriage because, heavens, they'd never even met the man, and to wait and think it over for at least a year. They have since agreed it was a good thing we didn't listen, because we've always had so many projects that they would hate to be responsible for throwing us a whole year behind schedule.

Three weeks later we bought a farm. We had been living in a one-room "utility" apartment. The kitchen was in a closet, the bed was in a closet, even the closet had closets. Opening the kitchen door meant you couldn't get in or out of the apartment; opening the window automatically tuned you in on the neighbor's fight with his wife. Gas rationing was about to shut off our only escape so we decided to spend our last tankful on a Sunday drive to the country.

We hadn't gone a mile before we were looking through the real-estate ads to see what small farms were listed. In less than ten miles we were agreeing solemnly that only fools buy the first place they look at. We were right. Our first place was a little white farmhouse on five and a half acres near Wheaton, Illinois, where tomatoes were ripening on the sill and the kitchen was sweet with the fragrance of baking bread.

"You wouldn't like to live in the country," Ed hazarded as we drove away. His voice was a study of disinterest.

"I would love nothing more," said I, my voice all squeezed together in an effort to sound equally casual.

"You would!" Ed shouted.

"Yes, yes!" I caroled back. That night we borrowed the earnest money from a friend, and we were back at the farm, signing papers, the next afternoon. If our jobs had not kept us in Chicago from nine to five we would undoubtedly have arrived for breakfast. Total time: twenty-six hours, for the second big decision of our lives.

Many of our friends in Chicago thereafter referred to Ed

as a "gentleman farmer," but anyone who works as long and hard as he did is no gentleman. He carried two part-time jobs as well as his wartime six-day week at the newspaper, and between us we tended two acres of truck garden and raised hundreds of chickens, rabbits, geese, pigs and ducks. There was need for careful scheduling. Ed did his work as libel editor for *Esquire* and *Coronet* magazines by spending most lunch hours at their editorial offices on Michigan Avenue. He also read batches of manuscripts as he commuted between Chicago and home on the Northwestern Railroad. His second extra job was in the Philosophy Department of Northwestern University, where he had been part-time instructor for many years; this work absorbed most of his Sundays.

My work record was only a poor imitation. I gave up my job at the *Times,* but held a kind of rewrite and editorial position with *Esquire-Coronet,* doing the work at home but reporting for weekly conferences in Chicago. I was also trying to get started as a free-lance writer, and there was housework and farm chores. Somehow we managed to juggle farm work and our four or five city jobs without any serious tangles. Except for the week end we had to take care of Squee G, the adopted member of our household.

Squee was a Chester White pig, first glimpsed when she was two days old and the farmer down the road was raising his arm to bash her brains out against the barn wall.

"Don't do that!" Ed begged.

"She's the runt, and the litter's so big she'll be squoze out. Won't live another day. What use you got for her?" the farmer asked.

Ed improvised hurriedly, "I'll take her home to my wife."

We put the little piglet on a formula of evaporated milk and corn syrup, supplementing it with orange juice and cod-liver oil. As for feeding times, we devised the simplest schedule of all—we fed her whenever she got hungry, which was about every two hours, night and day, simplifying this routine even more by parking her apple-box bed in the bedroom. The arrangement was congenial for all until Sunday came along, the day Ed regularly scheduled for work at Northwestern.

I had always gone along with him, but I couldn't leave Squee, and I thought it might be hard, especially in a farm community, to hire a baby sitter for a pig. So we *all* went to the university—Ed, Squee, and I, with sandwiches (not ham, out of courtesy to Squee!), formula, and a hot plate I used alternately to make tea and warm the piglet's bottles. We settled down in the office of the Philosophy Department and enjoyed a nice, long, productive day. I claim Squee is the only pig who ever went to Northwestern, at least in Philosophy.

Life on a farm contributed mightily to the success of our marriage. We never got bored with each other; there was always too much work to do. We seldom argued; somehow it's hard for two people on their knees weeding the onions, or hoeing corn when it's 95 degrees in the shade, to think of a clever retort, or for that matter, any retort at all. We never spent our money foolishly; after we'd paid for the new cistern or the last load of feed or the new roofing for the chicken house, we didn't have any left to spend.

The farm was also ideal for motherhood. My maternity clothes were cheap, durable, and all-purpose; I wore milkmen's striped overalls, with bibs which proved to be expansible beyond my wildest dreams.

When Hiram arrived, in 1944, and Johnny, in 1945, I found that five and a half acres and lots of animals was a pretty good formula for child-rearing. I cherish the memory of my husky little first-born, dressed, because of the heat, in nothing but a diaper, going through two barbed-wire fences and across a pasture full of cows, heifers and bullocks, so as to pay a visit to the neighbor. The back end of an eighteen-months-old boy crawling under a fence is one of the most beautiful sights in the world.

10

Children, farm work, writing, all took time. With only twenty-four hours a day to work with, the three activities often overlapped. It was a Friday when I strode into my weekly editorial conference at *Esquire*, weighing 180 pounds and causing a few worry lines to crack the beautiful pancake make-up on the slick chick at the door; Hiram was born on Sunday. I read and corrected manuscripts while I was in the hospital and at home learned to give the baby his bottle and read sheets of paper spread out in a semicircle around me. Our children have always known that "Daddy works and Mama writes," an implied comparison I can't help resenting. They were soothed to sleep by the click of typewriters and teethed on rejected manuscripts.

Eventually I hired a maid-of-all-work, and arranged with the farmer down the road to set up my writing headquarters in his spare bedroom. After that the two little boys staged two farewell and two greeting ceremonies every day. Daddy left for Chicago by car at seven o'clock. Mama and a sack lunch boarded a bicycle at nine A.M. and peddled down the road to the neighbors' farm. This involved a great deal of hugging, kissing and waving, both at seven and at nine. Mama was back home at four, Daddy at six—more hugging and kissing. We got out of all this what we put into it—a lot!

Looking back, I can see that our farm might have been good training-ground for a pair about to tackle private enterprise without private capital. We had met and conquered emergencies. There was the blizzard, for example, that left us powerless and hence heatless and waterless. But not hungry; I baked a veal roast in the fireplace, basting it with cups of snow. And in a way we had been in business for ourselves when we sold ducks, chickens, rabbits, eggs, sweet corn and strawberries.

Again and again Ed demonstrated a good shrewd business head by giving our produce away. But when our first big strawberry crop came in, he resolved to change. We had worked on hands and knees in the berry patch until our backs ached and our knees were raw. "I won't let my wife work like a slave," said the new, businesslike Ed, "for less than twenty-five cents a quart." That price, advertised on a handmade sign we hung over our mailbox, was about half what berries cost in the stores and brought in customers faster than we could pick. Ed was congratulating himself on the success of our first moneymaking venture when a sedan pulled into the yard and the well-dressed couple inside asked for two quarts of strawberries. The boxes, filled to overflowing, were well settled on the back seat when the woman exclaimed, "Oh my goodness, I left my money in my other purse. I only have thirty-eight cents!"

Ed waved grandly. "That's all right. Take the berries."

"We'll stop in with the twelve cents the first time we come back this way. . . ."

"Think nothing of it," Ed boomed heartily. "That's perfectly all right."

For a week my hard-headed businessman heard from me on the subject of letting his wife work like a slave for a total of nineteen cents a quart.

"They'll come back," said Ed.

"Ha!" said I.

The next Sunday afternoon they did. With them, the twelve cents. Ed was vindicated. He was so overjoyed that he dragged the couple out of their car into the living room and insisted they stay for a nice, big Sunday dinner.

"I *knew* they were honest," Ed whispered gleefully in the kitchen, as I busied myself preparing some four dollars' worth of provisions. "I tried to tell you, I'm a good judge of character."

iii

After five and a half years of marriage, Ed and I began talking about "security." We had paid off our debts. Barns, house, garage, had been remodeled and we had two cars. Ed held a top spot on a newspaper for which he had worked for fourteen years. In short we were comfortably, permanently, located. If *we* didn't have security, who did?

And then the most permanent thing of all, the rock on which our security was built, dropped out from under us. The newspaper was sold, and consolidated with another newspaper. The two staffs were consolidated, too, with hundreds of employees, from editors to copy boys, dropped in the process. There was the "first purge," then the "second purge," and old friends in the business began greeting each other with, "You had it yet or are you still in?" Ed, highest-salaried of the new legion of unemployed, was out of a job. So much for the "security" of big companies and high-salaried jobs.

What to do? That might have been the moment to go into business for ourselves. Daydreaming, we did talk about working as a free-lance writing team, Ed going afield for research and I writing at home. The few tentative letters we sent to magazine editors brought encouraging replies. But Ed, who had held three jobs at a time, had never in his life worked for himself. He was forty years old, and far less enthusiastic about trying things he had never tried before than he would have been twenty years earlier. Going into business was a total departure from living on salary checks. And the ghosts of what "they say" were leering at us—High Taxes, Labor Shortages, Big Business would squeeze us out, people aren't the same as their grandfathers used to be, it's too late, too late . . . We weren't quite ready to make the step. Ed went to work for the public relations department of one of the largest corporations in the world. We were back in familiar territory—someone else's payroll. It was an easy job and, because of the men Ed worked for and with, a pleasant one. Ed bought a dozen new white shirts and put on ten pounds. But after a year and a half he realized that an easy, well-paid job was not automatically satisfying, at least to him. He was out of his field; the present was far from invigorating and the future was vague. But now he was forty-two years old, and I was thirty-three. It was later than ever. Surely too late to change now.

We sat down in our living room on the farm, and talked it over. It was the first of August, and a hot, still day. We could hear the boys, playing together in the apple orchard. The hens clucked sleepily in the yard behind the house. Through the window we watched the sprinkler turning rhythmically, spraying a glistening circle on the green lawn. It was peaceful. We loved every bit of it. But we talked of leaving it.

"I've got a good job," Ed said. "It assures me of a salary, an expense account, insurance, eventually a retirement pension."

"But you don't really like it."

"Many men spend their lives on jobs they dislike far more than I do mine."

"Because they're afraid to let go. . . ."

We began to study our contemporaries, one by one, asking questions about them and about ourselves which we had never voiced so bluntly before. These men we thought we knew so well, were they really happy in their work, or were they simply holding on because they were convinced they were "too old" to risk changing? And how about their wives —how many of them ever wondered if their husbands really liked their jobs? How many of them knew full well that their husbands were unhappy, but didn't want them to change because they, too, were afraid?

The roll call was an eye opener. It led us to this conclusion: Most of the "successful" men we knew, the men who cherished "security," lived in such dread of losing their jobs that they never took a close look at them to see if they were worth keeping. And in this, the act of digging ever deeper into a rut, they were aided and abetted by their wives.

We might be foolhardy. The bright light of our courage might be like the last brilliant glow of the bulb just before it burns out. But we decided, that day, to crawl out of the rut while we were still silly enough to think we could. After all, we had once thought losing a job was the worst thing that could happen to us, and here we were, better off than ever. Why be afraid of resigning a job, just because we hadn't an idea in the world where we would go from there? "Security," we had learned at last, is what you carry around in your head, and the heart you put into using it. Well, what were we waiting for?

Thus we decided, with characteristic caution, that Ed should start the next day by declaring a deadline of October first as his last day with the public relations department. We turned to the next question—what to do after October first?

The quick and easy answer was to go back to work for a newspaper—someone else's. But as we talked, that summer evening in August, we agreed that we would not squander this perhaps-failing courage of ours. Whatever we had, stock certificates, farm, bank account, we'd risk it all; we'd go into business for ourselves. It didn't take us five minutes to decide what that business would be. Ed had been a newspaperman for twenty years. I was a writer. Our small business would be the only one we knew anything about—a newspaper.

"Our own newspaper!" I breathed. "We'd be our own bosses, at last. Work when we want, go fishing whenever we like . . ."

Ed took a turn for the practical. "Now let's see," he said, reaching for paper and pencil, "We'll figure out how much money we can raise. You have to have capital, you know."

First, we would sell the farm. The wartime housing shortage was not far behind us, and memory was still vivid of the realtors who had telephoned us, written us, and finally even inspected and appraised the farm, despite our sincere protests that we wouldn't sell at any price.

"Last real-estate agent appraised it at $18,500," Ed recalled. Carefully he headed the sheet of paper, "Cash Assets," and below wrote, "Farm, $17,000." "In case we have to make a quick sale," he explained. "Now, how about our bank account?"

I had received the monthly statement that morning. I found it and read off the balance. "$1,471.50."

Ed wrote down, "$1,400.00," saying, "Might be a couple of checks haven't cleared. Now, let's see, there's your writing."

I squirmed. Free-lance writing can be lucrative, but not necessarily when you need the lucre most. I thought uneasily of Fred Litten, an established author with some ten to a dozen novels to his credit. One year Fred's income came to $25,000 and he bought a beautiful home in a select Chicago suburb; the next year he earned $1,200. I had been making four or five thousand dollars a year. "But darling, I'm afraid to count on it," I objected.

"You've been earning that much every year," Ed said firmly. "No reason why you won't go on making at least that much from now on."

"But with a newspaper, will I have time to write?"

"Huh!" Ed was amused. "You'll have more time than ever, silly. Let's see, I won't put that down on cash assets, though. I'll start another sheet." He printed INCOME WE CAN COUNT ON at the top of another piece of paper, and wrote below, "$5,000, CP's writing." That was the very top figure, but then, why not be optimistic?

He leaned back and surveyed the list. "Back to cash assets. There's my General Motors stock. It's selling for 61, and I have 48 shares. That's $2,928. Then I have a little other stuff that would bring about $1,500." He wrote down, "Stocks, EWG, $4,500." He looked at me quizzically, sighed, and said, "Now, the next thing . . ."

"I know," I said quickly, "the stocks my grandmother left me. We could sell them."

Ed looked at me admiringly. He understood, and shared, my feeling about those stocks. We had started our married life together on a grand total of $22 (there has always been some disagreement between us as to how much of it was Ed's, how much of it mine!) but the inheritance from my grandmother had given me a sense of being protected no matter what happened. When the children were born, the stocks became even more important. All our earnings, even when Ed was holding three jobs at once, went back into our farm. We hadn't had that little extra every month with which to buy insurance policies or establish savings accounts; my stocks were our only insurance, our only savings, for our boys. Proper medical care, a good education— as long as I kept my securities my children's future was protected no matter what happened to Ed and me. *Sell* the stocks my grandmother gave me? The thought made me feel strangely hollow.

Ed was reassuring. "Don't worry, honey. Not a chance in a million we'd have to touch your securities. Except . . ." he grinned at me, "the Danciger."

My Danciger Oil stock was a standing joke. It, and some gold bonds of Rio de Janeiro, 1923, were something my grandmother had bought in a defiant moment to prove to my grandfather that she didn't need to consult him about such things. She had left me eighty shares, for which I got a quarterly dividend check of eighty cents and a good deal of unnecessary comment from my husband on the subject of marrying me for my money.

"We won't even write down your stock," Ed said generously. He totaled the figures on the "Cash Assets" sheet.

"Comes to $22,900." He kept studying the sheet. I came and looked over his shoulder, but rereading the column of figures didn't make it any longer.

"What do you think?" I asked anxiously.

"Oh, this is fine, this is fine," Ed said. "All we need is enough for a down payment, you know."

"We could borrow from my father."

Ed shook his head. "No, absolutely not. We're not going to buy a business if we can't stand on our own feet."

Twenty-two thousand, nine hundred dollars—we knew enough to realize that no daily paper would be small enough for such a pocketbook. We would buy a weekly, which probably meant living in the country. We thought we would have to work, and work hard, and we knew we had a lot to learn. Thus far we were on solid ground. But beyond that, we subscribed enthusiastically to every cockeyed notion about the weekly that fills the heads of big-city newspapermen.

A country publisher, we would have told you that August evening five years ago, does as he pleases. He sets his own hours and does a lot of fishing. He doesn't make a million, but through some quaint reversal of normal human instinct, he doesn't care. Money is less important to him than his principles, which direct him to expose important people, advertisers, etc., in fearless editorials. He is loved, respected, feared, and gradually becomes a pretty salty character with a tendency to say ain't.

Only one point worried us about going into business for ourselves in some small town—we thought it might be dull. We were used to the furious pace of a Chicago city room, where so often stories are written at breakneck speed, with a copy boy standing at your elbow to take what you write one paragraph at a time, sometimes even one sentence at a time. How could Ed jump from eight editions and two replates a day to one edition a week, without shriveling up and blowing away from disuse and boredom? From seventy editions a week to one a week—it stood to reason a weekly would be one-seventieth as stimulating as a metropolitan daily.

We were somewhat reassured by a former Chicago newspaperman, the only man we knew personally who had left the big city and bought a weekly. Ed asked him, "Jim, don't you find this once-a-week business kind of slow?"

"I thought I would," Jim replied. "But now I'd never go back to a daily. What I'm looking for is a real good buy in a yearly almanac."

So perhaps the pace wasn't too boring. The explanation was all that fishing. The small-town grocer, the country lawyer, the fellow with the feed and grain store—we could visualize them so well, whiling away the hours on the lake or riverbank, chatting around the old-fashioned stove, making their living without all the work and worry of the city. This life would be ours. Get out the paper, fish the rest of the week.

We dusted off one more decision that evening. As long as we were making the leap of going into business for ourselves, we might as well hurtle into the kind of spot we'd always wanted to live in. That meant the Pacific Northwest, somewhere in Washington or Oregon west of the Cascades, where the climate is mild, fishing is good, and you can play golf all year round.

Ed stood up, stretched, and grinned at me. My return grin was from the heart. We had decided, in one evening's time, to give up the bird in hand and go chasing after just one other bird in the bush—more than 2,000 miles away. And we felt wonderful about it.

Outside the boys were laughing together, calling across the pasture to their beloved neighbor. They had been born here. "Neighbor" meant only those people they had known and seen since the day they opened their eyes. "Home" was this house we had built, "dog" could be no other than the Airedale who was older than they were. Their world was safe and unchanging. Daddy goes at seven, Mama leaves at nine.

Listening to their voices, as confident as the chickens clucking in the yard, I felt one brief flash of panic. What decisions were we making, risking not only our world, but theirs? The step we were planning was tremendous, greater still because it could not be retraced. But was it half as big to us as the step they would have to take, unasked?

iv

An impulsive nature is an asset if you have four weeks in which to make a change sensible people wouldn't attempt in less than a year. Qualms about this project of ours tried to hop aboard but at the speed we were traveling they couldn't even get a toehold.

Ed had a job until October first. Two months, then, in which to sell the farm; to pack up possessions which in seven years had grown to fill a barn, a shed, a chicken house, a garage, a full basement, an attic, and a seven-room house; to investigate the weekly field in Washington and Oregon and select the newspaper in which we were going to sink everything we owned; to move, kit and kaboodle, across seven states, settle in a strange community and begin operating a strange business—at a profit!

But August, half our precious time, proved to be a loss. The farm was not sold that month, and we did not dare dismantle it for fear the bare bones of a house would frighten cash customers away. The first of September found us just where we were on August first—all bridges burned behind us and not the haziest plan of how to put up new ones.

Ed's two weeks of vacation began September first. That was the amount of time we had to make a 4,400-mile round trip to the Coast, and to pluck, like a needle in a haystack, a sound business venture out of an area covering, roughly, 70,000 square miles. Luckily both Washington and Oregon have publishers' associations, oases of information and sage advice. In charge the day Ed and I blew into Seattle from Chicago was the late "Pa" Kennedy. Pa was seventy-four years old. He had not been present when the first weekly in Washington was printed in 1852, but he hadn't missed much since that time. At the turn of the century he had assumed command of the Washington Newspaper Publishers' Association, a brotherhood of weekly publishers that had been organized even before Washington became a state. He had been fathering it ever since. In the early '20s he visited his "boys" in person, via a Model T Ford. Mrs. Kennedy sat in the back, calling, "Fritz, Fritz, slow down or you'll kill us all," while little daughter Jane bounced along beside him and cried out her delight at the breathtaking speed—of twenty miles an hour. When we first saw Pa he had been advising, championing, and scolding country publishers for forty years, and he wasn't about to stop, though many of the "boys" he had helped get started in their first newspaper were of an age to retire.

Ed and I, blissfully ignorant and boiling with questions, raced into his office. We expected to interview this Mr. Kennedy, whose name had been given us by national headquarters in Chicago. "We came to inquire about newspapers for sale in this state," Ed began. We had been breaking speed records. We didn't have much time. We had to get the information and move on. We would like to know. . . .

Pa's blue eyes studied us over the tops of his glasses. He cleaned, tapped, refilled his pipe, and then worked some time with a folder of matches getting it lit. He studied the pipe bowl, drew hard, grunted with satisfaction. Finally, with everything apparently in order, he spoke. "We're going to have some tea."

Ed threw me a look of bafflement, the husband-to-wife

look that means, "You try it this time, I'm not getting through. . . ."

"Uh, Mr. Kennedy," I tried gently. "You see, we have just arrived from Chicago, and we have a great deal to do, so if . . ."

"Dixie!" the old man bellowed suddenly. "Now what's keeping that confounded blonde?" The door opened a crack. "Three cups of tea," said Pa.

The door closed. Pa went back for another round with his pipe.

"We don't like to rush you, Mr. Kennedy. . . ."

Pa turned slowly, blinked at us, and replied, "I have tea *every* afternoon."

So we waited in respectful silence while the blonde, as unperturbed by Pa as he was by us, returned with three cups of hot tea and a plate of cookies.

"You're not in a hurry," Pa said at last. "I used to go out and see the boys in their own shops. I quit that. I make them come here and see me. Gets them away from work for a while. They're always in a hurry, too. 'Got to get back to the paper.' I tell them, 'Sit down. You don't have to work all the time. That's why I called you in here.'

"Now, about you two buying a newspaper. Maybe you can make a go of it. We never used to think a fellow could keep a weekly going if he wasn't a printer. You can't get out a paper without a printer, but it takes a good-size shop to pay for someone who can't do anything but write. It's always been that the publisher is a Linotype operator. Of course he's the editor, too, and the columnist and the news writer. Always used to do his writing right there at the Linotype machine, and a good many of my boys still do. Then he gets up and makes up the ads and runs the press, and his wife takes a turn at the machine. When the paper is printed, the man goes out to sell ads and printing, his wife catches up on the bookkeeping and phones for some news. But if they're both editors? I don't know."

He turned to Ed. "Newspaperman for twenty years, eh? Ever learn to set type?"

"We had about thirty Linotypes at the *Chicago Times*. But that wasn't my job. I never laid a finger on one."

"Make-up?" Pa asked. "Ever put type in a page, or make up an ad?"

"I was an editor, not a compositor. If I had touched a stick of type, the union would have called a chapel meeting."

"Know how to cast from a mat?"

"The stereos did that."

"Run a press?"

"That was the pressmen's job."

"Sell any ads?"

"We had a big advertising department."

There was a long, meaningful silence. Pa swiveled around slowly to face me. "You?"

"I write," I replied, feeling thoroughly ashamed of myself.

"Hrumph." Pa returned full attention to his pipe, which again was due for stirring up, cleaning, refilling and lighting. He puffed on it for a bit, cleared his throat, and then, in the kindest voice in the world, he said, "Times change. Maybe you can do it. I hope you can."

We went over the list of weekly newspapers for sale in Washington. Pa commented on each of them; in many cases he not only knew the publisher but the publisher's father. "That one's always for sale," he'd say. Or, "That don't gross enough to support you, not when you're going to have to hire a backshop." And when he thought it was a good sound buy, he'd say, "Cows and chickens. They got them in the area that paper covers. There's nothing more solid than cows and chickens."

We left Pa Kennedy's office with a simplified list of properties, arrived at by a process of elimination. For several days we visited the country print shops in Washington, and then we headed south and repeated the process in Oregon, where Carl Webb, chief of the Oregon publishers' association, steered us, as Pa had, from bad to good buys.

With only seven days left before Ed had to report back to work in Chicago, we drove to Snoqualmie, Washington. Snoqualmie was on Pa Kennedy's cows-and-chickens list; that was our first reason for looking into the newspaper there. And then the Snoqualmie Valley, the paper's circulation area, was beautiful—that was our second reason. It lies thirty miles east of Seattle, at the foot of the Cascade mountains. Heavy forests of fir and cedar cover the slopes above it and the ice-cold Snoqualmie River flows through its green meadows for some seventy miles before it meets and is lost in another larger river. North Bend, Snoqualmie, Meadowbrook, Snoqualmie Falls, Fall City, Carnation, Novelty, Vincent, Stillwater, Duvall, Preston, Cedar Falls—these were the communities along the river and in the hills above, where lived, we soon learned, some 1,800 subscribers, many of whom had been reading the paper for twenty-five years. It was a valley with a view, no matter which way you looked. Trees, lakes, brooks, rolling pastures, fish in every stream and an eighteen-hole golf course. All ours, for $30,000.

That was about the amount we had, on paper. The $17,000 we would get from the sale of the farm was hardly negotiable at this point. We hadn't sold Ed's stock. A bank balance of $1,400, that was the bird in hand. "We mustn't jump at this," Ed warned me soberly, in exactly the same tone of voice he had once used to say, "Only fools buy the first farm they look at."

Snoqualmie was bathed in sunlight the Sunday afternoon we drove out to see it. Seven hundred and fifty-two population, the signs at the city limits announced, but that didn't include the dogs, who were catching up on their sleep in the middle of the street. The business section occupied four blocks along the main street paralleling the railroad tracks.

There was a laundry, a café, a hay and feed store, two barber shops, a radio shop, a dry goods store, a hardware store, a drug store, three groceries, a bakery, and four beer taverns. In a little park between the street and the tracks was a beautifully carved and painted totem pole some ten feet high.

On a cross street, halfway between the center of town and the bank of the Snoqualmie River, was a smaller "business section." On one corner, the bank, with rose bushes six feet tall leaning against its windows. On another, a general store with a hitching ring still firm in the streetside wall, and next door, the post office. On the third corner was the Falls Printing Company, home, for more than thirty years, of the *Snoqualmie Valley Record*.

It was a white wood building thirty feet wide and forty feet deep. Two of the front windows guaranteed against illegal entry by a couple of nails driven at an angle through the window frames. Weather had faded the big black letters —FALLS PRINTING CO.—and had apparently driven half the sparrows in Washington into shelter under the eaves. A flagpole, without a flag or any sign of a rope to hoist one, was planted against the building. Although it was Sunday, a beautiful sunny day, and for miles around stretched a fisherman's, golfer's and hiker's paradise, the door to the newspaper shop was wide open. The reason was that the publisher was at work inside.

His name was Dale Krebs, and he had worked on weekly newspapers in Nebraska, California and Alaska before he bought the *Record* in 1944. He was a good Linotype operator, a good printer, and an old hand at the weekly game— all the things we weren't; yet he told us frankly that he wanted to sell out because he and his wife were just too exhausted to continue. We asked what questions our big-city minds could think up, and squinted thoughtfully at machinery we knew nothing about. But it was like the sunny Sunday afternoon seven years earlier when we bought the first farm we looked at. The Snoqualmie Valley was beautiful. The towns in it were small and quiet and sunny. The newspaper was interesting and the building quaint. We wanted it, all of it, and if the man who was trying to sell it had told us it was a bad bargain and we were headed for bankruptcy and a pair of nervous breakdowns, we wouldn't have listened.

I do remember noting, as we drove away, that it was too bad the owner had to be working on a Sunday afternoon.

"Yes, it's funny, isn't it," Ed mused. "Remember when we stopped at that newspaper in Deer Lodge, Montana, on our way out here?"

"The publisher was working alone in his shop, and that was a Sunday afternoon, too. . . ."

"Yes. S'funny thing . . ."

During final negotiations Ed showed the same shrewd business head that had brought us fame and fortune in the strawberry business. "He's *asking* $30,000," a Seattle newspaperman had remarked. "But what are you going to offer?"

"$30,000."

"Good heavens, man, don't you know how to do business? Two years ago his asking price was only $28,000. Now you go back out there and talk business. Nobody, but nobody, pays a man his first price."

Thus emboldened, Ed returned to Snoqualmie to "talk business," and the conversation went something like this:

Ed: What are you asking for it?

Dale: $30,000.

Ed: Well, that's your asking price. Now, what'll you take?

Dale: $30,000.

Ed: Well, I guess that settles that. O.K.

Our excitement overrode even this minor defeat. We were going to buy our own business, and in as peaceful a fisherman's paradise as we could have imagined. The Snoqualmie River flowed by only half a block from the back door of the newspaper shop. "We won't have to wait until the end of the week to go fishing," Ed said. "We'll catch a few during lunch hour."

"Lunch hour, ha!" I corrected him. "We're going to be our own boss. We can take more than an hour for lunch whenever we want to."

Ed grinned. "Gosh, that's right. I wonder how long it will be before I get used to taking it easy."

We needed earnest money, but the bulk of our capital was still in the pocket of the man who had yet to show up and buy our farm. In our own pockets were just enough funds to get us back to Chicago.

"Borrow from my father?" I suggested gently.

"I said, *no,*" Ed replied. "You know my feelings about asking favors of relatives."

"But we can't close the deal without making a payment!"

"I'll telegraph Nick."

Nick Raft is the only man I've ever heard my husband call "brother." Nick is a Greek, born in a village on the island of Ithaca. He had four years of schooling. When he was fourteen years old he left Greece to make a name for himself. He worked in Egypt, in Australia, finally in the United States. He always worked for himself, and knew everything we had to learn about "being your own boss." Once he had needed $1,000 to keep his business going, and the only man who would lend it to him charged him $400 interest on that amount.

Now Nick was in his forties. He owned the café which the men at the old *Chicago Times* affectionately termed the "Annex," and he could have paid spot cash for three *Snoqualmie Valley Records* without feeling the pinch.

"Does Nick know we drove west to buy a newspaper?"

Ed shook his head. "He doesn't even know we drove west."

But we sent the telegram anyway. It said simply: SEND FIVE THOUSAND DOLLARS FAST LOVE ED AND CHARLOTTE. We had a telegraphed money order from Nick in the morning.

Sunday, we saw the *Record* for the first time. Monday we returned to Snoqualmie and announced that "after thoughtful consideration" we had decided to buy the paper. Tuesday we met in a lawyer's office, presented our earnest money (thanks to Nick), and signed contracts. From the lawyer's office we went to our automobile, turned east, and began the 2,200-mile drive back to Chicago.

We were already well on our way to being small businessmen. We were in debt.

V

Our two weeks out west had been fast. But our two weeks back east in which we sold the farm, disposed of half our belongings and packed the rest, and headed for the Snoqualmie Valley, were faster. Ed was still working. Quite unexpectedly, so was I. At that most breathless of all times, a telegram arrived from a New York publisher which took the last of my breath away. They had bought a novel of mine, but wanted extensive revision—immediately. I wrote every day in the week for two weeks, often from nine in the morning until six at night, and mailed the finished manuscript to New York the day before we left for Snoqualmie.

Even the sale of the farm was breath-taking. It had been viewed and admired by a dozen couples for whom it was obviously just the right place; the only question seemed to be which of them would close the deal first. Then one Saturday afternoon a new family stopped in. There were too many of them for the house, the women recoiled at the suggestion of getting their hands dirty in the garden. They returned the next day with earnest money and a real-estate agent who had never before set foot on the place.

We had to sell. We had contracted to assume ownership of the newspaper on October first, and it was now October second. If the appraiser had been right, speed cost us $5,000, for the man who wanted to buy offered us $13,500, and there was the agent's commission. "I'll write a check tonight or I won't bother to come back," the man said. The capital which was to finance our plunge into business was suddenly cut down 20 percent and we hadn't even made a down payment. But we had no choice. We signed the papers that night. The next morning we called the movers.

Speed had its blessings; we didn't have time to think or say good-bye. Ed had lived in Chicago for fifteen years and I for eight. There would have been many sad partings if we had had time to make them. As it was, some of our friends didn't know we had gone until they began receiving copies of a newspaper they'd never heard of, printed in Snoqualmie, Washington. Our neighbors in the country planned a farewell party for us and collected money for a gift. We were somewhere in Wyoming and speeding toward Washington the night of the party, and the gift trailed along after us, parcel post.

Our last day in the Middle West opened with the arrival of the movers. A crew of five men spread out through the house while Ed and I raced from one room to the next, saying, "Pack that, leave that, pack that, leave that. . . ." By four in the afternoon everything we owned had been crated or jettisoned. Neighbors offered to put us up overnight but our minds were already out west and delay would have been intolerable. So, begrimed and bone-weary, we crawled into our car, Ed and I in the front seat, Hi and Johnny lying down on mounds of luggage and bedding in the back. At the back door, the only farewell committee eyed us silently—our seven cats and kittens, who like the house they guarded would have new owners in the morning. Dusk was falling as we pulled out of the driveway, past the dark pine trees we had planted, away from the home we had once said we would never leave.

We drove in near silence, the little boys fast asleep, and did not stop until we were out of the state of Illinois.

I kept thinking of the comment of another man in the

public relations department when he heard what Ed was going to do. "To try what you're trying, at your age," he said, "you have to have either an awful lot of money or an awful lot of courage." Then he grinned ruefully. "After working for someone else all my life, I haven't got either one."

I had a foggy but not a comforting notion of how long our money would last. The movers had estimated their bill at $400. We planned to repay Nick immediately, since he refused to charge interest. The down payment for the newspaper was to be $8,700. That added up to $14,100. We had netted only $13,000 from the sale of the farm and somehow we were going to have to eat and pay rent and buy gasoline until there was income from the business we had bought which came in after we assumed ownership and was therefore ours to spend. There were Ed's stocks, there were my securities. When they were gone?

As for courage—well, at our age, it was a matter of doggedly fighting it out because we were in too deep to back up. I knew that we might run out of money. I wished, and wished hard, that no matter what happened, we would never, never, run out of courage.

2

We were meeting our staff for the first time, with the former owner performing the introductions. In the back-shop, in a corner scientifically illuminated by one window and one naked electric-light bulb, was the printer, Mr. Jenkins.

Mr. Jenkins had spent most of his seventy-odd years in a print shop. Somewhere along the line his right hand had been caught in a press but there was no guessing it from the way that half-mangled member turned out work. Unfortunately Mr. Jenkins' disposition seemed to have fallen into the press also, and with far more damaging results.

When we were presented, the old man was feeding a sheet of blank paper into a small job press with one hand, sliding the printed piece out with the other. At our approach he threw us a quick sideways glance from under his green eyeshade and looked back at his work. Obviously a brand new set of employers was not sufficient cause to interrupt routine.

"Mr. Jenkins . . ."

The rhythm of the press continued unbroken. Swish, kachug, swish, kachug, the right hand over and the left hand back, at the rate of 2,000 printed forms an hour.

We had a try at it, thinking the new boss might succeed where the old boss had failed. "Mr. Jenkins? We're the new owners. . . ."

Scowling, the old man stopped the press. As he turned toward us, a particularly determined ray of sunlight forced its way through the dirty window and fell across his face. "Too cussed bright," he said by way of greeting. "I been waiting three years for a window shade."

"Glad to meet you," I mumbled appropriately.

That was our first meeting with one of the people on whom our immediate fate depended. We had inherited them, for better or for worse, from the old printer's eyeshade to the reporter's beautiful Spencerian handwriting. In our ignorance of country newspapering, we needed them desperately.

If we "inherited" the staff, they also inherited us, but hardly by mutual agreement, since we had been consulted, so to speak, and they hadn't. None of them knew that the newspaper had been on the market for a couple of years. Like magicians pulling the tablecloth off the table without moving any of the dishes, we had jerked the newspaper right out from under them, leaving them in the same spots but still rattled. What are these people from Chicago doing in a little town like this? What are they going to change? Will I keep my job—do I want to keep it, anyway? But except for Mr. Jenkins, whose welcoming address was as heart-warming as a good swift kick in the pants, everyone managed to choke back these questions and smile.

There was Chet, the teen-age pressman. Chet had sideburns and an acute case of being eighteen. He wanted to be a Y.M.C.A. director, to play the guitar, to write books, in fact to excel at a number of things which had nothing whatsoever to do with his job in our print shop.

There was Olga, the Linotype operator three days a week. To me typesetters were the faceless, round-shouldered men I had seen hunched over a battery of monster machines in metropolitan dailies. Not only was our operator a woman, but she was a smiling, middle-aged woman with gray streaks in her hair, wearing a housedress under a pretty flowered apron and looking for all the world as if she were about to mix up a batch of cookies.

There was Ort, the young advertising manager, ad salesman, and on Thursdays a one-man circulation and mailing department. Ort had graduated from the University of Washington only four months earlier, and had got married the same day. Commencement had dragged out longer than he expected so he got to his own wedding only because he crawled out of the auditorium on his hands and knees with his diploma in his teeth. His wife, Sylvia, worked in the bank across the street.

At the opposite side of the *Record's* "city room," which we reached by turning around right in place, was Hermia, the assistant editor, and wife of the local superintendent of schools. With a daughter away at college and a son in high school, she had decided, only five weeks earlier, to take a part-time job. Now suddenly she was confronted with a pair of strangers from back east. But she had been an expert mountain-climber. She had studied wild mushrooms until she knew the good from the poisonous. She had been thrown from horses and tossed off bobsleds and had successfully completed over forty years of life without even a smallpox vaccination. So she met this new emergency with perfect aplomb.

And last, there was Margie, the bookkeeper, who would have weighed a hundred pounds with her pockets full of type metal. Margie's husband was a carpenter, and the day we met, her four-year-old son, Jerry, was with her. Margie greeted the new boss and then tried to introduce him to Jerry.

"Say—Hello, Mr. Groshell," she admonished the little boy.

"Hello, Mr. . . . huh?" Jerry asked.

"Groshell, Groshell," Margie repeated vigorously.

"Hello, Mr. . . . Mr. . . . what, Mama?"

Margie shrugged her shoulders. "Oh, heck, just call him Ed," she said.

The introductions were complete. Now we were on our own.

ii

When we began in small-town business we received only two pieces of advice.

First, from the wife of another country publisher. "You've had an awfully good education," she told me. "You'll have to be careful. Don't tell people you've been to college, if you can help it."

I reasoned that if going to college was hush-hush, being a Wellesley graduate was downright subversive, so I kept my secret well. In time I discovered that as long as the *Record* was in the post-office boxes by 4:30 Thursday afternoon, no one would care if I'd been a don at Oxford.

So that first bit of advice was easy to follow. The second counsel came from a man who had owned a weekly news-paper for twenty-seven years. Following his sage advice proved to be impossible.

"Don't change anything!" the veteran publisher warned

Ed. "You're going to want to. You're full of enthusiasm and you're not quite broke. Also you've undoubtedly been storing up a million ideas and now that you've got your own newspaper you'll feel like trying them all out at once. Don't! You're out in the country now. Your readers are small-town people. They're used to the paper just the way it is and the minute you change it, even if the change improves it 100 percent, they aren't going to like it. Make up your mind to this—*for one whole year,* don't buy a dime's worth of equipment. Leave the shop building just as it is. Don't change a thing!"

As the days passed, we began to get a close-up of the building we weren't to touch, the newspaper we weren't to change, and the equipment we were to use just as it stood.

Even that first day in Snoqualmie I had noticed that the building seemed to need a new coat of paint. We soon discovered that what it really needed was a coat of wood. In time we learned it had been built in 1917 as a "temporary structure" on the builder's promise to move it off the rented lot inside of six months. But he didn't, so the landlord took over and the building had been "permanent" ever since.

It had a remarkable floor. It was made of wide softwood boards, black with thirty-two years of oil and grime and so worn the knots stood out like the veins on the back of an old woman's hands. It was springy; a heavy footfall on one end of a board gave the person at the other end the sensation of being flipped into the air. When the newspaper press got going, it bounced so hard pressman Chet looked like a speedboat driver rounding the last curve for the stretch. There were holes in the floor, too, but they had been neatly covered with tin cans hammered flat. These tin patches served two useful purposes: they kept the wildlife out, and they prevented us from peering underneath and discovering the truth about what was holding the building up.

"Central heating" was supplied by an oil burner near the press and a little black potbellied wood stove, which was indeed centrally located in the middle of the shop. It was a demon of a wood stove. Get near it and you broiled, move away and your teeth chattered; it isn't every heating system that guarantees a variation of thirty degrees Fahrenheit in only 1,200 square feet of building. And of course on that oily floor, in a room stacked high with every kind of paper, it was a fire hazard. We couldn't leave work at night until the fire had gone out, we all froze for a couple of hours in the morning until the fire was hot enough to send a few waves·into the far corners.

Luckily, these corners were not very far, and at times there were so many of us inside them that the combined heat of our bodies must have added up to an impressive number of British Thermal Units. Editorial offices, press room, job-printing department, paper storage, bindery department, stereo room, Linotype, make-up tables, stationery supplies, reception desk, library, newspaper files—all this and a lot more were jammed into a thirty-by-forty-foot plant. It hardly left room for people, and apparently on the theory that bipeds take up less room standing than sitting, some efficiency expert of a former day had seen to it that there were not enough chairs to go around.

This resulted in a grim, undeclared game of musical chairs. "I'm thirsty," Ed whispered to me one day as I walked past. "Would you bring me a drink of water?"

"Why?" I asked, all wifely concern. "Go get it yourself."

"I'm sitting on Ort's chair," he hissed, "and he's watching for me to get up."

"You might get Margie's. Isn't she about to go out for lunch?"

"She was supposed to two hours ago. But she won't give up."

If the heating system went back to Grandma's day, the plumbing would have done well to follow suit. The water supply, other than what came through the roof, was one cold-water faucet. Under the faucet, an old sink. Under the sink, a large pan, because it had been quite some time since the drainpipe had co-operated. A little water did go down the drain, to be sure. In fact, about half of it did. This made washing your hands something of a challenge. When you were through, half the dirty water would be in the pan under the sink. How to get rid of it? The trick was to empty it back into the sink so fast that you could rush the pan under the sink in time to catch the half of that half that hadn't gone down the drainpipe the last time. . . .

When Ed caught me at my little game, he commented dryly, "Haven't you heard about the man who tried to get to the door by dividing the space between himself and the door by half? He never got there."

"What am I supposed to do with the dirty water?"

Ed shrugged. "Throw it out the window."

"Is that sporting?" I looked doubtfully at the window by the sink. "And anyway, I don't think that one opens."

"Of course it opens." Ed put his hands to the frame and gave a mighty heave. The window fell forward, landing on the ground outside with a merry tinkle of breaking glass.

The lavatory, like the washstand, had the outward appearance of being modern, but at the smallest excuse it gave up the pretense and we were back in the Gay Nineties again. It was housed in a tiny outhouse next to the woodshed, separated from the main building by a few feet of mud. And of course it was cold, as poor little blue-lipped Johnny, age four, found out the day I stationed him out there and then forgot to go get him. He held the fort for thirty-five minutes before I remembered where he was and rushed outside, conscience-stricken, to retrieve him. The next week I went outside to get stove wood and my attention was called to the lavatory by the sound from within of little Hiram singing at the top of his lungs.

"Did you put Hi outside?" I asked Ed, back in the shop.

"Yes, I . . . ." He looked at the clock. "Great guns, that was an hour ago!"

The boys were too young to handle zippers and buttons but their parents' weaknesses were easier to cope with. After that neither child could be coaxed or beaten into going to the bathroom until he had stationed his brother in front of the clock inside.

iii

Ed and I had been reared on the forty-hour work week, with paid vacations, company health programs, pension plans, and the rest. As owners of our own business we discovered the seven-day week and the fifteen-hour day.

Inexperience, poor equipment, the wrong man in the right job, and a nest egg that was dwindling so fast a humming bird would have sneered at it—they all had something to do with it. Somehow, perhaps because twenty years of big-city newspapering were not entirely worthless, and because anyone can do anything if he works hard enough, somehow, we got the paper out every Thursday.

Mondays, Tuesdays and Wednesdays, Ed worked all day and most of the night; five hours' sleep was a luxury. To him the stack of newsprint in the corner near the big press was doubly important. It was the stuff we used to print the paper on, to be sure, but most every Wednesday night it was also his bed. We both looked forward to Sunday. That was the day we quit work at five o'clock.

The blessing of such long hours was that we had almost no time at home. For six weeks we lived in an auto court, where, thanks to its kindly owner, Mr. Hastert, we were both warm and comfortable. And cozy, especially when Hi and Johnny came down simultaneously with the measles, for what's cozier than four people in one room when 50 percent of the crowd is covered with spots and can't say anything but, "Mama, I'm going to be sick!"

Our room in the auto court was also the writing studio in which I completed the second revision of the novel,

Hear My Heart Speak, sold the month before. My contract read that the finished manuscript had to be delivered by November 15th. I had considered it "finished" after the changes I had made during our last weeks on the farm. But the editors wanted a revision of the revision, adding that they would like it by the first of the month rather than the fifteenth. It was no time to be a prima donna. I finished the book, with a pair of feverish and nauseated little boys furnishing the background music.

We rented a house, but we could not move into it until our furniture arrived by railroad freight from Chicago. Our luck held. The car containing our possessions was sidetracked in Idaho—Moscow, Idaho, of all places, and fie on the Russians—where it remained until an alert railwayman began to get curious about this boxcar he'd been seeing every trip for four weeks and the stuff was "speeded" on its way. When it arrived in Seattle, our bank account took another blow. The movers' estimate had been $400, and after only six weeks of owning our own business we weren't sure how we could pay it. Neither of us had drawn any wages. The procedure was quite the reverse; every week we had to take money from our personal account and deposit it in the company account so that we could write everyone else's pay check. I had received an advance payment for my novel, but that was the extent of my earnings from writing which Ed had hopefully listed under INCOME WE CAN COUNT ON. Salable writing is not produced by people who spend their time dumping rain water out of coffee cans. Notice that our furniture had arrived brought a whoop of joy and then a cry of dismay. The bill was for $882, and we had to present a certified check for that amount at the railroad siding before one stick of it would be released. We had already lost a month's rent we had given for a house we hadn't been able to live in. There was no choice. We paid.

Rental properties, in towns of six or eight hundred population, are houses the landlord doesn't want to live in himself and the tenants wouldn't either if they knew his reasons. Our house was small and dark. We stacked our goods in tiers and lived in cleared spaces in the center of each room. It was on a transcontinental highway. The big Diesel transports roaring by rattled the dishes in the china cabinet and if the windows were open we couldn't carry on a conversation in anything less than a screech. The place had been built twenty-five years earlier by a contractor with unfounded optimism about the weather, and was virtually without insulation. If stoked every hour, the old-fashioned coal furnace in the basement kept the rooms lukewarm but also fragrant with coal gas; heat and smell were inseparable. Coal, in western Washington, is only a step removed from peat; we hauled out more ashes than we put in coal.

But the house did have three bedrooms, which I felt we needed so as to put up a "live-in" housemaid. Hiram was at kindergarten every morning, but four-year-old Johnny needed all-day care which a working mama was in no position to give. My experience with our first maid was discouraging. She was good-natured, not to say jubilant. The kitchen resounded with sudden bursts of "Yes, Sir, That's My Baby" and "I Miss My Swiss, My Swiss Miss Misses Me," musical tendencies I put down to her bright red hair. When the boys were naughty she giggled, a reaction I would have understood if I had realized she was seeing them by fours and sixes. It took me three weeks to wake up, and it might have taken longer if the boys hadn't asked me, "Mama, why is Josephine silly sometimes?"

"Silly? How do you mean?"

"Like last night, when you and Daddy worked late at the shop. She made us go to bed real early. And then a long time later when we were sound asleep, she woke us up and turned on all the lights and made us get out of bed and play with our Teddy bears. It was twelve o'clock. We looked."

"That does sound kind of silly," I agreed, my throat feeling dry.

"Oh, that isn't the silly part," the boys chorused. "The silly part is, she was playing with the Teddy bears, too!" Sweet nursy, the darling Nana in whose hands I had been entrusting the physical and mental development of my children, had been tippling from dawn till dark.

She was succeeded by a young girl who got homesick and upbraided me for not staying home to keep her company, and another who had such a good time on her first day off that she forgot to come back. There were others. But the grand climax was Violet.

Violet gave no appearance of shrinking. She stood six feet tall and weighed upwards of 250 pounds. "I need a new pair of corsets," she confided the day I hired her, "and I got to get my hair curled. After that, you won't recognize me." She was wrong, though. Even with curly hair and her bulk contained and redeployed, Violet was unmistakable. Just her voice made recognition easy a block away and with your eyes closed. She had worked around lumber camps for fifteen or twenty years. Her gentlest tone was pitched to rise above the roar of a gang saw. "Don't you reach for that sugar bowl!" she would bellow during breakfast. "Want to get sugar diabetes?" The little boys tried replying at first, but they soon lapsed into unboylike silence. A word from either of them and Violet roared, "Hush up, you boys, your talk is making me nervous!" Ed and I took to sipping our breakfast coffee in the bedroom closet with the door closed, but we couldn't help but wonder what might be happening to the boys.

Violet had been a ranch cook in Montana. She fried everything except corn flakes, which she consumed at the rate of three boxes a week.

"I don't think I can afford to keep her filled up!" I told Ed.

"Just be thankful she likes corn flakes," was his practical reply.

During the war Violet had worked in the big local lumber mill. She sorted and stacked lumber as it moved along the "green chain," a kind of conveyor belt which carries uncured boards from saws to dry kilns, and she was one of the best men they had. Being used to throwing heavy objects, she attacked housework in the same way. She hated to get down on her knees, she explained, because it was so hard to get up again, so she dusted under our big double bed by lifting the whole thing—frame, springs, mattresses, blankets, and all—with one hand while she wielded a dust mop with the other. The only trouble was that her way of putting the bed back in place was simply to let go of it. One leg broke off in the crash. Ed repaired it, against Violet's thundering gale of apologies. Two days later the bed was back on the floor with two broken legs. This time, Violet explained in a tearful roar, all she did was lean on it.

Soon after, a living-room chair suffered the same fate.

"I can keep mending the furniture," Ed objected, "but about two more of her apologies and I'll be deafened for life. You'll have to fire her."

"Who, *me?*"

"She's a sport. She only picks on things her own size."

"Yes, but what if she tripped and fell on me?"

"Oh, all right. . . ." Ed is five feet six and he hadn't been getting half as much nourishment as Violet. But he took me and the boys to the shop and went back home to fire her. We've never had a housekeeper "live in" since.

iv

The first Sunday afternoon we worked in the shop was also our first Sunday afternoon in the Valley. We naïvely believed that this was a very unusual way for people who are their own bosses to spend a week end. Therefore, I was amazed when the office door opened and a woman walked in, nodded in a friendly way, and as if this were a perfectly normal time to do business, opened her purse and said she wanted to pay a bill.

I couldn't help asking, "How did you know we'd be here today?"

"How did I know!" Her eyebrows shot up in surprise. "Why, I've lived here for years. I know editors work *all* the time."

Those were prophetic words. Sundays, nights, beautiful sunny Saturday afternoons. Perched on the high wooden stool at the front window, I watched the family down the street step into their car and head for the early show. Saturday nights I counted young couples driving past on their way to the dance. Sunday mornings it was the older couples, in shiny best, walking home from church. People came into the newspaper office whenever they saw someone there, to pay a bill, or tell us about a tea party, or write down a want ad. No matter how late it might be, nor what day it might be, they never seemed surprised to find us there.

We spent our first Thanksgiving in the shop, and it was our first holiday without a customer. "They're all at home, stuffing themselves with roast turkey," Ed said dryly. "What are *we* going to have for Thanksgiving dinner?"

"What can we fry?" I retorted.

Ed was gathering pages of a booklet we had printed. The children were crawling around on the floor salvaging pieces of type metal. I had undertaken the job of paying the bills.

No matter how carefully I checked the figures, the sum we owed remained twice the sum we had in the company's bank account. I tried again, but there was no melting the cold heart of the adding machine. At last I called to Ed. "Darling, we'll have to give the company account another transfusion. I can't pay the bills."

Ed said grimly, "I guess I didn't tell you. A couple of

days ago I put the last of our personal account into the company account. The blood bank is dry."

"You mean, this balance here, which won't cover half our bills, is all we have in both accounts?"

Ed nodded. "I've already sent my General Motors stock to a broker. We should have the money Monday."

We owed $21,000 to the former owner of the paper, and $5,000 to our friend Nick. Twenty-six thousand dollars in debt and we were being forced to sell securities just to meet regular expenses. It was a nice thought for Thanksgiving. I looked helplessly at the pile of bills. Many of them were for two or three hundred dollars. Many were a month overdue.

As usual, Ed read my mind. "Don't worry, darling," he said, patting my shoulder, "we'll work out a system. . . ."

We did, and it was a system we followed for many months afterward. I started with the bills filed under the *A's,* and continued writing checks until our bank balance was used up. The next month, I started with the *Z's* and worked backward. I liked this, because we had fewer creditors with names like Xantippe and Yarborough and Zip than we did at the front of the alphabet and I seemed to be making great strides toward solvency. The flaw in the system was one which creditors under the *M's* were quick to point out— they were in the middle of the file and I never got that far. So every third month I began with the *M's,* and worked in both directions.

We did celebrate Thanksgiving, in a way. We didn't get home until eight o'clock and our holiday dinner consisted of pork chops served on the oilcloth-covered kitchen table. But we didn't set the alarm clock. "I'm my own boss," Ed said, shaking his fist at the little black clock. "I've got to get used to taking it easy, see?"

The day after Thanksgiving a woman came in to pay for a classified ad. I recognized her as the customer who had come in our first Sunday in the shop and commented sympathetically, "Editors work *all* the time." She wasn't sympathetic today.

"This place is never open any more," she said tartly.

"Oh, but we're here almost all the time!"

She shook her head. "No, you're not. Place was all locked up."

"I'm so sorry. When did you come?"

"This morning."

"We were a little late," I said apologetically. "But we worked all day Thanksgiving, so we didn't set the alarm clock and we didn't get here until almost nine o'clock."

She shrugged. "Well, if you don't care whether you get your money or not, it's all right with *me*."

V

As the sage publisher of twenty-seven years had feared, we ignored his advice completely. We began changing things the moment we walked in the door.

We changed the appearance of the paper, using pictures until our monthly bill at the engraver's topped former publishers' engraving bills for a year. We went out hunting for news and features, until the paper grew from eight to ten pages, ten to twelve, twelve to fourteen, and finally to an unprecedented eighteen pages a week. Of course the resulting production costs were unprecedented, too.

The job press, Mr. Jenkins' pride and joy, had been second-hand when it was purchased by a former *Record* publisher in 1923. We wrapped it in a shroud and bought an automatic press to replace it. The new press cost $2,200, but the sale of Ed's General Motors stock had revived us, so we went even farther; we also purchased a brand-new type cabinet, the cost of which we'll remember forever because it was one dollar a pound—price $550, weight, 550 pounds.

"General Motors is high at 61," Ed said, "so it's a good time to sell. And it's a good time to buy the cabinet, too, because the salesman tells me they're bound to go up." What a blessing that we could not look ahead! A few months later the stock we sold at sixty-one dollars a share was divided and two shares issued for every one; the price for the new shares soon climbed to 89. Ed was right about the type cabinet, though. In no time the same piece of equipment was selling for $700. "See, we made $150," Ed cheered, until he went to a sale of second-hand printing equipment and saw the same cabinet sold for $350, and not empty like ours, but full of type. And what was ours but second-hand, now and forevermore?

We had new panes of glass put in the windows, which released a good deal of cardboard for active duty, and we called in the roofing company, so that fifteen coffee cans and the publisher's wife were rendered obsolete. We raised the wage scale for everyone in the shop. Everything was bigger and better—shop, equipment, salaries, the newspaper. "Making improvements is good business," was Ed's theory. He was a little shaken, but not really dismayed, by the fact that every week we were paying out more than we were taking in.

This error in management was not obvious while our personal bank account lasted. The sale of Ed's stock also concealed it for a while. But I had an occasional twinge of uneasiness, and a few weeks after Thanksgiving I asked our bookkeeper, Margie, to show me some figures I could understand. Here, then, is our first financial statement as owners of our own business:

Total amount paid to Charlotte and Ed Groshell from Oct. 1 through Dec. 18: $243.86. Amount loaned to the company from the Groshells' personal bank account, for period Oct. 1 through Dec. 18: $1,000. Balance in the company account: $256.00. In other words, it had cost us only $500.14 to work for twelve weeks. In the same period of time our shop staff of eight, some working only part-time, had received $4,294.60 in wages.

It's not surprising that a few interested citizens in Snoqualmie were giving odds of twenty to one that the former owner would get the business back in less than a year. We would have bet that way, too, if we'd been able to scrape up something to bet with. And then, in time for Christmas, we had a windfall.

Months earlier I had received a communication from a company interested in buying shares of Danciger Oil stock. It was a printed form, mailed to all stockholders, offering to buy at par value. My eighty shares would have brought only a few dollars. It was this, not foresight, which made me refuse to sell. "I've had my Danciger stock for a long time, I might as well keep it," I said. "Who knows, they might strike oil someday." The next time anyone bothered to write me about my oil stock, it was to inform me that the company had been reorganized. I had to sell whether I wanted to or not, my eighty shares would now bring me $2,000, and please to reply "without delay." I don't know about the other stockholders but the only delay on the part of the one in Snoqualmie was caused by the fact that mail didn't go out until five o'clock that afternoon.

Christmas was wonderful. It was our first day off since we had become country publishers three months before.

Of all the treasured possessions we left behind in Illinois, I had missed only one—my piano, a gift from my grandmother on my fifth birthday. I am no pianist. I play by ear, right heel thumping and head bobbing. But without any kind of a musical instrument, I felt lost. There was only one thing I wanted more than a piano, and that was an old-fashioned church organ.

It was late Christmas Eve when the boys and I came home from the shop. There, in that dark, unloved house, was the most beautiful little reed organ I have ever seen. It had been made in Lebanon, Pennsylvania, in the '80s, had come west via ship sailing around Cape Horn, and in the fashion of its day was carved from music rack to candle holders. Ed had found it in the little Congregational church in Carnation, a town fifteen miles to the north, and he and our young ad salesman, Ort, had used the local furniture store's pickup to go down and get it.

There had been a problem to hurdle—the store had some last-minute deliveries to make.

"But if you'll deliver the stuff, you can have the truck," the owner agreed, so Ed and Ort had spent a busy Christmas Eve toting refrigerators, living-room suites, and automatic washing machines all over the Valley so as to race fifteen miles to Carnation and fifteen back and bring me my Christmas present.

They grinned proudly and asked, "Do you like it?" I replied instantly by shedding buckets and buckets of tears.

By New Year's the *Record's* new publisher and his wife were showing symptoms of battle fatigue. The red of our eyes vied with the red on the ledger. Our nerves stood up like quills on a porcupine's back; a friendly pat on the back and we'd come up swinging. And then, when we were almost broke and almost broken, the weather stepped forward to minister the coup de grâce.

The storm broke on New Year's Eve, and didn't let up for two months. When the Valley was reeling from the impact of a heavy snow, eighty-mile-an-hour winds came along to drive that snow into giant drifts. Then came sheets of freezing rain, and the thermometer would plummet to five or ten above zero and stay there until it was time for more snow. Old-timers began talking about 1916, when drifts reached the tops of telephone poles. But to housewives, living in homes that had not been built for such Middle Western winters, and to every local businessman, who wondered how he could keep going and who would ever get to his place if he did, it was no time for reminiscence. It was a hard, daily fight.

The roads were alternately ice-covered, flooded, or blocked with snow. Ice and falling trees frequently pulled down power and phone lines, at such ideal times, from a repairman's point of view, as two o'clock in the morning. Our little local phone company, with one aging pickup truck and a crew of four, raced from one "case of trouble" to the next. They worked in five and six feet of snow, seven days a week, and apologized because they could not work all night since they were the same crew that had to make repairs in the daytime. One blizzard cost the company eight to ten thousand dollars. But the storm of 1950 went on for a long time. It wasn't one blizzard, it was several.

Telephone repairmen were followed or preceded by a haggard and dogged crew from the power company. In one week six poles went down, a big transformer dropped through a meat market and another crashed though a car, and countless lines went down in areas so snow-bound the weary linemen had to walk two or three miles before they could start to make repairs.

One night a fresh storm hit just after dark. Ice pulled down the hospital's power and telephone lines. At the time a patient with pneumonia was in an oxygen tent in a critical condition; yet the hospital had neither power nor any way to call for help.

Two men in the waiting room raced down the hill to the Snoqualmie Fire Hall and blew the siren. In a few minutes there were six firemen at the hospital, the oxygen tent was attached to a portable light plant, and seven more firemen were standing by at the Fire Hall in case they were needed. No fireman left his post until the power company crews had finished repairs.

A dairy farmer named Ed Leitz was one of the true heroes of the endless storm. He had 125 cows, which were of course milked by machine and watered by an electric pump. When a particularly vicious siege brought down the power lines, he and his hands milked the 125 cows by hand, though they were eight hours doing it. Then they carried the milk, each can weighing a hundred pounds, through waist-high snowdrifts to a point some hundred yards away, where the road had been cleared so that the milk truck could pass by. A county road-scraper tried to open the road to the farm. It slipped off the road and came to rest in a ditch near the Leitz barn. The men could see it every time they struggled through the snow with a hundred-pound can of milk.

One cold, bleak, Wednesday night, at the height of a blow, the Linotype broke down. The Linotype is the heart of the print shop. Few country shops have more than one, and that usually a model that is apt to go into a decline at any time. So when our machine quit cold the night before publication day, with columns and columns of type still to go, we were in a truly desperate situation. And the weather didn't help.

At two in the morning (Yes, a Linotype operator was working then, and it wasn't the first time by a long shot!) Ed made a long distance phone call to Tom Dobbs, publisher of a weekly paper in the next county. After Ed had described the symptoms, Tom said, "I think I know what's wrong. Put your operator on the wire."

Ed called Ralph to the phone. Ralph was printer, Linotype operator when Olga wasn't there, pressman when Chet wasn't there, and foreman of a backshop force which was automatically reduced 33⅓ percent whenever someone stayed home with a head cold. Ralph had chosen the worst winter in thirty-four years to move to the Snoqualmie Valley and join the *Record* staff, a fact that may have crossed his mind that blizzardy midnight when the Linotype broke down. Ralph took over the receiver. "Now, first do this . . ." said Tom. Ralph went back to the machine, carried out Tom's instructions, ran back to the phone and asked, "Yes, what next?" Tom's voice from the next county continued, "Now do this . . ." And thus, at two in the morning, with one man standing barefoot on a cold floor at one end of the line, and two others racing from Linotype to telephone at the other, the repair was made and we were back in business. All the while Ed was eyeing the blizzard raging outside, wondering at what stage of disembowelment the Linotype would be when the phone went dead.

One of the worst blows of the winter also came on a Wednesday night, and when Ed rose in the morning from his bed of newsprint he looked out on streets blocked by snowdrifts four to six feet high. Most members of the staff lived at least two miles away, and a glance at the great Arctic outside convinced Ed that they couldn't possibly get to work.

The "shift" began at eight o'clock. About ten minutes to eight Ed saw an odd procession making its way toward the shop. At its head was the superintendent of schools, a six-foot-three-inch Norwegian. He was breaking trail, with great kicks and flourishes of his size-thirteen boots. Behind him was our assistant editor, barely recognizable as a journalist in a costume of ski pants, sweaters, boots and lumberjacket. And right behind *her* was our little bookkeeper, also swathed to the earlobes, carefully falling in and out of the super's big footprints. They had walked two miles through some of the deepest snow in the Valley, and they made it right on time.

"I didn't think you'd come to work today," Ed said, all choked up with admiration.

"What?" the women exclaimed together. "Not come to work *on Thursday?*"

We suffered less because of the weather than many other businessmen. We didn't have to stay up all night to keep the pipes from freezing—we didn't have any pipes. Snow stood on the inside sills even with the windows closed and locked, but that doesn't bother a person who has been arranging coffee cans to collect rain. Other local businessmen were worried about digging out driveways so that oil trucks could get in with fuel oil. Not us. We didn't have a furnace. And as for the "conveniences"—due to age and ill temper our facilities had frequently been anything but convenient so what matter that the first day of the storm they froze up tighter than Nisqually glacier and remained that way until spring thaw, when we removed the crockery, shattered and split at every seam, and gave it suitable burial.

The only member of the *Record* staff humiliated by the

weather was Ort, who liked to do the right thing the right way and had a tendency to blush. As luck would have it, both Ed and I were out on an errand the wintery afternoon that little Johnny decided he couldn't wait until he got home. Ort, doubling as baby sitter while he drew up his ad schedule for the next week, knew of only one lavatory in the vicinity that was inside and functioning—the one in the bank across the street. So, four-year-old John in tow, he went to the bank and asked one of the tellers if it would be all right, would they mind . . .

"Go right on in," the teller said, "through that office and to the right . . ."

Ort opened the office door, only to see that a meeting of the board of directors was in process within. "I . . . the little boy . . . excuse me . . . he . . ."

At that point Johnny straightened out the president of the bank, the vice-president, the cashier, and five members of the board of directors, as to just what it was he had to do.

"Come right in," the bank president said quickly. "Right straight through, and to your right."

The board waited respectfully while Ort and Johnny walked over their feet. "Excuse me, uh, us," Ort mumbled, red-faced.

"That's all right, think nothing of it," the bank president reassured him.

Errand accomplished, Ort and Johnny retraced their route, once more pushing past directors and officers of a chain of seven banks.

"That's all right, think nothing of it," the president said heartily. And added with the touch of true hospitality, *"Any* time."

During that first winter the rigors of life at the shop were far more bearable than the comforts of home. The house, being innocent of insulation, simply could not be heated by the puffing and belching coal furnace. We joked about rushing the milk bottles into the refrigerator so that they wouldn't freeze and blow their tops and we most certainly did rush ourselves into bed to keep from doing the same. Since we had no maid, the children had to stay with me at the shop. A typical day ended about eight or nine o'clock at night, when we bundled the weary boys into the car and crawled six miles home over icy roads. Because of snowdrifts, we couldn't drive close to the house. We had to walk a hundred feet along a narrow path half-lost under the snow that had fallen or drifted across that day. And since there had been no one at home to stoke the furnace, the house awaiting us was always literally below freezing.

The two little boys, speechless with hunger and fatigue, would be propped up on the sofa under several layers of blankets while Ed headed for the basement and I for the kitchen. With our driveway blocked by snow, the only fuel deliveries we could get were the ones Ed made on his back. It wasn't carrying gunny sacks of coal through snowdrifts that broke the publisher's back; it was the fact that in our furnace the contents of the sacks didn't give any more warmth than if he'd piled them in the middle of the highway and lit a bonfire.

One Tuesday night the house was so cold I put the boys to bed fully clothed and in sheepskin-lined hunting jackets. During the night, Ed got up every two hours and went to the basement to rebuild the fire. By the time he made his last trip, at 4:30 in the morning, he had poured into that furnace all 200 pounds of coal which he had so laboriously toted into the house only eight hours before. But the temperature had finally climbed to seventy. He lay down for one more nap before the alarm went off.

When we got up at six o'clock, the inside thermometer read 29 degrees. The water pipes were frozen; we couldn't squeeze out enough for a pot of coffee. We couldn't even start a fire in the fireplace—we'd burned everything but the furniture the night before.

"This is it," I announced. I pulled the children out of bed, steered them into the car, and all four of us headed for an all-night truckers' café on the highway. "Black coffee, all the way around," I called to the waitress, "and make it strong."

An hour later, warmed and fed, I telephoned the auto court. Mr. Hastert had a vacant cabin, yes, but what had happened?

"Hold it for us, please," I said fervently, *"we're coming home!"*

vi

Spring came, all innocence and flowers, and smiled upon us scarred and battered survivors of winter. On a lovely Sunday afternoon, I insisted Ed quit work and come for a drive.

"You've never even been on a road that wasn't a direct route from the house to the shop," I said. "Get your nose off the grindstone and take a look at the mountain, and the hills, and the woods."

Ed allowed me to drag him from work when it was still two hours shy of Sunday quitting time. He settled down in the back seat of the car, to enjoy, in perfect relaxation, his first sightseeing tour. Mount Si, the 4,000-foot mountain which looms over the Snoqualmie Valley, looked particularly beautiful in the clear spring sunshine. Its base is only four miles from the print-shop door but we had never had time to explore the gravel roads which lead to it. I headed that way, exclaiming every hundred yards about how lovely it was and how wonderful to get out at last.

A jog in the road brought us right up under the mountain. I stopped the car. "Look, oh look!" And I turned to share the ecstasy with Ed. Yes, it was wonderful to get out of the shop. He was fast asleep.

That same month we had an earthquake. It lasted less than a minute and it came at three o'clock in the morning. Six months earlier, I would have awakened instantly, but when I slept now it was a sleep no earthquake could touch. Ed was awake, reading copy in the kitchen. He rushed to the bedroom, shook me, and called, "Honey, wake up, hey wake up, we're having an earthquake!"

No response.

"Honey, you've *got* to wake up. It's an earthquake. Gosh, it makes the hair on the back of my neck stand right up."

"Well, wet it and brush it down," murmured his wife, "and go to sleep."

Thus the grandeurs and terrors of Nature went unnoticed as we battered our way from Thursday to Thursday. If we let some experiences go by, it was because we were in the throes of the still bigger experience of surviving.

"I know what you're going through," said a fellow businessman by the name of Ote Sloan. "I went into business for myself, and all my friends began crying, 'You'll never make it.' But I did. I kept her going and I paid her off. And I'll tell you this—if you can stick it out for a year, you've got a chance. If you can last for three, the guy you bought from will never get it back from you. And if you're still here five years from now—boy, they'll have to shoot you to get you out of here."

The only sign of spring that cheered me was the first writing check I'd received since we took over the paper. It was for $21.38, hardly worth the rapt look on Ed's face when he pulled it out of the envelope.

"You know," he said thoughtfully, "I've been thinking of building a wing onto the print shop."

"What are you saying?" I exclaimed. $21.38! My poor hubby was cracking under the strain.

He nodded. "This old building is too small."

"Ever heard of money? That's the stuff we never had enough of and now we don't have any of."

Ed's gaze was fixed on some exciting vision just over and beyond my right ear. His eyes actually shone as he said, "Yes, inside of a year, we'll have part of a new shop building, inside of two years we'll have a home of our own, and inside of three the shop building will be three times as big and all new." He brought his attention down to earth, and me. "You with me?"

"Only because I'm used to you," I snapped.

"You could have done a lot better than me."

"After what I've been through with you the past seven years I haven't got the strength to break in a new one."

"Then we're together. . . ."

The memory of Ed and the strawberry business shot across my mind. "Darling," I began uneasily, "have you figured . . ."

But he wasn't listening. He had picked up a piece of scratch paper, and he was sketching the way the new *Record* building would look.

3

If you own a little dairy, your work day centers around the moment the co-op truck stops to pick up the milk. If it's a bakery, you labor day and night for the moment you take your product out of the oven and place it for sale on the front counter. The single point of time more important to the fellow with a little business of his own than any other second, or minute, or hour of the day, is the moment he actually delivers.

Our witching hour was 4:30 Thursday afternoon. By then the afternoon mail had been distributed, and everyone who came to the post office expected to find his *Record* tucked into the mailbox along with his letters. No praise for the publisher if he had got the paper out early, for Mrs. Jones is going to make only one trip uptown and that when she can pick up letters and paper at the same time. But down with the publisher if the paper is late. Who can wait around the post office with dinner to get on the table by 5:30? So for us, 4:30 Thursday afternoon was the point at which one week ended and the next began.

But on one particular Thursday, early in our lives as country editors, the paper was late. Four-thirty came, and not a paper ready for delivery. The clock ticked on to 4:45. The tiny lobby of the post office was crowded with people waiting one minute more before they gave up and went home.

The silent ones, leaning against the wall, the chatty ones in little gossipy groups, were all keeping wary eyes on the door through which the papers would come. Behind the counter the postmaster and his assistant were waiting, too, starting into animation whenever the door opened, subsiding into silence when they saw it wasn't the boy with the armload of papers. Four-fifty, 4:55. A few people detached themselves from the group and walked across the street to the *Record* office.

"Not out yet?"

"Sorry . . . Just a few more minutes . . ."

They went back to the post office. "Just a few more minutes," they relayed. "Lady at the *Record* office said, just a few more minutes."

Five o'clock . . . a handful of papers were ready for delivery. There were only ten or fifteen of them, out of the hundreds addressed to the Snoqualmie post office alone, all marked for subscribers whose names began with *A,* but I grabbed them and ran to the post office.

"Here's the paper now!" someone exclaimed.

I, the editor of only a few months, had to explain to this subscriber of perhaps twenty years, that this was only the beginning of the *A's* and it might be some time before the rest could be delivered. Naturally the subscriber I drew to explain to had a name that began with *T* or *Z* or *W*. And naturally he was about ten feet tall with lots of muscles.

"I been waiting thirty minutes," the man said, leaning over me, "and now I got to go home without my *Record*. How come?"

I looked up at him helplessly. Postmaster and assistant were leaning so far forward across their counter they were in danger of falling face down into the lobby. Everyone in the post office was listening. Faces I knew by sight but not by name were turned toward me and they looked about as friendly to me as the man with the pin does to a butterfly.

What to say? The truth was long and involved. For two days every piece of our machinery had vied with every other to see which could break down loudest and stay in pieces longest. But could I tell this indignant subscriber who had paid his three dollars a year and was asking nothing more than that we give him what he paid for—could I cry out, as I might have, "Our Linotype is broken and our saw is broken and our router is broken and our press is broken and our folder is broken and pretty soon the owner will be, too?" No. All I could manage was a strangled two-word explanation: "Mechanical difficulties."

The man's face changed instantly. The "I want my money back" expression vanished and was replaced miraculously by one of throbbing sympathy. "Mechanical difficulties," he repeated, shaking his head sadly. He turned to the little cluster of listeners at his elbow. "Mechanical difficulties," he said again. They sighed and clucked. "That's too bad," one woman murmured, patting me on the arm as she walked out of the post office and headed for home. They left the post office quietly, nodding or smiling tenderly as they passed. Two minutes earlier they wouldn't have wasted a nickel for powder to blow me up. "Mechanical difficulties"—and they looked as if they were ready to send me flowers.

As the months passed, through painful experience we came

to understand and appreciate this Open sesame, to the hearts of our readers.

Sometime, some place, there may have been a country newspaper shop which owned new equipment. But after five years in our own shop and a good bit of nosing around in other people's, I've come to the conclusion that country editors have been the greatest antique collectors in the world. Because they won't, or can't, change, half of them still are. Much of their machinery is obsolete; new parts have to be custom-made, a process so expensive that many publishers resort to the baling-wire-and-chewing-gum type of repair. Naturally manufacturers don't offer training courses in maintenance of equipment they haven't made for thirty years, so printers in country shops have to learn by experience, a euphemism for "Let's try it this way and if something crumbles, that was the wrong way." If there are three printers present when the press falls apart, there will be three different theories about how to fix it. Sometimes the only catastrophe greater than having the press break down is having it repaired.

Our first "mechanical difficulty" struck when we had been in business only two or three weeks. The newspaper folder, somehow discerning we were on deadline, gave one last monumental squeak and collapsed in a torpor. No amount of coaxing could arouse it, there were 300 papers still unfolded, and mailing time was literally minutes away. So we organized assembly-line fashion and folded and trimmed 300 newspapers by hand. The superintendent of schools stopped in to say hello to our editor (his wife), and seeing our predicament, rolled up his sleeves and joined the line. The postmaster was afraid we wouldn't finish on time so he raced over to the shop and folded papers, too. "I'll work overtime tonight," he grinned, "so Uncle Sam won't be gypped out of my services." And he did.

If the mailed edition of the *New York Times* were late getting to the post office, can you imagine the postmaster of New

York City rushing over to help get the paper out? The superintendent for a district which includes the schools of four towns has an important job, and he was no more obliged than the postmaster to worry about getting the paper out on time. But when the last *Record* was folded, addressed and mailed, he straightened up, looked at the clock, and exclaimed, *"We made it!"*

The veteran publisher who advised us "Don't change anything!" had inspected our shop, and had certainly recognized that by using our equipment we were depriving the junk dealer of a very nice haul. But he patted the old press lovingly, and commented, "You can still squeeze a good many dollars out of this. . . ." He squinted at the folder, and said, "Well, she's not new, but they haven't made many changes in the past twenty-five years." When he got to the Linotype, he was almost ecstatic. It was only twenty-three years old. "Why it's the newest of the old models!" he exclaimed.

Ed's idea, to which he held stubbornly despite all good advice, was that newer equipment would mean more production, a better product, and happier employees. He was right on the first two counts. It took Mr. Jenkins to show how wrong he could be on the third.

The old printer's greeting our first day in the shop had been a gruff complaint about the light in his eyes. "We'll fix that," said Publisher Ed, all bounce and cheer, and he spent the best part of our first Sunday in the Valley installing a new window shade. First I washed the window, which took some time, since only cold water was available for this unprecedented attack on a rare old collection of grime. Ed's job of putting up a pair of sockets took time, too, because at the first blow of the hammer the window frame had some kind of a seizure and had to be repaired before the shade could go up. At last it was done, and we could hardly wait to see Mr. Jenkins' sour face sweetened by a smile of appreciation.

Five days later we were still waiting. Finally Ed called it

to the old man's attention. Mr. Jenkins' expression of appreciation was brief. "I wondered who was messing around in my department," he grumbled, and turned his back.

Mr. Jenkins' "department," now brighter than it had been when he said it was too bright (No, he never pulled down the new shade and howled when anyone else tried to.) consisted of two hand-fed job presses and a kind of slanted desk on which he assembled type. One of the presses was covered with an old sheet and hadn't been used for years; it was referred to as "the old one." A bill of sale we later found in the file revealed that the "new one" had been bought twenty-nine years earlier and was listed as a second-hand "rebuilt" machine then.

"What we need," said Ed, "is an automatic job press." Miraculously a salesman turned up to second the motion. He had been summoned not by us, but by Mr. Jenkins, whose letter he showed us:

> *Dear Salesman,*
> *When you were here last time you asked me to get in touch with you if anything comes up here. Krebs sold out to some guy. He wants to buy some presses. Hope you get here in time.*
>
> **The Old Printer,**
> *Si Jenkins*

The purchase of an automatic job press was our first major improvement. It cost $2,200 and as I have said it did awful things to our bank account. It was an even harder blow to the status quo. First, the unused and unusable press had to be transferred into the shed outside. Goodness knows how they had moved it into the shop twenty-nine years earlier, but we had to knock a hole in the wall to get it out of the building and knock another equally large opening into the shed to move it in there. Now there was room for the new press, but we sensed that the sagging floor had been waiting for just such an opportunity, so we had a cement slab poured and the machine was set up on it. Meanwhile production had virtually stopped while we paid hourly wages for sidewalk engineering.

At last remodeling was done, the press was installed, a flip of the switch and this marvel would perform. Only trouble was that no one knew how to run it.

Least of all Mr. Jenkins, who had all but ordered it. He eyed it warily, and no matter what the printing order, insisted on using the old familiar hand press. Ed tried pep talks, though the mental hospitals of this state are full of publishers who have tried to cheer Mr. Jenkins. He hired an expert job printer from Seattle to come out to Snoqualmie and give instruction to Mr. Jenkins. This foray into higher education cost us hourly wages for the Seattle man, and time and a half for his pupil. Gradually the old man began to show some interest. "Never saw the press I couldn't handle," he grumbled one day, and we knew his enthusiasm had reached a fever pitch. Ed and I sighed with relief. Our investment in this new machine and in training our printer to use it were not to be wasted after all.

Ed and I were in Seattle buying supplies the day Mr. Jenkins actually used the automatic press for the first time. It was an order for five thousand printed form letters, and when we got back from the city, well after quitting time, we found Mr. Jenkins standing guard while the press clicked along merrily. He was grinning like a schoolboy. He had met the challenge of this monster and he had won. I had never before seen him laughing and smiling, and I never did again. Because when I picked up one of the letters as it came off the press, I saw, to my horror, that it contained a bad typographical error. Four out of five thousand had already been printed, 4,000 sheets of highly costly wastepaper. All as lost as the wages we would have to pay for the printer's wasted time.

Mr. Jenkins froze when I pointed out the error. Without a word he turned off the press, picked up his coat and hat, and walked to the door.

Ed and I looked glumly at our fine new press. "We were warned not to change anything," I said at last. "But we did, and look what happened."

"But it's *time* to make changes. Look at that old press."

"Look at Mr. Jenkins."

"The difference," Ed said feelingly, "is that you can still buy parts for the press."

Mr. Jenkins snarled even louder after that. We knew we would be helpless without a printer, and we had been told so often and so feelingly that it was impossible to get good help we were convinced there just wasn't anyone to replace him. I walked a wide circle around him and Ed held grimly to a laugh-it-off policy. But Mr. Jenkins did not like his insults to be ignored. Eventually they grew so pointed that Ed yelled back. There was a brief interchange of words recorded simultaneously by the hackles at the back of my neck and the seismograph in San Francisco. Then Mr. Jenkins strode out, coat over his arm, and in furious silence extended his hand for his check.

He had quit or he had been fired—the point was too delicate to establish right then. At any rate, he was leaving. I made out his check with a shaky hand. Mr. Jenkins snatched it, glowered at me, walked out and slammed the door.

Ed emerged from the backshop. Silently we watched our only printer cross the street and disappear around the corner. "I had all I could take," Ed said at last. "But what are we going to do now?"

Pa Kennedy, the Publishers' Association man, had made it clear that editors and writers are something a country newspaper can do without, and his opinion of our importance was certainly being borne out. The traditional printer-publisher could have stepped into Mr. Jenkins' shoes. We could not. We'd have to go on being the copy boys and hope and pray we could find another Mr. Jenkins.

Many years ago there was a floating population of printers, of varying degrees of skill and sobriety. They stayed a few weeks, perhaps a few months; they had no money, no wives, and no references. Ed and I had assumed that the organization of the printing trades had been the death of the tramp printer. After Mr. Jenkins left us we discovered there were still tramps aplenty, and oddly enough they all wanted to work for us.

Mr. DeMarco issued forth from the nearest saloon the same week Mr. Jenkins departed. "Got any work?" he asked, his little red-rimmed eyes fixed on the idle job press.

He was wearing a pair of brown trousers, a dark-blue suit coat with sleeves which ended just above his bony wrists, and a straw hat. His face was as haphazard as his costume; the features should never have been thrown together in the first place and were simply making the most of a bad situation. His smile was wide and friendly, but it seemed to be directed at someone standing just behind and to the right of you, and his eyes had the same trouble deciding what to light on.

"What can you do?" Ed asked.

This question delighted Mr. DeMarco. "What can I do?" he laughed, beating his chest hard enough to raise a cloud of dust. "Man, I can do everything. I been printing for thirty-five years."

Mr. DeMarco looked as if he had been drinking just a little longer than he had been printing. But we were smarting under a sense of our own inadequacy. In Chicago Ed would have handed Mr. DeMarco a dollar or two and told him to run along. Instead he said, "You're hired."

"I think he drinks," I whispered to Ed when our "new" printer (who hadn't been new since Teddy Roosevelt was leading the Rough Riders) was out of hearing.

"If drinking makes a printer out of you," Ed hissed back, "I'd better try it myself."

"But do you suppose he's sober enough to work?"

Ed said grimly, "Drunk or sober, he'll turn out more work than we're doing with that press standing idle."

"Hey, Ed!" It was Mr. DeMarco's voice, happy and beery.

Ed blinked, muttered something, but aloud, with cheery little grace notes in his voice, he called, "Coming . . ."

Mr. DeMarco was standing next to the press, his rummage-sale straw hat held delicately in both hands. All he wanted to know was, "Is there a place to hang my hat?"

Ed reached for the hammer, pulled a nail out of his pocket, and with two blows drove it into the wall. "Yes," he said solemnly, "there is."

Mr. DeMarco hung up his hat. "Thank you." And then he went to work.

Ignorant as I was, I thought you had to be able to focus to be a good printer. Mr. DeMarco was never sober, but in all the work he did for us he never made a mistake. He was good-natured—in fact he was practically de-natured. We didn't expect to see him from day to day. Yet every morning he showed up, all smiles, hung up his hat, turned back the sleeves of his suit coat, and went to work.

"You like to drink?" Ed asked him one afternoon in the conviviality of the back room.

Mr. DeMarco burst out laughing. "I can read the label on a whiskey bottle," he chuckled, "just running my finger tips over it with my eyes closed."

The little old hand-snapper was the kind of press Mr. DeMarco had undoubtedly used when he learned the trade, and he seemed to know it intimately. He was rarely in condition to drive a car, walk a straight line, or sign his own name. But he could print.

On Friday Ed confessed, "I wish we gave out pay checks at the end of the month instead of every week."

"What do you mean?"

"Today's payday. What do you bet tomorrow we'll be looking for another printer?"

And we were. When the checks were dispensed that afternoon, Mr. DeMarco looked distastefully at his and asked if he couldn't have it in cash.

"Figuring on coming back Monday?" Ed asked, with remarkable calmness since we both had the "this is the end" feeling about looking for another printer.

"Monday?" Mr. DeMarco mused, trying hard to peer into an era removed from the present by so many hours and so many beers.

Ed said earnestly, "I'd like to count on you. . . ."

"You got a nice shop," Mr. DeMarco countered. "A real nice shop. And I like you, Ed," he added, in a conciliatory way.

"Thanks, Mr. DeMarco," Ed replied. "You've done a good job this week."

That brought on Mr. DeMarco's widest grin. "I *told* you," he said, slapping himself, "I told you, I can do anything!" That had been his first cue, and that was his exit line. We never saw him again.

To our intense relief, Mr. DeMarco's successor was a respectable family man. He didn't like to drink, he didn't like to smoke.

"You see, we've been worrying needlessly," Ed told me. "This man is the kind that shows up every Monday morning and stays on one job for year after year. Our help problems are over."

"He doesn't seem to move very fast."

"He's just efficient," Ed explained. "A good man can get a lot of work done without appearing to work hard at all."

It soon was clear that our family man was efficient like a two-toed sloth, who never wastes a motion either. He didn't like to drink or smoke, that much was true, but most of all he didn't like to work. His ambition was to be a foreman, he told us. Luckily for us he had been in the trade so long that the printer in him sometimes turned out a lot of work before the foreman woke up to what was going on and put a stop to it.

"I'm no superman," he repeated several times a day, "I'm no world-beater." From then on, we called him Superman.

I met Superman's family on a bitterly cold morning in mid-winter. The little frame building was anything but cozy, but the Linotype operator was setting type with frozen fingers and the associate editor was calling for news despite her chattering teeth. The round iron stove was our only defense against frostbite, so I was doing my best to co-operate with it. The cord wood was buried under a fresh snowfall. I dug around, found an armload, staggered back into the shop with it, stoked the potbellied little monster, went back out again.

I was busy in this race against death by freezing when our printer entered, and with him, a smiling little woman and a teen-age boy with an unnerving resemblance to his father. All three clustered around the stove. All three watched with superb disinterest while I fed the fire, went outside, stumbled through drifts to the woodpile, dug out another armload, and returned.

"Sure is cold," commented the boy, whose muscles bulged under his letterman's sweater.

"My, you have a lot of running around to do," said the printer's wife.

I dropped the armload of wood with a clatter. "Working warms you up," I said pointedly.

The printer shrugged. "No use me trying to run a press until you get the shop warmed up."

"There are two jobs that were promised for today."

He shook his head. "I'm no superman," he said, and that retired the side.

Ed was out on an errand. By the time he got back my temper was throwing more heat than the stove. I described the scene in detail and wound up hotly, "Are you going to keep an employee who lets *me*, the *boss's* wife, do janitor work while he sits and warms his hands?"

"Can you run the job press?" Ed asked quietly. "Can you turn out good printing?"

My case against Superman collapsed. It was true—as long as we could not do the job ourselves, we'd have to be janitors and like it. I grinned. "All right, darling. I'll carry the wood for him and I'll love, honor and obey him."

"Hey, that last line is wrong," said the publisher. *"That* one's for me, remember?"

ii

In the spring we had our first try at backing a worth-while civic project. We had already supported such annual events as the "Heart drive" and the "Cancer drive," by printing both news stories and editorials. But when the county blood bank reported that there was a critical shortage of blood designated for use in the Snoqualmie Valley, the situation was different. In this case there was no big national organization to launch a drive and meet the emergency. No big-city dailies would print appeals to their readers to give blood for the Snoqual-mie Valley. The Valley's one service organization, a Kiwanis club, stood ready to sponsor a drive for blood, but there was only one way they could reach the people they had to appeal to, and that was through us. This was our first chance to perform an important public service. We decided to throw the entire weight of the *Valley Record* into a campaign for blood.

Ed conferred with Kiwanians, and worked out ways and means. Each week, a coupon was printed on page one of the *Record* and those willing to give blood were urged to fill it out and mail it to the *Record* office. We did this "urging" with the longest stories and the biggest headlines the front page would hold, and we repeated it every week until Blood Donor Day. Coupons were returned in every mail, and when the blood bank nurses arrived at the doctor's office where they were to set up shop, they found donors waiting at the doorstep. Housewives, loggers, teachers, merchants, came at the rate of twelve donors an hour.

Ed was one of the local businessmen who left his shop long

enough to give a pint of blood. When he got back, Superman was waiting for him.

"Just wanted to tell you, I'm quitting," he said laconically. "But I never walk out on anybody. I'll finish out the week."

It was Wednesday. . . .

"But I thought you liked the shop," Ed objected.

"I do. I don't have nothing against you *or* the shop."

"Then, why . . ."

"We don't want to live here. We like sports, and there's nothing here you can do."

Ed looked at him dumbly, not at all sure he had heard right. But the man was serious. "People come from hundreds of miles around for the sports we've got here!" Ed protested. "Two of the best ski areas in the state are only eighteen miles away. Lake fishing, stream fishing, right in your own backyard, and in less than an hour you can get to salt-water fishing. We've got a beautiful eighteen-hole golf course. The hunting is terrific—they took 575 deer out of that woods right over there in only two days' time. There's so much horseback riding we've got three riding clubs in this one valley. Hiking—why, there are beautiful mountain trails all around us. There's an archery club, if you like that. We've got an indoor swimming pool, free for anyone who wants to use it. Basketball, baseball—we've got leagues organized for all ages from grade school up through businessmen. Sports? Sports! Where could you find more sports?"

Superman shook his head. "You don't have no bowling alley."

For a few hours we had been glowing over the success of the blood donor drive. At Superman's announcement the glow faded, leaving us cold with a sense of failure.

"No printer!" I exclaimed. "*Now* what will we do?"

Ed shook his head. "I wish he'd told me before I gave that pint of blood," he said dryly. "I feel like going over there and getting it back."

It was the first time we had been too gloomy to talk. Ed

leaned on the desk and stared out the window, as if a sober, reliable, experienced printer were due in on the 8:45 bus. I kept looking at my watch, trying to remember what it was I was going to do at eight o'clock. It came to me, and I broke the silence. "The blood bank is about to close. I'm going to go over and talk to the doctors and nurses, and get material for this week's story." Ed nodded silently and I left, trailing clouds of despair.

When I walked into the doctor's office I was the picture of a professional mourner who has filled up one tear vial and is having trouble holding up production until she can find another. One of the local women who had been assisting bounced across the reception room. "Look, here's another one!" she cried joyfully. "Maybe we can break a hundred, after all."

"I came to get facts for a news story about the drive. . . ."

"Carol! Martha!" she sang out. "Look, come here, here's another." She grabbed my arm and began pulling me toward the doctor's office. "Oh, I almost forgot." She stopped. "How long ago did you eat?"

At that my face must have become more doleful than ever, because I hadn't eaten since noon and she had just given me something more to be unhappy about. "I had lunch about twelve o'clock. . . ."

"Wonderful!" She looked curiously at the notebook and pencil I was clutching against my empty and growling stomach. "What's *that* for?"

"Do you wish to give blood?" This was a nurse, in white uniform.

I was suddenly ashamed. For weeks I had been telling everyone to give blood and yet I had never thought to sign up myself. But it wasn't too late. "Yes, I certainly do." Instantly I felt better. I was so elated by this chance to make good that I forgot all about Superman.

The nurse looked doubtful, and when the doctor took my pulse he looked even more so. "I don't know," he said. "You seem to be awfully tired. . . ." Then came the routine question, "Past illnesses?" and that did it, for I had had rheumatic fever as a child. The doctor shook his head. "No, I don't think so. . . ." Then he smiled. "I know how hard you two are working. I didn't turn your husband down, but I'm afraid if I took one more pint of blood from the Groshells we wouldn't get our paper this week."

The nurse led me back to the reception room. The sense of failure I had brought from the print shop returned full force, and to it was added an unreasonable feeling that by not giving blood I had failed again. Mechanically I asked questions, and got the facts I had come for. Ninety-five pints of blood in one afternoon. Nine rejections. A wonderful turnout, the drive was a tremendous success. . . . It would have been cheering news to anyone less determined to be unhappy.

I expected that when I got back to the shop Ed and I could enjoy our misery together. Ed was right where I'd left him. Leaning on the counter, staring out of the window. But his expression was very disappointing. He looked happy.

"I've been thinking," he burst out the moment I came in. "Remember this?"

He held up a sheet of paper. There were penciled scribblings on it, lines, squares, a few arrows. It was the rough plan for an addition onto the print shop which he had drawn the afternoon I received a writing check for $21.38.

"I thought you had thrown that thing away."

"It's a design for adding onto the building."

I nodded wearily. "Yes, I know. That's the 'new wing' you were going to build for $21.38."

"Huh!" With that he dismissed me and looked back at his plan. "The bottleneck in our production is that newspaper press," he said. "Since it prints only two pages at a time, it costs us twice as many man-hours to get the paper out as we would have to spend if we had a four-page press. But this little old building wouldn't hold a four-page press. Therefore, we've got to add onto the building."

I said glumly, "Impossible."

Ed looked up. "Why?"

"We haven't got any money."

"We'll figure something out."

I shook my head. "Anyway, we have more immediate problems than a building we can't afford for a press we can't afford either."

Ed was so lost in his new plan he actually looked surprised. "What problems?"

"Our printer is leaving. We haven't got anyone to replace him."

Ed shrugged. "Oh, something will work out. . . ."

"No, it won't, it's impossible. . . ."

Ed looked at me narrowly. "That's the second time you've said that," he said, and he took a good look at my face. "Say, you're feeling low, aren't you? Let's go get something to eat."

"But can't you *see* it's impossible!" I wailed. "As if we didn't have enough trouble and then . . ."

Ed took me by the arm. "Let's not talk about it until tomorrow."

"How can you talk about adding onto the building when we don't know how to meet the payroll? How can you . . ."

Ed had me out the front door. "Tomorrow," he said gently, "it will all look different tomorrow." He opened the car door and pushed me in. "We're going to get a good hot meal. After all, you shouldn't have to cry on an empty stomach. . . ."

In the morning it was a different world, indeed. A frantic world, since it was Thursday and we were fighting the weekly battle to get the papers into those post boxes by 4:30 in the afternoon. But a world not as bereft of hope as it had appeared the night before. When the last *Record* had been delivered, and the Linotype operator and the bookkeeper and the apprentice and, yes, even Superman, had said, "Good night," Ed took my hand. "Now," he said, "let's sit down and talk."

We'll expand! That was the program Ed wanted to launch now that we were short of printers, equipment, prospects and

cash. Like Marshal Foch at the Battle of the Marne, Ed figured that since our center was giving way and our right was
pushed back, there was nothing to do but attack. First, we'd
buy still more new equipment. Second, we'd knock the back
wall out of the print shop and build an addition of equal size,
so that our floor space would be doubled. Third, we'd buy a
big, four-page newspaper press.

He admitted gracefully that financing could be a problem.
We owned nothing we could borrow on. We lived in a rented
house—no collateral there. Nor could we take out a loan
against the shop—our contract with the former owner for-
bade it until we had paid him every penny of the $30,000.

"Of course, we could borrow on your stock," Ed said ten-
tatively. "We did it once last fall, we might do it again. Borrowing on it isn't like giving it up."

Hadn't we promised, before we went into business for ourselves, that we'd throw everything into it in order to succeed?
The stock was for the children, but the business was, too. I
would be penny-wise indeed; in fact I would be cheating my
children, not protecting them, if I clung stubbornly to a
handful of stock certificates and let a $30,000 property go
down for the third time. My heart was in my throat but I said
quickly, "We need more cash than we can raise by borrowing
on my securities. We'll sell them."

Ed looked at me quizzically. "Sure?"

"I'm sure."

"Then," he said with a deep sigh, "we don't have any problems at all."

"Just that same old problem."

Ed grinned. "Yes, I know. Where are we going to find a
printer? That will work out, too."

As if by prearrangement, a stranger crossed the street,
peered at the sign over the door, FALLS PRINTING COMPANY,
and walked in. His suit was a twin to Mr. DeMarco's, the coat
being dark blue and the trousers brown. But his hat wasn't

straw, it was a gray felt and looked like the door prize at the Salvation Army. On his feet were a pair of tennis shoes.

"You the owner?" he asked. His voice had a crack in it.

"Yes, sir," said Ed. "What can I do for you?"

The man put one elbow on the counter, leaned on it, and looked moodily through the windows. "That's the way it usually is. Town like this always has a little print shop, maybe a newspaper, tucked away on some side street. Never find 'em on the main street. I was coming through from east of the mountains. The fellow that gave me a ride said, 'I'm going to Snoqualmie. Where you headed?' I told him, 'I never been there but Snoqualmie's as good as any. You can let me off there.' I knew there'd be a print shop." He turned to Ed. "You got any work?"

He said his name was Anton Toski, and it wouldn't have fitted him better if it had been his own. In five minutes Ed had hired him. "O.K., Mr. Toski, eight o'clock in the morning." Our new printer tipped the old felt hat, grinned toothlessly, and went out the door.

Ed wheeled toward me. "See? I told you everything would work out all right. He's reliable. He didn't even ask for an advance."

"Ha! When he hasn't even worked? He doesn't look good to me."

Ed said stiffly, "He's not as drunk as Mr. DeMarco."

"No," I retorted, "nor as sober as Superman."

Mr. Toski appeared promptly at eight o'clock in the morning, which Ed took as such a good omen that he immediately telephoned a builder and asked when he could start work on an addition to the shop.

The "wing" we built wasn't really a wing at all, but a 30 x 48 addition directly behind the old frame building. It was made of fireproof cement blocks, with steel reinforced-concrete floors and lots of aluminum-framed factory windows, and was larger than the aged parent building to which it was

75

attached. We knocked out as much of the back wall of the old plant as we dared, and *voilà,* one big *Record* office, brand-new at one end, thirty-three years old at the other. An angle-worm is also made up of two parts but he can't claim to represent two different generations.

The little potbellied stove was replaced by a modern furnace, and at this point one of our readers set up a wail. "What have you done with that darling little stove? With all the changes you're making, it won't look like a country shop any more."

I mumbled something about making it a better place to work, but she continued to shake her head. "I liked it the way it was," she said. "It was so quaint."

That lady's kitchen, her "workshop" as the printing office was ours, contained such "quaint" items as an electric range, an electric refrigerator and an automatic coffeepot.

The new fireproof addition to the shop was completed in May. The question then was to locate the type of press it had been built to house. We heard of one in a community some thirty-five miles away. The owner might sell it or he might not. So on a lovely spring afternoon, the kind that lightens the heart and softens the head, we drove over to talk him into it.

We were in our eighth month as country publishers, but thirty minutes after we'd arrived in a shop whose owner had been in the business for fifteen years we were pointing to his $3,000 press and saying, Wrap it up, we'll take it. We had no difficulty talking him into selling it, but we guessed we'd have considerable trouble talking him into giving it away.

"Consider it sold," Ed said grandly. He turned to me. "Honey, you write a check while I telephone the Castagnos and see if they can move the press to Snoqualmie first thing in the morning."

I tried to make the look I threw him a two-sided affair. To the owner of the press it was supposed to say, "I write checks for $3,000 every day and twice on Fridays," and to my husband it had to mean, "Are you nuts?" We had been expanding, all right, just as Ed had planned. We had new equipment, a new building, but the last of the money we had raised by selling my stock would do little more than cover the week's payroll. Luckily we had gasoline credit cards, for between my purse and Ed's wallet we couldn't have bought enough gas to drive back to Snoqualmie.

With more desperation than skill, I managed to draw Ed aside. "I've said a dozen times that we could turn to my father if we had to. Don't you think this is the time?"

Ed nodded. "I've tried to work out some other way, and I can't. If I could borrow from the bank . . ."

"On what?"

Ed frowned. "That's just it. The car, maybe."

"Ha!" It was an economy model Chevrolet, almost a year old. It had cost only half as much as the press when we bought it new.

"Or on the print shop . . ."

I shook my head. "You know what the contract says."

"I don't suppose your publisher is about to send you a million dollars for your novel?"

"Remember that advance last October? Remember, I wrote and asked for another $500 on account, and we used that up when we had that big shipment of newsprint in February? I won't get any royalties for five months."

"Will you call your father?" Ed asked dolefully. "Tell him we'll repay him just as fast as we can."

My father left New England in 1914 and has been an attorney in the state of Washington ever since. I telephoned his office in Seattle. "Hello, Daddy?"

"Charlotte? You in Seattle?"

"Well, no. We're in a print shop in White Center. We just found the newspaper press we need."

"The what?"

"Newspaper press. You know, to print the *Valley Record* on."

"Oh. Thought you had one. How are the children?"

"They're fine. Say, Daddy, I don't suppose you could lend us $3,000?"

Slight pause. "For the press?"

"Yes. It's just what we need. But we're broke."

"I can get the money for you. Come out to the house and we'll talk it over."

"We have to rush back to the shop."

A professional tone crept into his voice. "Have you drawn up the proper papers?"

"Do we need any?"

"Good night . . ." Pause. "Now, look, when did you first see this piece of equipment?"

"About an hour ago."

"When do you plan to have it shipped to Snoqualmie?"

"Eight o'clock tomorrow morning."

Very long pause. Then, "Just one more question. When do you want me to send you this check for, uh, $3,000?"

"Can you get it in this afternoon's mail? We've got to pay for the press right now and we've only got fifty dollars in our account."

My father dictated the sales contract over the telephone, and sent the check, but the incident left a mark on him. His telephone calls had always opened, "Hello, there, how are the boys?" but now they began, "Hello, there, how's that press of ours?"

The press weighed ten tons, and that, plus her size, made moving day a memorable event not only for us but also for our local transfer company. The company is a family affair, owned by Rem Castagno, his three sons, and his brother Frank; the rest of the staff is made up of all their wives. The Castagnos are not big men but they were all apparently born with sixteen-inch biceps. When it comes to moving printing presses, it doesn't matter how big the door is, the press is always a little bit bigger. Before the Castagnos could slide the black giant onto their big flatbed truck, they had to knock the wall out of the shop where she stood. But Ed had been foresighted and our new building had a back door big enough to admit an aircraft carrier. With ease the Castagnos transferred our new press from the back of their truck to the floor of the shop. I would as lief lead a blind elephant down the basement stairs as try the job they accomplished so smoothly.

The first Thursday we printed the *Record* on our big new press she went into action with a roar. She is, one repairman later assured us feelingly, the noisiest press of her kind he had ever run into in twenty-five years in the business. Wham, squeak, kerthump, pow—Ed and I had to shout at each other over the terrible din but we had never been happier in our lives. The sound is as comforting now as it ever was; it means she is running. The only time the noise bothers us is when it stops.

No subscriber was more interested in the big press than a man named Bill. Bill is a logger. He subscribed to the *Record* the week he discovered that buying it at a newsstand cost him ten cents a copy but a year's subscription came to only five cents a copy. He had never bought it at the newsstand, either, but he knew a bargain when he saw one; so one Saturday afternoon he came into the newspaper office and slapped his three dollars down on the counter.

The next week we got the big press, and the week after that, we got subscriber Bill. "I paid in my three dollars," he explained, "and right after that the editor went out and got hisself a big new press. I figure it was me bought the press, so can I go back and watch it run?"

Bill was working nights at the time, and supposedly slept days, but some alarm system deep within him seemed to be hooked up with the newspaper press because it never got rolling but that Bill showed up at the door. Once he fell into a barrel of scrap paper but he managed to stay out of the machinery and so week after week we let him into the backshop so he could see "his press" at work.

The great gallumphing racket of it tickled his ribs. He

laughed and laughed, doubling way over and slapping his arms across his chest. "Ain't that wonderful?" he kept exclaiming, laughing till he cried. "Ain't that press of ours plain wonderful?" And when Ed, whom he called "Mr. Editor," passed near enough, Bill would reach out and slap him lovingly on the back.

"Now we got that press," he said, giving Ed's back a tap that nearly sent him to the floor, "I know what we ain't going to have no more of. No more of them there mechanical difficulties."

4.

It was a peaceful, sunny day, our first Friday as owners of a weekly newspaper. "The day after paper day," as our two sons quickly learned to identify it, and we were tasting for the first time that wonderful Friday feeling. On Fridays the country publisher is so relieved that for just one day his eternal optimism rises above his eternal fatigue. The sensation is senseless but strong, something like that of the 195 survivors of the Charge of the Light Brigade, who were undoubtedly so amazed at coming back alive that if the general had said, "Well, chaps, let's try that Balaklava routine again this week," they would have agreed affably.

Our first Friday was the day we first came face to face with one of our subscribers. He convinced us that life in the country would be all peace, quiet and neighborliness—and two months later proved that for real peace and quiet we should have picked Cicero during a gang war.

We had driven into Seattle to buy paper supplies, and it was well after five when we returned to the shop in Snoqualmie. I raced across the street to the grocery, Ed began unloading the car. He was standing at the door trying to balance several reams of paper in one hand and get the key into the lock with the other, when a kindly voice said, "Here, let me help you. You got too much of a load there."

Over the top ream Ed peered at a slight, gray-haired man whose blue eyes blinked cheerily from behind a pair of rimless spectacles. The man was fifty to sixty years old and was dressed in worn work clothes and a leather jacket. "You're the new editor," he said. "Say, that was a real good paper you put out yesterday. I read everything in it. I always do. I been a subscriber to the *Record* for a long time. I'll hold them things while you open the door."

I came back from the grocery to find that Ed and the gentle, smiling little man had unloaded the car and were talking, hands in pockets, like farmers on a street corner Saturday afternoon. The country editor and the faithful subscriber—they fitted perfectly into the peaceful scene. The dogs were asleep in the street, the sparrows were settling themselves in their nests under the roof, and down the block a group of eight or ten children playing Run, Sheep, Run, froze at the shrill call, "Jim-mee! I told you, come in and wash up for dinner. . . ." I sighed contentedly. Thank God for peace, I thought to myself, thank God for old-fashioned neighborliness, and thank God for a place like this in which to bring up our children.

"I want you to meet this man," Ed said as I approached, and I could see he was feeling as sentimental as I. There were introductions, thanks, hand-shakes. Ed and I were dewy-eyed with the conviction that we were the luckiest two people in the world.

As the little man turned to go, I said, "Tell me your name again. I don't want to forget it."

He smiled shyly. "Walter Peden," he said, and hands in pockets, strolled across the street. At the corner, he turned and waved.

Walter Peden is dead now, but it is certain that neither Ed nor I will ever forget him. He lived in a little house in the woods some five miles from town, in a settlement called Ernie's Grove. He kept some chickens, a dog and a cat. His only income was from the sale of eggs and perhaps from a small pension, yet he fed his animals well and the reason for his second appearance at the *Record* office was that he knew he would soon "owe for the paper" and he insisted on paying rather than waiting for a bill. His affection was strengthened by the fact that he, too, had "worked on the paper"; the former publisher had once hired him to stack stove wood in the back yard. To him, Ed was always "Mr. Editor." To Ed, he was "that nice, friendly little man, the one who helped me."

One day early in December Walter Peden came into the office and said he had to talk to "Mr. Editor." His problem, it developed, was that his cat had kittens. There were four of them. He couldn't afford to feed them all but he didn't have the heart to get rid of them.

"You could chloroform them," said Ed, the practical man.

Walter Peden winced. "That's killing them. I couldn't do it."

"Or take them to Seattle, to the humane society."

His eyes narrowed. "They *say* they find homes for them. *I* don't believe it. They'd kill them, for sure." His voice cracked. "They'd kill them," he repeated shakily, "those cute kittens . . ."

"Well, but after all . . ." Editing a paper had never called for so much in Chicago. Ed was wondering if he was expected to pull out a handkerchief and dry the little man's eyes when

Walter Peden suddenly pulled himself together and said cheerily, "I want to buy a want ad."

"Want ad?"

"About the kittens. Put it in like this: 'Wanted, a good home for four nice little kittens.' And then put down my name, and my address. They'll have to write to me, I don't have no phone."

Ed wrote the advertisement on a classified-ad blank. Peden checked it carefully, finally nodded his approval. He took a dollar bill from his pocket and when Ed handed him the change, he said, "Now I got $4.58 left, to live on for the rest of the month."

The rest of the month—but it was only December 6! Ed protested, "Here now, you can pay me another time. If I had known . . . Here . . ." and he tried to return the dollar bill.

Peden waved it aside. "I been worried about those kittens," he said brightly, almost gaily, "and now you took a load off my mind. I won't let you put an ad in the paper if you don't let me pay for it." And Ed couldn't change his mind.

That classified ad appeared in the *Record* that week, and the next week was included in news dispatches wired all over the country by the United Press. Perhaps, sometime between Thursday afternoon and the following Monday morning, someone replied. Perhaps not. In any case, on Monday morning the four kittens were still in their box in Walter Peden's shack in Ernie's Grove, and no doubt the little man started the day by feeding them, and his pet dog, and his two or three dozen chickens. Since it was Monday, Ed and I were in the shop in Snoqualmie, already mired in the problems of getting out another edition on Thursday.

We'll never know who it was—the effect of the announcement was so strong we can't remember whether he was blond or dark, lean or fat—but about eleven o'clock the front door of the shop burst open and a man demanded, "One of you guys going out to Ernie's Grove and watch the shooting?"

"The shooting?" Ed repeated, as if after fourteen years on a Chicago tabloid he'd never heard the word.

"Shooting?" our associate editor inquired politely, looking up from the story she was writing about a church rummage sale.

"I just seen another patrol car go past. Boy, half the cops in the state must be out there. One of them ought to catch up with him."

"Who has been shot?"

"*Who? Who?* Four different people, that's all. Four. They got them all at the hospital."

"But who did it?"

"Walter Peden . . ."

Ed turned to me. "Not our subscriber," he said. "Not that nice, friendly little man."

"Well, ain't you going out to see it? Write about it for the *Record?*" the man demanded impatiently.

"Are you going out there?" Ed asked.

"Who, *me,* with old Walt shooting from one side and ten million cops shooting back from the other? I'm not nuts," and our informant took his departure with a gay, "S'long . . ."

Ed and I looked at each other. Shootings are routine in Chicago, and the photographers and reporters and rewrite men and copy readers and editors who handle them almost daily have no more sympathy for the people who get shot than they have for the people who shoot them. Walter Peden's insane shooting spree was just the kind of story that makes a big city editor rub his hands together with glee, a "real good story," the kind that sells papers. What a difference now! We had been in the Valley only three months, but we already knew in our hearts that to a small-town editor, no "real good story" can ever be routine. We knew the killer, and newcomers that we were, when we learned the names of the men he shot, we found we knew them, too. (Gunman and victims, they were all subscribers!) We had lost our objectivity. To us this wasn't a "real good story," it was a tragedy.

There was another difference: Metropolitan city rooms contain thirty to a hundred telephones, our "city room" in Snoqualmie had one. We kept it hot that day. We called the local office of the state patrol, and the town marshal, and the hospital, and those residents of Ernie's Grove who had telephones and were in any condition to answer them. With each new development we made a series of long distance calls to the Seattle papers and the United Press. Not for remuneration—all we got out of it were some hearty thanks and an even heartier telephone bill. But Ed was still a newspaperman with an unalterable compulsion to rush a page-one story onto page one, even someone else's page one. And this being Monday, our paper wouldn't come out for three days. So we worked our fool heads off to give our story to everyone else. We didn't leave the hot, sticky telephone all day Monday, and slowly the story of mild little Walter Peden took shape.

There were only fifteen dwellings in Ernie's Grove then, but at ten o'clock Monday morning, when Walter Peden stepped out onto his front porch with a single-shot .22 rifle in his hands, several of his neighbors were on hand to see him. There was Leah Fitzgerald, standing at the window of her house watching her husband, George, go to their car for a quick trip to town. There was George Fitzgerald, who drove the car a few yards down the road so as to pick up a neighbor, C. F. Johnston; he was sitting in the car when Peden came out onto the porch. And there was Johnston, who had asked for a ride to town.

Mrs. Fitzgerald knew about "Old Walt's" gun. He had found it in a garbage dump, polished and repaired it, and she had given him cartridges for it so he could shoot crows and squirrels. Like most of his neighbors, she considered the little man "queer but harmless." She was still musing at the window when Peden raised the gun to his shoulder, aimed at her husband, and fired.

The car window next to George Fitzgerald exploded into

bits. Losing her head, Mrs. Fitzgerald ran out of the house toward the car.

"Stay where you are!" her husband shouted. "He shot me in the arm. The old guy is nuts and he'll shoot you, too!"

While she stood in the road, too bewildered to obey, neighbor Johnston came out of his house and headed for the car. George Fitzgerald called a warning, but it was too late. Peden fired again, and Johnston dropped, his face covered with blood.

Peden slipped another bullet into the .22. Paralyzed by panic, Mrs. Fitzgerald knew she was next. But just then a dog walked onto the scene. It was Peden's own dog, a nondescript, friendly hound with big eyes.

"There you are, you damn Democrat!" Peden yelled suddenly. The dog turned toward his master, and wagged his tail. Peden aimed, fired. Mrs. Fitzgerald saw the dog drop, and then her bewilderment ended, and she ran for the house.

That was the beginning, but before he was captured three hours later, this "harmless little man" with the .22 from the garbage dump had shot four men, one of whom, state patrolman Paul Johnson, died that night. The final insane touch was that he also shot his chickens and another dog. For he was insane, of course. "A little bit nuts, but he wouldn't hurt anybody" was the way people had described him before the tragic day, though afterward the same people said, "Everyone knew he was crazy. That's why he had to leave Oregon. He was declared insane down there so he moved up here to keep from being locked up. . . ."

"Strange no one realized he might be dangerous," Ed reflected in discussing Walter Peden with one of the local residents of Snoqualmie. "But if he'd never done anything, no one could have guessed. . . ."

The man laughed. "He'd been carrying that rifle around under his shirt for two weeks—everyone knew that. Couple years ago, when he was living over there in that boarding house across the tracks, one of the other boarders woke up in the middle of the night with Old Walt's hands on his throat trying to choke him to death. Everybody knew about that, or a lot of people did. He'd been in the nut house down in Roseburg. If a guy's dangerous in Oregon, how come he's O.K. to be loose in Washington?"

"Why didn't you report all this?"

The man shrugged. "I don't go messing around in other people's affairs. I got troubles enough of my own."

"Incapable of comprehending the peril he would face by trial or of assisting in the preparation of his own defense"— that was the judgment of three psychiatrists and two police officers, and Walter Peden was committed to the state hospital for the insane at Steilacoom. But he never forgot the "local paper" or Mr. Editor. He became our first subscriber in an insane asylum, though not our last.

However dark and twisted his other thoughts, on the subject of his *Record* subscription he was lucid until the day he died. Our first letter from him, written in the asylum at Steilacoom, said he was sure his "paper was about up"; a dollar bill was enclosed and his letter explained that was all he had but he'd send the rest soon and "please don't stop my paper." Later he wrote us from Medical Lake, which, like Steilacoom, lies north of King County in which our Snoqualmie Valley lies. "Dear Mr. Editor," a typical letter said, "I find you sent me the wrong statement. The one I got was for three dollars and your paper says $3.50 outside of King County. The lady that was tending my chickens wrote me that everything of value had been taken from my place. I have no way of knowing what was taken. There was a new sixty-four dollar Gruen watch, a violin that was probably one-hundred years old, a new waffle iron, radio, and several things I valued as keepsakes. I had lots of clothes, and my laundry mark 1175 I have had for twenty years. I have been well and hope you folks are the same. . . ."

During the examinations before he was committed, Walter

Peden had said several times that he "got sick in 1931," and that date, the point at which he felt himself sink into the terrors and bemusement of insanity, apparently remained with him, the one image that kept repeating itself in his nightmare. For his letters, carefully penciled on lined writing paper, were always carefully dated. The month changed, the day changed, but the year was always the same—1931.

I've said that shootings were routine in the city room in Chicago, but Walter Peden's brief reign of terror in a valley 2,200 miles away jarred a dozen Chicago newspapermen out of their apathy and brought us three letters and a telegram. The United Press dispatch had quoted "Publisher Ed Groshell of the *Snoqualmie Valley Record*" and included Ed's reference to the classified ad he had written for Peden. Two or three of Ed's old friends at the *Chicago Sun-Times* were leaning on a UP teletype machine Monday afternoon when the story came in. When Ed's name was ticked off they let out a simultaneous whoop and in a matter of minutes the copy was being set in the composing room. The next morning Ed got a telegram from one of them: "MY WIFE WANTS ONE OF PEDEN'S KITTENS. . . ." There was more irony to the request than that Chicago newspaperman knew. More than we knew ourselves, until a day or two later, when we discovered that when gentle little Walt took up his .22 that Monday morning, the first of his victims were those four little kittens he had been so worried about.

ii

"No point in lining up a correspondent out in the Snoqualmie Valley," Ed had replied to the United Press representative the day he was asked to work for the wire service on a "string" basis. "That's country out there. Woods and farms and little towns of a few hundred population. Nothing'll ever come up worth phoning you about. . . ."

Our second week on the job a girl married her brother

(adopted, of course) and the happy couple settled down with their mutual mother-in-law. Not long after, two men were apprehended carrying cartons of cigarettes out of a local store; they explained they had to do it because they were broke and their little kids were hungry. When we took over the *Record* a dozen other interesting events, or arson or murder, for that matter, may have been bubbling hotly under the peaceful surface, but we had yet to meet Walter Peden and still clung innocently to our conviction that nothing ever happens in the country.

"If I only had one good story," Ed moaned that first Thursday morning. "Something with a twist, something for page one. . . ." Only minutes thereafter, a woman walked in and announced she had seen a flying saucer.

Flying saucers were not being scoffed at in October of 1949. Ed was pleased at having a feature story for page one and assumed that our readers would be even more pleased at seeing it there. He was not prepared for what happened.

The woman who reported seeing the flying saucer was a redhead, and when she stormed into the *Record* office the next morning she was a mad redhead. That story made her look ridiculous, she told Ed, and she didn't like it and she wasn't at all sure she liked him, and she didn't mind taking fifteen minutes of his time to tell him why.

"I'm sorry," Ed finally managed to say. "But I hope you will continue to read the paper. . . ."

"Are you telling me I should cancel my subscription?" she blazed. "I've been taking this blamed sheet for twelve years and I'm not going to quit now," and she departed, slamming the door behind her.

There was a sharp snap like the ping of a bullet. A long crack appeared across the upper pane of glass. Ed and I stared at it thoughtfully. I was thinking—how often do country publishers have to patch up the door to the customer entrance?

Ed said mildly, "She didn't like the story."

I shook my head. "Our first complaint."

Ed frowned at me. "I don't like the sound of that. You don't suppose this, uh, this type of conversation is the usual thing? I mean, if one of our readers doesn't like this story or that story, she, or he, simply stamps in here and lets the publisher have it between the eyes?"

"The publisher . . ." Colonel McCormick, and William Randolph Hearst and John S. Knight. Publishers, as we had known them, are swept from their limousines into private elevators and up to luxurious suites which 95 percent of their employees, and 100 percent of their subscribers, never even see. They are dignified and inaccessible, and since the two qualities are inseparable, they have armies of secretaries and receptionists to see to it that they stay that way. Publisher Ed's only protection from *his* readers, it appeared, was the counter in the front office and whatever speed and agility he might develop.

"Publisher," he muttered, staring moodily at the spot where the redhead had been. "She came in and told me about seeing the flying saucer. She brought the story in herself."

"She didn't object to your using the story. It was the way you wrote it."

"Where did she study journalism? How many newspaper stories has she written?"

"She's a subscriber," I said brightly.

"You mean everyone who pays three dollars a year automatically knows how to run this newspaper?"

I grinned. "Look, darling," I said as soothingly as I could, "I'm a stranger here myself. . . ."

At the end of our second week, we had our second visitation. It had been an eighty-hour week, too, with the monotony of long hours broken only by a scene or two with our honey-tongued printer, Mr. Jenkins, and two or three mechanical breakdowns. A man we had never seen strode into the office waving the previous day's edition of the *Record* and demanding to see "the new editor."

Ed owned up, rather reluctantly, I thought, from my safer position behind the roll-top desk. In tones that made the walls bulge the man announced that the club he belonged to was just as important as any club in the whole Valley and the sooner we woke up to that fact the better off we'd be.

Ed had been getting an average of four hours' sleep a night. The customer was always right—we had agreed on that—but Ed's face had the relaxed expression of the man who has just been pole-axed by his grandmother.

"Our club can do you a lot of good," the man continued, leaning across the counter. Instinctively Ed backed up. Just as instinctively, I came out of my hole and stood beside him. The man glared at us both. "*Or*," he said, lowering his voice in a threatening sort of way, "*or* we can do you a lot of harm."

Ed and I exchanged looks of purest stupefaction. "But we printed the article about your club," Ed finally choked out. "It was in the paper this week."

"Look!" the clubman shouted, opening up the *Record* and beating it soundly with the back of his hand. "It's on the back page! I wanted you to put it on the front page!"

At this point Ed seemed to be getting no co-operation from his vocal cords. I knew that my husband had a breaking point, and I began to suspect we were approaching it a good deal faster that I liked. So I began chattering about editorial judgment and favoritism, news values, etc., ending by quipping, I hoped good-naturedly, that of course it was late to change yesterday's paper.

This was supposed to be the humorous touch that would make friends of us all, but our subscriber would have none of it. "You ruined the story this week," he replied, baring his teeth, "but from now on, *you'll know what to do!*" With that he left. Just in time, because Ed was showing signs of coming to life. The circles under his eyes were taking on a purplish, quivery look.

"He didn't break a single pane of glass!" I caroled, with terrible cheeriness.

That man left the Valley shortly afterward, but he wasn't crazy, as I suggested hopefully that afternoon. Nor even unusual, for he was only the second of our readers who filed in those first months and either praised or denounced us. "You changed everything around. I liked it the way it was," and from someone else, "We just about stopped reading the paper, but now you've made so many changes, we're enjoying it again." "There wasn't enough North Bend news this week," would come hard on the heels of, "Why print so much North Bend news? Don't you think the other towns are just as important?" And on to the most baffling remark of all, "Since you took over, there's just too much news in the paper, a person doesn't have time to read it all. . . ."

Compliments were many and complaints few, but one word of criticism threw us into a fit of blues that twenty of praise couldn't pull us out of. The Indians hereabouts used to cure all ills by lying in a steam house until they could no longer stand the heat and then plunging naked into the icy waters of the Snoqualmie River. After a few months in business for ourselves Ed and I knew just how they must have felt; we'd made the same trip from hot to cold a hundred times. It was a treatment which killed as many Indians as it cured, a hopeful thought for our future.

Not that all our first experiences were shadowed by our first difficulties. Nothing could obliterate the new joy of living in the country and doing business in a small town. The people of the Valley would have been amazed to know how often delight settled too suddenly in big lumps in our throats, and more amazed still at how little it took to do it. Among the delightful "firsts" was our first church supper, when we realized the advantage of living in a heavily Scandinavian community. The ladies were obviously accustomed to feeding loggers and each plate contained the average daily nutritional requirements for a man eight feet tall.

There was our first meeting with a local minister. He was a man of the cloth, all right, but that day it happened to be a bright-red logger's shirt. A big pipe bobbed in his shirt pocket like a baby kangaroo in its mother's pouch, and the rest of his outfit consisted of an unclerical assembly of knee boots, work pants and disreputable felt hat. The pipe was soon between his teeth and he was leaning over the counter, legs crossed, hat on the back of his head.

I didn't realize it, but he was making a formal visit. As he left, Ed said, "It was nice of you to stop in at our place."

The minister grinned. "I have 'a place,' too. Why don't you return the compliment?" and with a friendly wave he was gone. The Snoqualmie Valley version of the ministerial call, praises be.

Then there was the day we were asked to keep a certain news item out of the paper.

A little woman with gray hair and a timid voice asked if the new owners were in.

"I am one of them," I said, introducing myself, "but my husband is here, too. I'll call him."

"No, no, please . . ." she said quickly. "I'll have to, that is, I'd prefer to, talk to you."

She spoke rapidly, as if she wanted to get it out before her courage was gone. No need to ask her whether she wanted to discuss something privately. But in a shop thirty by forty feet, housing six to eight men and women with good ears? We would have had more privacy at a Chicago policemen's ball.

I steered her around the corner and behind the big newspaper press.

"Two years ago," she began in a choked-up whisper, "my daughter got into some trouble . . ." and she told me, in all its tragic detail, of a local scandal in which her family had been involved. I was a stranger to her, and worse yet, a stranger from "Back East." Yet she confided in me, because she thought that if I knew the whole story she could ask me to strike out indirect references to it which might pop up in news items from time to time. I can't think of a better way to guarantee complete coverage, with pictures, of a family scandal in a big city than to tell the city editor all about it and ask him to keep it out of the paper. But others beside that little woman have put themselves in our hands and with equal confidence that we would rather protect than expose them.

When the veteran publisher advised us to "change nothing," he had emphasized that 1,800 subscribers indicated excellent readership and therefore people liked the paper just the way it was. We thought the paper could be improved. Most of our innovations brought new subscribers and compliments from the old ones. Some of them got us into trouble.

First, we began copying news items out of *Records* of ten, twenty and thirty years ago, and reprinting them as a kind of amusing backward glance into the past. The former publisher was still in town, and he advised strongly against it.

"I tried running that kind of feature when I was on a paper back in Nebraska," he said. "And then one week the 'Twenty Years Ago' column included an item about a wedding. I didn't know the couple had broken up, and there was a lot of talk, and the husband was still touchy about it. But I found out when the man came into the office and told me if he ever caught me alone outside he'd beat me to a pulp. I believed him. I never ran a 'years ago' item again."

Ed and I hastily issued orders that wedding stories were to be included only if it could be definitely established that bride and bridegroom were still happily married, and to each other. Some references have had to be rubbed out since, but so far no reader has come in to do the same for the editor.

Our second innovation was a "baby column." Birth announcements had been scattered all through the paper. We gathered them all together in a page-one column headed by a cut of a stork and entitled, The Tri-Corner. It was a popular feature, and we have continued it to this day. But once a typographical error brought the direst threat of all, "I'll cancel my subscription!"

Every press day was frantic. Sometimes the printer with his

eyes on the clock did a careless job and the proofreader did a worse one. One Thursday four lines of type from a news item on the other side of the page were inserted by mistake into a birth announcement in The Tri-Corner. The result read: "A bouncing baby boy was born April 11 to Mr. and Mrs. Covin Johnson, Mr. and Mrs. Alfred Dart, Mr. and Mrs. Lloyd Fitzhugh, and Mrs. and Mrs. Jerry Townsend, who were on their way to Seattle to attend a lodge meeting. He weighed eight pounds, two ounces, at birth, and reportedly looks just like Daddy. . . ."

I answered the telephone when the mother called. She tried to sound angry, but she had just managed to say, "I wish to cancel my subscription" when she began to cry. "I was going to take the clipping and put it in my baby's book," she sobbed. "Now I can't, it looks so silly."

"But you can still put it in the book. Just take a scissors and cut out those extra lines."

"It will *show!*" she wailed. "What will people think, when they see I had to cut something out?"

In the next week's *Record* we carried the birth announcement a second time, but without the extra parents, so that our subscriber would have a correct, whole clipping for her baby's book.

Illness is news in a small town, yet the *Record* had carried no list of patients entered and discharged from our little hospital on the hill. It's a beautiful hospital, with twenty-one beds, and nurses who really believe that keeping patients happy is part of their job. When we asked for a report every week, they agreed enthusiastically.

They made up the list, writing in parentheses "Boy" or "Girl" after the names of maternity cases. Before we began The Tri-Corner and interviewed the mothers in person, these little parenthetical notes were especially helpful. Relying on them, I wrote a birth announcement to the effect that Mrs. Jane Worthington had given birth to a baby girl. But "Mrs." Jane Worthington was an eleven-year-old girl, which was what the obliging nurse had tried to tell me when she made up the list, and the telephone call from her father that night was something I'll never forget.

"I've been trying to laugh about it," he said, "but I end up madder every time. I can take a ribbing, and I'm sure going to get one. But what about my little girl? How will she feel when she gets out of the hospital and goes back to school?"

"Mrs. Jane Worthington gave birth to a baby girl!" he exploded anew. "Good night, there *is* a Mrs. Jane Worthington, all right. She's my daughter's grandmother and she's seventy years old. And how do you think *that* sounds?"

He demanded a "retraction," which I agreed to write if he wanted me to, but when I pointed out that further reference to the mistake would only point it out to every reader who had missed it in the first place, he said simply, "Skip it," and that was all I could do, except apologize.

But the name of Jane Worthington was seared into my mind, and when the hospital list appeared some months later with the name "Mrs. Jane Worthington" on it, I knew instantly it was an error and it was one I wasn't going to fall into again. So I corrected it, stating that Jane Worthington, eleven-year-old daughter of the Walt Worthingtons, was in the hospital this week. . . .

This time it was her grandmother, hospitalized because of a heart attack.

iii

He was a young man and I knew instantly, a shy one. He opened the office door, hesitated, looked around the office, and obviously relieved to see no one but me, proceeded slowly to the counter.

"I wanted to put an ad in the paper." He looked at me hopefully. "But I don't know how to say it."

I realized he meant a classified ad—people in our Valley always do when they talk about "putting an ad" in the paper;

sometimes it's "want ad," but never "classified ad." Though we were then the greenest country publishers in the state and I probably hadn't composed as many advertisements as he had, I realized that "I don't know how to say it" was my cue to offer to write it for him. So I hastened to assure him, "Oh, don't let the wording worry you. I'll figure that out. You just tell me what it is you want to sell."

He looked a little uncomfortable. "Well, it isn't that I want to sell anything," he said. "What it is, I just got back from the service. I'm not married and I live with my sister and brother-in-law. What I like to do is dance. I don't know any girls around here so I thought I'd put something in the paper, asking for a dancing partner."

I was to compose an advertisement for young girls. He looked like a clean-cut type but I felt uneasy nevertheless. "I, well . . . Look here, wouldn't it be better to get out and meet some girls, and choose a dancing partner yourself? You don't know who might answer your ad."

"It don't seem like there's any place *to* meet girls."

"Through your sister and brother-in-law? Surely, among their friends . . ."

"That's just it," the young man said mournfully. "Their friends are married. All they talk about is their new television set, or their new baby, or how to pay for them."

The young man sounded intelligent. I had to suppress a sympathetic grin, and at that moment the dangerous desire to play Miss Lonelyhearts was born. "Oh, I see . . ." I reached for a classified-ad blank and a pencil. "How about this?"

> "WANTED: *Respectable young man, just out of the service, would like to get in touch with a girl who enjoys dancing. . . .*"

He read it slowly, out loud, and I was rewarded by a great big smile of relief. "Gee, that's swell!" he said. "I couldn't figure out how to say it."

"Now, there's one more thing," I said, every bit the helpful auntie. "Your name and address, if you want them to answer by letter. Or your telephone number, so they can call you."

"I wouldn't want to put my name on it," he said quickly. "I'm new here—it wouldn't mean anything, anyway. I was planning, well, to put the *Valley Record* phone number on it, and you take the calls."

Flushed as I was with the desire to comfort and counsel, I could not ignore the red light that suddenly began flashing off and on at the back of my mind. Nice as this young man looked, strong as my instinct was to pat him on the top of his head, I didn't like the idea of screening young girls for him. "No . . . o . . . o . . ." I said, "we have an editorial policy (well, we did, after that) against taking telephone calls of that kind. Isn't there some other telephone number you can include in the ad?"

"My sister and brother-in-law have a phone," he said doubtfully. "8732. . . ."

"Good . . ." and before more complications arose, I hastily wrote that down. He should have informed me that he wasn't going to tell anyone, even his sister and brother-in-law, about placing the ad.

The replies didn't come to our office, so I have no way of knowing whether the young man got the results he expected. I am here to say, however, that there were results for Ed and me which we didn't expect at all.

The "dancing partner" ad attracted a lot of attention. It was a little island of excitement in a full page of pigs for sale and baby sitters wanted. Everyone wanted to know who had placed it. Some telephoned the *Record* office. "Sorry, I cannot give out that sort of information. . . ." I said again and again, feeling sillier every time. The more resourceful picked up the little local telephone book and ran a finger down the columns of telephone numbers until they came to 8732. It isn't really a chore, in a small town.

The brother-in-law! A married man, and he has such a cute

wife and they always seemed to get along together. . . . The young man was new to the community, all right, but the brother-in-law wasn't. He had lived here for years and had a lot of friends. They all wondered why he was advertising for a dancing partner and they didn't mind asking him. He was mad enough to break the editor in two and throw the pieces over Mount Si, and when he turned up at the *Record* office he looked big enough to do it.

I went to the backshop to find Ed. "*You* talk to him," I whispered. "You explain how it happened."

"Oh, no," Ed said feelingly. He was holding onto the edge of the big newspaper press as if he thought I would try to tear him loose and drag him up front. "You're in charge of dancing partners. You composed the ad, you were the one that was all sympathy. Go on, now, do your job. I hereby appoint you Editor In Charge of Dancing Partners."

"Coward," I hissed. "How can you be so heartless?"

"He's not so likely to hit a woman," Ed assured me.

I made a face and went back to the front office. Ed's prediction was correct. The unfortunate brother-in-law looked as if he wanted to slug someone but he held himself down to a few words, selected at random from what I guessed to be a pretty full vocabulary. Then he left. I thought that was the end of it.

It was, as far as the *Record* was concerned. But I heard indirectly that it went on for some time at No. 8732. If the brother-in-law was angry because everyone thought he had advertised for a dancing partner, his wife was even angrier; she thought he had, too.

iv

Friday was sometimes a bad day, simply because it came after Thursday. This one promised to set a record.

The night before we had received an unusual number of "Thursday calls"—telephone calls from readers who found something they didn't like and couldn't wait until we had had a good night's sleep to tell us about it.

The last of these had come at midnight. I stumbled through the house, murmured a dazed "Hello?"

A man's voice, against the soothing obligato of a juke box, demanded that we do his printing order all over again.

"Didn't we give you what you ordered?" I asked.

"Yes," said he, "but now that I seen it I don't care much for the color. So you've got to do it over again, if you want any more business from me."

That was the comforting thought I slept with for the rest of the night. It was still with me early Friday morning, when an angry subscriber braced me on the street corner with, "I brought my daughter's picture in to go with her engagement announcement and you didn't put it in the paper. I'm going to cancel my subscription if that's the way you run things."

"But Mrs. Westlund," I replied, "we didn't receive the picture in time to get it in this week's paper."

"Don't hand me that!" she burst out. "I took the picture to the *Record* office myself, at ten o'clock Thursday morning. I know you don't print the paper until Thursday afternoon!"

My efforts to explain about the time involved in mailing a picture to an engraving plant and getting the engraving back moved her neither to pity nor understanding. As she reminded me several times, "I've been taking this paper for eleven years, that's a lot longer than you two been around here."

In the morning mail was a litle pink slip from the bank. It informed us that our account was overdrawn in the amount of $97.48, requested that we make a deposit immediately, noted that they would have to charge us one dollar for breaking the bad news.

"We print these slips for them," Ed said sadly. "We sell them seven slips for a cent, and buy them back at a buck apiece. How are we going to get ahead that way?"

"And today's payday!"

I meant for everyone else, of course. Neither of us had received a pay check since we bought the business. Stocks, savings account, everything was gone. We hadn't been able to repay my father or even start payments to Nick. There was only one resource left—the children's war bonds. If we cashed them, we could cover the deficit and the payroll.

"There are those bonds. . . ."

Ed looked at me sharply. "The boys'?"

I nodded.

"Do you want to cash them?"

"I'd do anything else first."

"So would I," Ed said firmly. "We'll pray something good comes in, on Monday."

"And I'll make out pay checks, as usual."

"Absolutely." Ed grinned weakly. "You don't suppose we could talk them into cashing them some place else, like, for instance, San Antonio, Texas?"

There were other diversions that day, and it didn't help to reflect that two previous *Record* publishers had gone blind, three had gone broke, and one had stepped from our editorial office into a private asylum.

Promptly at five o'clock Mr. Toski shut off the press, washed up, and appeared at the front desk to minister the coup de grâce. Once he had his pay check in hand, he beckoned to Ed and in a hoarse, conspiratorial whisper, he announced, "I got to quit. I got to get out of here."

"What are you talking about!" Ed exploded.

Mr. Toski's hands closed convulsively on the pay check. He looked over his shoulder, out the window, then back at Ed. "They're after me again," he said, the crack in his voice widening audibly. "Them gangsters."

He explained that he had worked with the cops seventeen years before, but They (the gangsters) hadn't forgotten. They hounded him. They had come close to killing him, but he always got away. He thought he had given them the slip, moving out to the country like this. But someone had squealed on him. Night before They had thrown a stink bomb into his hotel room. That showed They meant business. Next it would be, well . . . And he really liked our place, too. Liked the shop, liked us. But he had to get away, fast. . . .

With that the hunted man and his terminal pay left the *Record* forever. We watched through the window as he fled across the vacant lot and turned sharply into the open door of the nearest tavern.

"Mr. Toski," Ed commented dryly, "is one of those people who just can't stand prosperity. I should have known what was up when he came into the shop with a new pair of yellow shoes and that bright-blue felt hat." Out of curiosity, we telephoned the hotel in which the stink bomb had allegedly been thrown.

"No, no," said the proprietor, "this place smells the same as usual."

Ed turned to me. "Don't ask me, '*Now* what are we going to do?' I don't know. But you look tired. You need a change. Take this order of letterheads and envelopes down to the Congregational church in Carnation. The drive will do you good."

"It's five o'clock."

"The minister just called me. He'll be there for another hour at least."

"You do it. You're more tired than I am."

"That's just it. I'd fall asleep at the wheel."

So with the printing order in the back seat, I headed down the Valley.

The town of Carnation is a farmers' town. It has a population of six hundred, and a main street guarded in those days by a drug store, a hardware store, a dry goods store, a lumber yard, two restaurants, two groceries, two taverns, a barber shop, a Grange general store and a bank. The bank had already furnished the setting for one of our best news stories.

One Thursday morning a lone youth stepped up to the teller's cage, handed the teller a brown paper bag, and barked, "Fill it up." The teller found herself looking down the barrel of a rifle, so she complied. The young man ran out of the bank, jumped into the car he had parked handily at the curb right outside, and drove away.

Bank manager Joe Brown ran outside, leaped into his own car and roared after him. A garageman named Bob Lawson saw the commotion. He got into his car, picked up the postmaster, Buss Anderson, and joined the chase.

A mile or two down the road, Buss Anderson got out to put up a road block. Whenever Bob saw someone near the road he stopped, shouted the news, and asked him to put up a blockade.

The drama came to a sudden end, for the bank robber had made a poor selection both of getaway cars and getaway routes. He got as far as the foot of a steep hill, where his old car boiled over and gave up the chase. There Joe Brown overtook him. Armed with nothing but indignation, he demanded the money and the gun. The boy obeyed without a murmur. Bob Lawson arrived to witness the surrender. Robber and pursuers turned around and went back the way they'd come, Joe Brown and the paper bag of money heading for the bank, Bob Lawson and the unhappy youth for the town jail. It was our first press-day scoop, for we had the story in the paper and had delivered the papers to Carnation before most of the local residents knew there had been any excitement in town that day.

Nearby the town of Carnation is the Carnation Milk Company's beautiful experimental farm, the home, during its infancy, of what is now the second largest canned milk company in the world. The Carnation Farm gave the town its new name, and the Carnation Company, in memory of the wife of the founder, financed the construction of Carnation's Nan Fullerton Stuart Memorial Chapel, a Congregational church. That was my destination on the black Friday when

Mr. Toski left and we were once again fresh out of printers as well as fresh out of funds.

I found the minister in his office, a cubbyhole which had apparently been filled, like Montezuma's throne room, with papers, books, pipes and Bibles, and then stirred up with a spoon. In the midst of this scholarly disorder sat the Reverend Walter McGettigan. He unfolded, grinned and shook hands.

"Here's your stationery," I said, thrusting it at him. "Ed thought you might want it tonight."

"Good. Swell. Glad you came down. Let me show you around."

"Oh no, I can't take the time. I've got to hurry back."

"Mm . . ." The minister studied me briefly. What he saw was a woman with circles under her eyes and a costume she had apparently leapt into from a distance of six feet. "Mm . . ." he repeated, while I jittered from one foot to the other and muttered something about, "Have to hurry back."

"You like to play the organ?" he asked suddenly. He knew about my Christmas present, the little reed organ, for it was he (and the church board) who had sold it to Ed.

"Love to!"

"Ever play a Hammond?"

"No . . ."

He nodded. "You could. There's a beauty in the church. I'll show you how to turn it on."

"No, really, I couldn't . . ." I backed up. The suggestion that I do something other than work threw me into a panic. "I've got to hurry . . ."

The minister said firmly, "Forget it. So far you haven't completed a sentence without the word 'hurry.' Now, come on . . ." and he took a firm grasp of my arm and half-led, half-pushed me out of his office, down the walk, and into the church.

"Here's the light switch," he explained, "and here's the

key to the organ. You hold this button down, so, and this one here, so, and then you let this one go. Now, there's the foot pedal, to make it louder, and you press some of these things down over here. . . ." I was probably murmuring something about hurrying when he ambled out, whistling. At the door, he called over his shoulder, "Turn out the lights and the organ when you're through. And remember where the switches are, for the next time you come. The church is always open."

The interior of the chapel was cool. Twilight through the stained-glass windows cut softly across the shadow. One light shone over the altar, another across my hands, groping over the organ's intricate keyboard and miraculously finding a tune. Luckily no bona fide musician was within hearing distance, for I had no music, and was too rusty to have been able to read it if I had. I began with the hymns I could play by ear, moved from hymns to symphonic themes, and then, more daringly, into tangos. I didn't play well because I don't know how, but the organ has beautiful voices, even in the key of G. With each tune I sought and found, some inner knot came untied, some invisible wire loosened. This was sleep for the weary, drink for the thirsty. I played for an hour, and by the end of that time I knew we had been right to buy the *Valley Record*. I knew we would make a go of it. That man who had hauled me out of bed at midnight to complain about his printing order? Well, I could see his point of view. And the woman who bawled me out because her daughter's picture wasn't in the paper? After all, I shouldn't expect her to understand the mechanics of putting out a newspaper. Mr. Toski's departure? Another and better man would come along. . . . My fingers landed gaily on the bright fast notes of "Yankee Doodle," and I wound up my hour at the organ in a blaze of chords and runs.

I turned off the organ, flipped the light switch, and suddenly rather sheepish, wondered if the not too religious selection I had just polished off had carried beyond the church and into the minister's study. I all but tiptoed toward the car. But I need not have worried. Through the open window of his office I heard the Reverend McGettigan whistling. And what was he whistling, but "Yankee Doodle."

V

Driving back to the shop I resolved to pass along my feelings to Ed. I would scoop up my optimism, the light-headedness and cheer and hope that had burst upon me, and somehow pour it over him, like dumping a bucket of water on his head.

I was gathering up my burden of joy when he met me at the door of the shop.

He was grinning broadly and for some reason he didn't look tired at all. "I just came back from North Bend," he said. "Called on one of the businessmen I'd never met before. He ordered some salesbooks from us. And you know what? On my way out another fellow in the store told me a traveling salesman from the same salesbook company was in last week, offering to sell the same books for less than we charge. You know what the businessman did? Told the salesman he didn't know us personally but he always deals locally if he can. He said he understood we were dealers for the salesbook company and he had no use for someone from the same company trying to undercut us. And then he threw the salesman out of the store and told him never to show his face in there again!"

We looked at each other speechlessly. Maybe everything was going to be all right, after all. . . .

"There's something else. Here." Ed handed me two envelopes that had come in the afternoon mail.

One was a note from a reader in California, written on the back of the yellow subscription statement: "Dear editor, I don't see any use in renewing my subscription to the *Record*. I haven't lived in the Snoqualmie Valley for fifteen years. I don't recognize the names in the paper any more. Nothing in the news interests me. Enclosed is my three dollars for the paper for another year."

The second letter was from a subscriber, too. The envelope contained three one-dollar bills and an application for a money order, carefully filled out by our subscriber, who also sent us a note saying, "I am sending a money order to pay for my paper this year. . . ."

"A 'money order. . . .'" I looked at the application and giggled. "Both of these letters are wonderful. Maybe they're a sign. I was just thinking, everything is going to work out all right, after all. . . ."

I was interrupted by the sound of the job press coming to life in the back room.

"What was that!"

Ed's grin was wider than ever. "That," he said, bowing slightly toward the sound, "is our new printer."

"You're joking. Who could you have found so fast? And who would be working at 6:30 at night?"

"He's doing those wedding invitations the Smiths wanted in a hurry," Ed said in a superior tone of voice. "Go look."

I approached the back room fearfully. There by the press was a tall thin man with a long face, sad eyes and drooping shoulders. He was reading one of the wedding invitations he had just printed, and he didn't look up. Posture, expression, even the cut and color of his old black suit, spelled gloom. Suddenly his voice broke out in hysterical protest. "It won't do! It won't do!" he cried, and it was lucky I wasn't carrying anything or I would have dropped it. "*Mrs.* and *Mrs.* W. O. Smith invite you . . . No, no!" His voice rose and fell like an air-raid siren. "No, it just won't do!"

He wheeled toward me. "Here, you a proofreader?" he asked, his voice plummeting to a despairing rumble.

I nodded, silently accepted the invitation he handed me. "Then read that again," he ordered.

I hurried back to the front office. "Here," I whispered to Ed. "He says to read it again."

Ed nodded. "I heard him."

"What's his name?"

"I think he said Bill."

I sighed. "Just Plain Bill."

"Here, you read this thing, too."

So we both read it, and finally considering it perfect, Ed went back to the backshop. "These are fussy things to correct," he said, in a friendly way. "It's hard to spot the errors."

Just Plain Bill exploded in high C. "You got to read them until you go mad!" he shrilled. "Mad, mad, mad, I tell you!"

"Yes, indeed . . ." Ed retreated quickly. In the safety of the front office he slowed to a halt. We stared at each other. I could see he was trying not to laugh, and I was nearly bursting too. "Mad, mad," Ed whispered, and that did it. We ran outside, slammed the office door, and treated those citizens of Snoqualmie who happened to be nearby to the sight of the weary publisher and his weary wife leaning on each other and laughing until they cried.

5

Is it possible to be a free-lance writer, a good mother, and a help to your husband in his business, all at the same time? That was the question I began asking myself a few weeks after Ed and I and our junior partners, Hiram and John, took over the newspaper and print shop in Snoqualmie.

I had been so confident, back in those salaried, debtless days in Chicago, when our only fear about going into business for ourselves was that we would be bored with so little to do. The week we bought the *Record* I wrote Barbara Brandt, my literary agent in New York, a glowing letter about our new venture and wound up with, "Despite my new duties as publisher, I'll have as much or more time for writing than ever. . . ." I couldn't understand her reply at all. She said she would be able to lend me some money and she forgot to congratulate me.

I can't prove that a writer needs brains or talent, but I did find out for sure that a writer must have time to write and a place to write in.

I tried working at the print shop, and after two days concluded I'd do better in the path of a stock-car race. That was the point at which I retreated to the gravelike stillness of the auto court, where the two little boys were recovering all too rapidly from the measles.

When we leased a house, I set typewriter and notebooks on the bureau in the bedroom. Those were the days of the red-headed housemaid whose rendition of "Yes, We Have No Bananas" went through the walls like a bullet through butter. I fled to a room in the basement. Ed's "leisure time" began when he got home from the shop around midnight, but he cleaned the room thoroughly, covered its peeling walls with bright Indian blankets, and carried tables and chairs downstairs so as to provide me with a quiet, pleasant place to work.

And it was quiet, even when the mighty Violet came, though her every footfall made me wonder if *this* was the time she'd plunge right through to the basement. The disturbance was the old-fashioned coal furnace. It smothered everything with soot. I blew and brushed, but still there was a gritty sound as I rolled a piece of paper into the typewriter and every morning I could write my initials in the sticky black dust that had settled on my manuscripts overnight.

I worked in the basement for two or three months. And then one morning I blew off the soot, dusted the typewriter and the stacks of notebooks and packages of paper, wiped the dirt off the pencils, sat down on the chair, and burst into tears. I must have been expressing myself pretty clearly because Ed heard me upstairs in spite of Violet. He hurried down the basement steps. "What happened?"

I answered sensibly, as crying women always do. "I tried, and I can't!"

"Can't write down here?"

I nodded.

"Well, for gosh sakes," he said, pulling a clean handkerchief out of his pocket, "dry off and we'll get you out of this hole."

"You're so sweet to me!" I wailed.

"That's all right, kid," he said, the very spirit of comfort. "I can't afford to have anything come between you and this little old typewriter, you little gold mine."

Ort, our ad salesman, and his wife Sylvia, lived in a cottage on the river. For a while I rode my bicycle to their house every morning and wrote in their living room, or on their lovely patio above the water, until the two of them returned for lunch at noon. Later my "studio" was the house of Ralph, Linotype operator, pressman and foreman. I worked on the front porch there until it was lunch time for Ralph and his wife Jeanne, who, like Ort's wife Sylvia, worked for the local bank. For a while I traded houses with a baby sitter; she came to our house to take care of Johnny, I drove to her house to write. The table in her kitchen was the only available desk, but it was frequently laden with buttered toast, jam, cheese, and various interesting tidbits of food. At first I put everything away. Then I made a fortunate discovery: It was a lot quicker, and much more enjoyable, to eat it up.

"Aren't you glad you married someone whose work is so adjustable?" I asked Ed. "Think what it would be like if I were a pianist, and you had to provide me with a grand piano."

"Think of what it would be like if you were a Linotype operator," was Ed's reply.

Writing had never been a hobby. It was my profession, just as newspaper work was Ed's profession, though both of us would blush at using the word and would be far more likely to say, It's a way to make a living. On the farm my income from writing paid for chicken feed or roofing or the new septic tank. There was no basic difference in spending it on newsprint or Linotype parts. In fact we counted on it, and that was our mistake. From the fateful day in August when Ed listed "CP's writing" under INCOME WE CAN COUNT ON, all through the blackest winter of our lives, I didn't earn a cent, other than the $500 advance against royalties received in September and spent before we even assumed ownership of the newspaper. Six months later two small checks came in for radio rights and magazine reprint rights on articles I had written long, long before. They totaled less than a hundred dollars and in our advanced stage of financial decay were no help at all.

"You're my little gold mine," Ed repeated loyally, though month after month passed and that Writing Income, CP, was still just around the corner.

The day the big newspaper press was unloaded, a local businessman strolled by, surveyed the new equipment and the new building it was going into, and commented, "Only here eight months, and you've already got it made. Boy, this print shop must be a little gold mine."

Ed looked at the man with genuine surprise. He almost asked— How did you know my wife's name? "Do you really believe we're paying for all these improvements out of company earnings?"

Now it was the storekeeper's turn to look surprised. "How else?"

Ed spoke of the sale of our farm, of the stocks we had sold, and of the loans we had made.

The businessman had a good head for percentages. He had been envious at first, but now he was openly sympathetic. "Look," he said, "you can't keep that up. You can't run a business that isn't paying its own way."

"But we're expanding."

"I can see that," the man agreed. "But you're in awfully deep. How are you going to pay it off?"

"I have got a gold mine, just as you said. My wife. She's a free-lance writer."

"Free-lance writer?" the man asked. "What's she write?"

"Everything," Ed said, with pride so disproportionate to what I can do, and for that very reason so wonderful, that I never know whether to kiss him or stick a gag in his mouth. "My wife is a great writer. She writes books, magazine articles and short stories."

The man was impressed. "You mean she gets *paid* for that kind of stuff?"

No matter how little time I had for writing, I never quit altogether. Before we went into business for ourselves, I had worked on a regular nine-to-five schedule. But now it was an hour here, two hours there, wherever and whenever I could find a place to set up my typewriter. I've always felt scornful of people who talk about writing by "inspiration"; so often they write little if at all. But if three paper companies, two printing supply houses, and a couple of ink plants breathing down your neck is not inspiration, what is?

In April my first novel was published. I received letters of congratulation and a number of desperate program chairmen asked me to speak. A club in Carnation, fifteen miles away, offered to pay my travel expenses if I would make a speech for them. Then the largest department store in Seattle asked me to appear in their bookstore for an autograph party.

This was acclaim, all right, though I would gladly have traded it for credit at the local grocery. The autograph party worried me. My wardrobe had a left-over look. Without a new dress, I was sure to look just like a writer who hasn't sold anything for eight months. An autograph party in Seattle— that was no place to have my morale showing. There was one way to outfit myself inexpensively. I bought yard goods, a pattern, and went to the local dressmaker.

At every fitting I was bubbling over with excitement about the event for which the dress was being made. I picked up the finished product the day before I was to go into Seattle, and by then I couldn't control myself. "My novel was just published," I confided. "That's why I wanted this dress. They

114

are holding an autograph party for me in Seattle tomorrow."

She was instantly enthusiastic. "You're going into Seattle tomorrow?"

"Yes," I said, wondering if she hadn't grasped the meaning of what I told her. "You see, there's to be an autograph party, because of the publication of my novel. . . ."

"That's just fine!" she exclaimed. "I need some gray suit-lining real bad. I've been hoping I'd find someone who was going into town. Get it at Frederick's basement, if that won't take you out of your way. Shall I give you the money now, or pay you when you bring it to me?"

Ed kept talking about his little gold mine, my agent continued to file my rejection slips away quietly, and eventually some of my manuscripts did not come bouncing back. June was the glad month which dissolved my growing suspicion that the good Lord meant me to be something other than an author, probably a spot-welder. A magazine article was sold in June, television rights on my novel were purchased in July, and in August a magazine bought one of my short stories. At last we were back to "Daddy works and Mama writes," and letters from my agent were no longer written on stationery with a black border. From now on, perhaps we could count on Writing Income CP, after all. Three hundred dollars here, five hundred there—things were as they had been, except for a slightly altered attitude on the part of the author. Once the big thrill of selling an article or story was the moment I opened the magazine and saw my work in print. Now the great moment I trembled for was the day I opened an envelope from my agent and pulled out a check.

In August I met the editor who had bought my novel. He was calling on all of the publishing house's authors on the Coast. With only one book behind me, I was probably the newest and greenest. Undoubtedly I was the most anxious to please. I wanted him to take back to New York a good impression of this new writer out in the state of Washington. I felt that my whole future depended on it. I wanted him to see and remember the Snoqualmie Valley, too, so even though it was a rainy afternoon, and late afternoon at that, I insisted that Ed and I pick him up in Seattle and drive him out to see Snoqualmie Falls.

It was after dark by the time we got there, and raining harder than ever. But I led on relentlessly. At the spot where a high wire fence keeps sightseers from falling off the cliff and into the river, we stopped.

"What a beautiful sight!" I exclaimed. "A 268-foot drop. See the tremendous spray, listen to the roar of the Falls. . . ."

The editor said, "I am really awed. . . ."

It was a fine evening, I thought. Ed agreed that our guest had seemed quite impressed. "He even *acted* impressed," I insisted, visualizing all those books he would soon be asking me to write. "Did you notice how he kept studying me, you know, as if he were interested in what I was thinking?"

If he wasn't interested, he was at least extremely curious. A few days after I showed him Snoqualmie Falls, a friend from the East stopped in for a brief visit and of course that called for a trip to the Falls, too.

This time, it was daylight. There was no water over the Falls; there hadn't been for weeks. It was the dry season, and the power company above the Falls had erected a dam so as to force what water there was down through their plant and the giant underground turbines which generate our electricity. The "roar of the Falls"—that had been water the plant released at the bottom of the falls. The 268-foot waterfall I had seen and described so vividly—it just wasn't there.

There were two possibilities. One was that the editor thought I was crazy, and that was bad enough. The other was that the editor had seen the Falls, too. I shuddered. That was worse, much worse.

116

My own writing and my work at the shop could not go along together without an occasional knock-down, drag-out fight. But they were not basically incompatible. Motherhood was something else, however. I began to wonder what kind of a mother I had become the day our son Hiram disappeared.

It was a Friday in mid-winter. The school bus took Hiram to kindergarten, we deposited little Johnny at a baby sitter's, and left instructions with Ort, our ad salesman, to call for Hiram at noon and drive him to the baby sitter's house to join John. Then we left for Seattle, little dreaming that one of the worst storms of the winter was about to break.

Heavy snow began to fall about ten o'clock, and it was driven by a hard wind. The schools were filled with the hundreds of children whom the big yellow school busses had brought in earlier. By afternoon the roads the busses had to travel would be dangerous, perhaps impassable. The superintendent wisely ordered that youngsters be packed back into the busses and returned to their homes.

Hi was an enthusiastic member of the North Bend kindergarten. He loved his teacher. He loved the routine, from the first roll call right on through the daily treat and the "rest period" ("Heads down on the arms, children, eyes closed . . ."). The day he first walked out to the school bus and rode off with the "big kids," I stood in the doorway weeping senselessly, as mothers do when they are suddenly aware of important landmarks. I thought that was the moment when my elder son began his education. The same evening I discovered it was the beginning of mine.

"So you started out with roll call?" I asked, lapping eagerly at every drop of information he would give me about his first day at school. "You mean Mrs. Rud called the names and everyone had to answer either Present or Absent?"

And little Hi said patiently, "Mama, they could only answer Present."

I recognized my deficiencies right then, but luckily his kindergarten teacher was more of a man than I. There was, however, a tremor of self-doubt in her voice a month or so later when she telephoned and began the conversation with, "You know, I *do* want to answer all the children's questions, at least if I can. It isn't that I'm trying to dodge any issues. . . ."

"No, I'm sure you aren't. Is there some problem? Has Hi caused trouble in class?"

"Not at all. It's only . . . Well, has he told you about the starfish?"

He had, many times. There were lizards, guppies and caterpillars in the kindergarten window zoo; a recent acquisition had been a starfish. The full force of Hi's five-year-old curiosity had been turned upon the creature, dry and rigid as it was, and I had been pelted with questions concerning its respiratory, circulatory, digestive and nervous systems. "Yes, indeed, he's told me about the starfish."

"Well, has there been any one question he's brought up particularly? I mean, something he wants to know more than anything else? You understand, I'd tell him, if I only knew. Or perhaps you have some idea where I could get the information?"

"Yes, there is one question he keeps repeating."

"Yes?" she said eagerly. "And do you know the answer?"

"He wants to know how starfish breathe."

"Breathe!" Silence, followed by an audible sigh of relief. "Oh, thank goodness! I thought he said *breed!*"

To Hi, one of the happiest aspects of school was getting there. How dull education would be, if only walking distance from home. Even the first morning, when I stood weeping in the doorway and watched the big yellow bus carry my child from babyhood to boyhood, Hi's one emotion was delight; he rode away without a single backward glance. Before the teachers caught on and put a stop to it, Hi, and later his little brother Johnny, used to hop onto the school bus that took the longest ride around Robinhood's barn, arriving home some thirty minutes later than they would have had they taken the proper bus.

That first winter the bus past our house was crowded, and so Hi, being a kindergartener, was not entitled to a seat. "But I always sit on the same girl's lap," he said. "Her name is Lou Ann."

"Is she pretty?" Ed asked.

And once again Hiram had to be patient with his elders. "How would I know, Daddy," he asked with sweet reasonableness, "since we're always facing the same way?"

The day Hi disappeared during a snowstorm, he and Lou Ann were undoubtedly riding tandem, as usual, as the school bus retraced its route and dropped the children off at their homes. The complication was that Hiram's mother wasn't at home to greet him.

When the school bus stopped to let Hi off, the driver, a quiet young man named Joe, was quick to notice that the house looked deserted. "Is your mother home?" he asked Hi.

Hi replied instantly, "My mama is never home. She's always working."

"I wouldn't like to leave him here alone," the driver said, and asked one of his adult passengers, a teacher also homeward bound, to check. Mrs. Neeley got off the bus, struggled through snowdrifts to the front door, rang the bell. No response. She peered through the window, and found the house in its customary homey condition—dark, cold and empty.

"No one home," the teacher reported. "Perhaps Hi can tell you some place else to drop him off."

But Hi, who had developed a convenient memory even at the age of five, had no such suggestion to make. All he could think of was that he was going to get one of the best rides on the school bus he'd ever had.

It was certainly the longest. Our school district covers an area some thirty-five miles long and three to ten miles wide, and Hi was lucky enough to be on the bus that covers 103 miles every day. He climbed hills and mountains and followed the course of rivers. He went all the way to the summit, where the Snoqualmie Pass cuts through the Cascades. Every time a child got off the bus, Hi's delight in his remarkable situation grew. He got a seat all to himself. Eventually there was even a vacancy right behind his hero, the driver, Joe. Joe talked to him, and gave him chewing gum and candy, and the party got more exclusive at every stop. Later Hi claimed he had been "awful worried," but the truth was that for three hours, through one of the worst blizzards in forty years, he had had one whale of a good time.

Ed and I, mooning over some greasy piece of outdated printing equipment in some supply house in Seattle, imagined that our heir was safe and warm in the kindergarten room, presiding at the starfish display or trying to talk himself into a second cookie at treat time. Meanwhile word that the schools were closing caused a general alarm at the *Record* office.

"I was supposed to pick Hi up at school at noon," Ort exclaimed, "and take him to the house where Johnny is staying."

"There's no one at his house," said our assistant editor. "He must be all alone."

They telephoned our empty house. "No answer," moaned the editor. "But do you suppose Hi is old enough to answer the phone?"

Ort said grimly, "If I know Hi, he would, if he were there. *Where is he?*"

For the next three hours editing and selling interfered very little with the search for Hi. Ort in his car, and Hermia, the assistant editor, on the telephone, covered the territory, thoroughly arousing teachers, school officials, friends and baby sitters.

Through it all the superintendent of schools held calmly to the correct solution. "I bet Hi is happy and safe and perfectly well cared for," said the big red-headed Norwegian who had dealt with a good many boys of all sizes.

"But where is he?" our troubled staffers asked.

"Where would you be under the circumstances, provided, of course, you were a small boy? Riding the school bus, of course."

Hi's bus completed its world tour about 1:30 that afternoon, and when it crawled out of the storm and back to headquarters, the last of the fleet of ten busses to complete its run, the superintendent was waiting in his car.

The orphan of the storm emerged, his face sticky with candy and his cheeks puffed out with chewing gum.

"What were you going to do with him?" the superintendent asked bus driver Joe.

"I was going to take him home with me, and give him something to eat while I called you."

"Thanks, Joe, but I happen to know where he belongs," said the super, hoisting our supremely happy son into his own car. Thus Hi was delivered to the *Record* office, where Ort took over. By the time Ed and I returned, the only remnants of the crisis were the worried lines on the faces of our ad salesman and our assistant editor.

I write a column for the paper called The Last Word Department and I decided to devote it the next week to thanking Joe for the care he had given my boy. From his first concern about leaving the child in an empty house, to his final plan to feed and house him in his own home until parents could be routed out, it seemed to me Joe had shown thoughtfulness well beyond the call of duty. I mentioned the idea to our assistant editor.

She approved heartily of such a column, but there was a note of reservation in her voice. "Perhaps I should tell you about an accident we had here two years ago," she said, "because it's something you might want to keep in mind when you are writing about Joe.

"We've had an excellent school-safety program in this district, and no one person has done more to develop it than Sergeant Baker, the head of the state patrol unit for this area. Everyone calls him 'Bake'—I'm sure you've heard of him, if you haven't met him. Well, Bake is largely responsible for the wonderful safety record in this district. We've had only one fatality. A little boy ran into the street behind a school bus, the bus backed up and killed him. It was a terrible tragedy, doubly terrible because the boy who was run over was Sergeant Baker's son.

"It wasn't the bus driver's fault—no one thought or said it was. But the driver was stricken. He said he would never drive again; the superintendent had to order him to get back in the bus, to drive away. He was, and is, a good driver, a careful driver, and he's wonderful with children. But I'm sure he lives under the shadow of that accident. He'll never get over it, though he has forced himself to stick with his job, not to run away from it.

"I thought you ought to know all this, because that driver was Joe."

iii

Hi's "disappearance" pointed up the question: was the life we were forced to lead fair to our children? We had thrown *our* own bank accounts and nervous systems up for grabs, but what were we doing to *them?*

In the first place, both little boys had developed the well-groomed appearance of Huck Finn after a couple of weeks on the raft. Their mother had no time for sewing, mending or cooking. Admittedly, they didn't seem to fade on a diet of foods I could prepare in fifteen minutes. But "home cooking" aroused a clear picture in their minds of Mama racing into the house, turning on every burner on the stove, and covering them all with frying pans. "My wife is a good cook," I overheard Ed say to a friend. "A real fancy dinner takes her fifteen minutes, but an ordinary meal she can fix in a hurry."

Clothing? Well, it was clean. I did the washing at night, and more than once hung it out in a back yard illuminated by the headlights of the car. But I had no time for mending; the boys wore jeans and T-shirts until the ratio of holes to whole cloth shamed even their mother. In desperation at the end of a year, I sent a box of mending to a seamstress; it contained twenty-one pairs of blue jeans with the right knees gone. But if the holes in their clothes exposed too much body to wind and weather, at least our sons' heads were doubly protected; before I ever got around to shooing them into a barber shop both little boys seemed to be peeking out from under O-Cedar mops.

There is no "home life" for youngsters whose father works at the shop seven days a week and whose mother pedals an Addressograph instead of a sewing machine. But thanks to the total absence of domestic help—and I refuse to classify Violet and her predecessors as "Help"—our little boys enjoyed a special kind of home life in reverse; their parents were never home, it's true, but the boys saw a lot of us anyway because they were so often at the shop.

They ate in the print shop and sometimes slept in the print shop. The country publisher's wife who showed how efficiently a woman can combine motherhood with her job was the mother of a friend of ours, who breastfed her hungry baby while she was working at the Linotype. I'm not a typesetter and my "babies" were in jeans. But the meals I provided for them often came from packages of lunch meat, a loaf of bread, and a carton of milk, served on a clean sheet of newsprint spread over a bank of type. If an afternoon nap was indicated, they were bedded down on a stack of newsprint in the corner and covered with coats and sweaters. When I saw Ed tuck them in and lean down to kiss them "good night," while the job press banged out a lullaby, I felt very close to that country publisher's wife of forty to fifty years ago.

I chided myself for neglecting my children, especially after Hiram's three-hour bus ride, a direct result of not having a mother home where she belonged. Actually Ed and I spent more hours with our children than most so-called normal parents ever do and the environment, greasy, inky, noisy as it was, probably didn't hurt them a bit. They gained in independence what they lost by having the nest pulled out from under them. Long before they could read they knew how to answer the phone and write down the number we were to call back. Whenever I felt cold cuts in cold bread with cold milk alongside was an inadequate diet, I sent the two of them out to a restaurant, where they ordered their own meals, paid for them, left a tip and brought back the change.

They were five and seven years old when we launched them on this particular wave of independence, and after they had disappeared around the corner, Johnny holding Hi's hand, some remnant of the maternal instinct quivered through me and I began to worry. After ten or fifteen minutes I visualized them in tears in the restaurant, hungry because they didn't know what to say and sobbing, We want Mama!

I abandoned typewriter and telephone, raced to the restaurant, burst through the door and all but cried, "I'm coming, darlings, everything is going to be all right!"

The two cherubs were up at the lunch counter. They turned beaming, mustardy faces toward the door, but the smiles faded when they saw who it was.

"Did you have to come to *this* restaurant?" asked seven-year-old Hi.

But five-year-old Johnny was kinder. "That's all right, Mama," he reassured me. "You could sit over there, at the other side."

We felt it was good training, so when the boys were in school we continued it. Ed bought each of them a meal ticket in a café in North Bend. The boy who had made his bed every day, fed the cats and dogs, and completed all chores both at the home and at the shop, was allowed to go "uptown" (people hereabouts never go downtown) for lunch on Friday. They agreed to the plan enthusiastically and the Friday lunches continued for some time, presumably without a hitch.

Three years later the boys confessed that their first lunch "uptown" had not been altogether successful.

"They gave me such a big menu!" little Johnny explained. "I just couldn't read all of that, about steaks and things, but I could read 'turkey,' so I asked for that. Boy, I must of pointed at Thanksgiving dinner, or something. The waitress brought me soup, and then a big platter covered with turkey and mashed potatoes and gravy, and a dish of peas, and salad, and then for dessert a big chocolate sundae."

The recollection made him sigh deeply. "I remembered what you always said about the Clean Plate Club. I ate it all up. When I got back to school I went to the boys' lavatory and threw up. There was only one boy in there that knew. Kenny. Do you suppose he remembers? Do you think he will tell?" Three years later, he was worried.

Hi grinned. "Now that you told, John, I might as well tell what happened to me. I was sure excited all week, thinking about going uptown on Friday. When Friday finally came, I was just awful excited. The minute the bell rang I jumped up from my desk and I ran all the way to the café and only stopped once to catch my breath. I had been thinking all week what I was going to order, I didn't even have to look at the menu. I had a chiliburger, a glass of milk and cherry pie with ice cream, only I learned you call that à la mode. It tasted so good I just gulped it down, and boy, was I full. Then I ran most of the way back to school. I got there just as the bell was ringing—for the end of morning recess! I had been so excited I had gone uptown for lunch at ten o'clock in the morning! Oh boy, but the awful part was, when they did ring the bell for lunch, and I was stuffed like a fat sausage.

"I didn't know what to do. I talked about it with my friend

Fritz. We decided the best thing to do was pretend to be sick. So that's what I did. I spent the lunch hour up in the nurse's room. Whew! That was close, though!"

Sometimes independence had to be curtailed. When it led to hitchhiking, for example. Hi was still a kindergartener the Saturday afternoon a Model T Ford pulled up in front of our house and he stepped out and waved good-bye to the man and woman on the front seat. I had left him at a friend's house for the afternoon—a house, incidentally, that was a good two miles from ours.

"You were supposed to stay at Billy's until I came for you!"

"I felt like coming home."

"But who brought you?"

Hi said matter-of-factly, "I don't know. I was hitchhiking."

He had wanted to come home, so he came, and by the most practical means he could think of (especially practical since it did not involve announcing his departure to Billy's mother). He had walked out to the highway, taken up his station facing the line of traffic, and made appropriate gestures with his thumb. He confessed that the first two cars passed him up. The Model T was the third one he signaled.

"But don't you have any idea who the people were?" I repeated, because the make of car indicated they weren't going far, and I wanted to phone and thank them. "Do they live some place nearby?"

"Oh, no," Hi said positively. "They live way down the other way, in the opposite direction from here. But I told them to bring me home first and then go back."

That was Hi's first and last hitchhiking and perhaps it was just as well to have it out of the way before the age of six.

At its best, the independence thrust upon the smaller partners in our enterprise was their willingness to do things other children aren't expected to do, simply because they could see they had to be done. They learned, in other words, to rise to the occasion.

There was the Saturday afternoon I bought two big

chickens from a nearby farm lady, thinking Ed would be home in time to butcher them. The inevitable phone call came; someone had to have his printing by seven o'clock that night, and Ed, being publisher, was the lucky fellow elected to stay down and finish it.

I can pick a chicken, draw it, cut it up, and cook it, but I can't take its head off. On the farm Ed and I occasionally dressed forty to fifty chickens in a day, but it was Ed who brought the ax down and I who stood by with gritted teeth and closed eyes. So I looked helplessly at these two stout Rhode Island Reds. My idea of having an old-fashioned Sunday dinner wasn't much of an inspiration if Ed was to spend Sunday morning doing the dirty work.

"What's the matter, Mama?" young Hi asked.

"I was just wishing there was some way to get these chickens butchered, so Daddy wouldn't have to do it in the morning."

"Can't you do it?"

I shook my head.

"Are you afraid?"

"No, it's not that. It's, well, I just can't. . . ."

Hi squared his shoulders. "Then I will."

Single file, we headed for the woods in the back of the house, where the end of a log offered a good chopping block. First in line was Hi, carrying the extremely dull Boy Scout hatchet I had selected as a suitable weapon; faint heart that I was, I wouldn't let him use Ed's double-bitted ax because I could picture him taking the chicken's head off with one side and cleaving his own with the other. I followed, holding a squawking chicken in each hand. And Johnny, all awe and admiration, brought up the rear.

Hi said, "I've got to hold the hatchet with both hands. Could you hold the chicken?"

The hen looked at me balefully as I adjusted her on the end of the log. Hi said a little shakily, "O.K., Mama, I'll do it now. . . ." which was all the signal I needed to close my eyes. He brought the hatchet down. But the chicken was a sturdy beast and the hatchet was dull and the executioner was only seven years old and feeling a little queasy. So it took several more blows, and when I opened my eyes I said, "Hi, when you butcher this next chicken, see if you can't do it with the first blow. Bring the hatchet way up high, and swing it down with all your strength."

Hi nodded. His round face looked grim. I held the second chicken in place. Feet apart, hands gripping the handle tight, Hi swung the hatchet up. I didn't see him bring it down, but I heard the mighty blow and with my hands clamped around the other end of the chicken I even felt the vibration. I looked, and found that this time Hi had done a fast, neat job.

I sighed, but no louder than he. "I'm sorry I couldn't do it," I apologized. "I guess I'm just a sissy, the way I closed my eyes when you used the hatchet."

"Oh, that's all right, Mama," the little boy said. "I closed mine, too!"

iv

The modern mother is endlessly patient, lest she "reject" her children. She shields them from knowledge of financial or domestic worries, lest they lose their sense of "security." She puts her children's desires ahead of her own, lest in her selfishness she "frustrate" them. And if the beast in her occasionally gets the upper hand, she suffers from a sense of guilt. I had been in and out of enough textbooks to know all this, but when we bought our own business my distinguishing mark as a mother was not patience, nor protectiveness, nor unselfishness, but fatigue, and if I had any sense at all I'd have a guilt complex a mile wide.

Our children knew nothing of domestic problems, because those first years we weren't domestic enough to have them. But they overheard a great deal about other worries. Was there enough money in the bank to cover the payroll this week? The cost of engravings and the volume of advertising and the most recent repair bill for one of our priceless mechanical heirlooms—they heard all of it. They emerged with a healthy respect for work, and with understanding of the sweat and tears behind their allowances and moving-picture money from which model parents would have sheltered them zealously.

Hi was all of six years old when he first asked, "Daddy, did we get enough advertising this week?" His way of describing the villain in a moving picture he and Johnny had seen was, "He was a bad man. He killed people, and he didn't even pay his bills!" The boys observed from the very start that their tired parents were even more tired on Paper Day; boisterous and meddlesome as they might be six other days of the week, on Thursdays they walked quietly and kept their voices down.

I remember vividly the day when I felt my nerve endings were sticking out all over me, like spikes on a mine just waiting for some passing craft, like a small boy, to touch them off. Hi and Johnny came bouncing into the house. "Will you come out and play with us?"

"No, not now."

"Aw, come on, Mama. . . ." and they began dancing around me, chanting, "Come on out, come on out. . . ."

I should have forgotten my worries, ignored my headache, and bounced along with them, the endlessly cheery, patient, model mother. Instead I snapped, "I won't play and I'll tell you why. I'm tired and I'm mad!"

They stopped in their tracks. But instead of feeling rejected, they were immediately sympathetic.

"Why didn't you say so in the first place?" Hi said brightly. "Come on, John, quit worrying Mama."

"That's all right, Mama," little Johnny said tolerantly, and hand in hand the boys tiptoed out of the room. Their mother was a human being, after all, and just as snappish as anybody else. They accepted the fact, not resentfully, but with understanding, and thus learned to think of someone else. If that's being "rejected," so be it.

Nor did it hurt them to work at the shop themselves. Once they were both old enough to be in school all day, the boys frequently took the school bus to the shop, rather than to our house, and spent the afternoon sweeping floors, burning wastepaper, sorting out leads and slugs, and collecting sweepings of metal for the casting machine. We didn't pay them. We gave them money for other things, many of them less deserving of pay than what they did at the shop. At the shop they were to share the load as partners, and we would not put a price on that.

Nor did we say, "You must work so many hours. . . ." If they were to learn anything at all from this experience of ours, let it be that the man who is his own boss gives up the inalienable right to quit work on the last second of the last minute of the forty-hour week; he works until the work is done. The measure would not be "How long?" but "How good?" More good training—and we stuck to it, though their help often enabled us to do a job in just a bit more time than it would have taken to finish it without them.

We did not preach about "responsibility." When Hiram's music teacher reported a conversation with him, we discovered we didn't have to.

Explaining that she wouldn't hold classes during the summer vacation, the teacher told Hi she planned to take a trip.

His instant response was a deep sigh of envy, and the remark, "I'd sure like to travel to faraway places."

"Like . . ."

"Like Texas or California," the little boy said.

"But you're pretty young," the teacher said. "I'm sure you'll take many trips when you're older."

Hi said solemnly, "No, I'll be running the print shop for my Dad."

"But even if you do, he'd let you leave sometime, if you asked him, so you could travel to, er, Texas and California."

Hi shook his head. "No, I couldn't do that," he said positively, "that would be letting my dad down."

It was Hi's own idea to make improvements in our circulation department. In Chicago he had seen newsboys selling papers on the street, and the picture stuck. "You got to go out and *sell* papers," said the seven-year-old, and he put a bundle of *Records* under his chunky little arm and went out onto the street.

"Getcher paper!" Hi shrilled, waving a *Record* over his head. *"Valley Record,* ten cents. Getcher paper here!"

The dogs sleeping in the middle of the street raised their heads and blinked. The swallows nesting under the eaves of the general store swooped to cover. Three white-haired men standing in front of the post office turned their heads slowly, and stared.

"Paper, paper, getcher paper . . ." Hi disappeared around the corner, manfully hawking his wares, Chicago style. He covered the town. When he got back to the shop he was more puzzled than unhappy. He hadn't sold a single paper.

"I don't understand, Mama," he said. "I yelled *Valley Record* but everyone already had a *Valley Record* under his arm. This must be a different kind of a paper than they have in Chicago."

V

On a warm summer day the banker across the street smiled pleasantly and said, "Hello, Ed." As far as I could determine that was the only reason that after only nine months in the Valley my husband began talking about building a home of our own.

"We don't want to spend another winter in a rented house," he said.

I agreed noisily.

"But why spend thousands of dollars buying someone else's old house when for the same amount of money we could build one ourselves?"

"Now wait a minute. . . ." He never sounded that logical

unless we were headed for more debt. "But how will we *pay* for it?" I was beginning to wish that the Powers who were overseeing our affairs would write me some new lines.

"Why, honey," Ed said in a puzzled tone of voice, "we haven't even got a house plan. There's *lots* of time."

That was about the first of July.

Have you ever observed a husband and wife planning their little love nest together? He wants a white house, she likes hand-split cedar siding. She thinks those California-style car ports are darling and he shouts back that in this climate they're impractical. She has always dreamed of having a living room with windows running from ceiling to floor, he claims the kids will kick holes in them in less than a week. He is looking at costs, she is looking at those color illustrations she's been clipping out of *Better Homes and Gardens*. "We can't afford it!" he cries, and she retorts, "What's the use of building a house if you can't have anything you like?"

Despite these few mild differences of opinion, Ed and I shared a primitive urge to live in a home of our own, and so we called in an architect to resolve our problems.

Actually, we called in two. The first one devoted our conference to a philosophical monologue about an architect's duty to his clients. For an hour he explained that he didn't care about money, his desire was to build a home for us that expressed our personalities. Listening to his dissertation, I tried to imagine what kind of house would express Ed's personality and mine at the same time, considering how beautiful had been our accord on the subject of the house so far. Ed listened, too, with so much patience I concluded he must be asleep. But he finally broke in. "Would you mind giving us some hint," he asked gently, "as to what this house that expresses us is going to look like?"

"I see Arizona sandstone," the man began, "with perhaps a wide sweep of tile. There will be rough cedar, but just enough, not too much. And the lines will be clean, the western line, simplicity but grandeur . . ."

"Thank you for coming out," Ed said. "I'll get in touch with you when we feel like getting expressed."

The next architect came with a builder. Studying a tentative plan, the builder said it would cost $8,500 and the architect said it would cost $19,000.

"Someone," Ed commented acidly, "is allowing a pretty wide margin for error."

It was now the first week in August. We had the land, two acres of meadow right at the foot of Mount Si. Gray crags pierced the clouds 4,000 feet over our heads. The ice-cold Snoqualmie River flowed between us and the mountain's base. Behind us lay pastures and groves of alder and fir. It was peaceful, but it was accessible, for our land fronted a county road and would be kept clear by county equipment should we have another bad winter.

"What's this road called?" Ed asked the real-estate agent.

"This is the North Fork Road," he said. "Keep going you come to the North Fork of the Snoqualmie River."

"Ah, then the river in front here between us and the mountain is the North Fork?"

"No, that's the Middle Fork."

Ed scratched his head. "Then why isn't this called the Middle Fork Road?"

The realtor said patiently, "Because the Middle Fork Road is two miles east of North Bend, it goes around the south side of the mountain."

Ed asked, "South of the mountain! Isn't there a South Fork Road?"

"Certainly."

"Where is it?"

The realtor was beginning to sound harassed. "Why, right over there," he replied, and I swear he pointed west.

We checked with our neighbors-to-be along the road, and they all agreed that we were on the North Fork Road. We loved the location so much Ed wrote an editorial about it. He sang praises of the view, and no one took issue with him.

But he also referred to the name of the road, and that nearly cost us a subscriber.

One complaint was good-natured. Deo Reinig, an old-timer with a twinkle in his eye, came into the office to straighten us out. "You better find out where you're going to live," he said. "The North Fork Road is the one that runs past *my* place."

"Then what's the name of the road past *my* place?"

Mr. Reinig shrugged. "I don't know. But it's not the North Fork Road. That's been in front of my place ever since 1890."

"All our neighbors think they live on the North Fork Road. Some of them been living there for twenty years."

"Newcomers," said Mr. Reinig, chuckling. "But at least I'd like to think the editor knows where he is."

Another reader registered bitter complaints—with everyone but us. Reports came back to us that Mrs. O'Hara had no use for the new editor because he'd only been in the Valley nine months and he was already trying to change the names of roads.

After that we kept our address out of the editorial column, but we kept on loving the place, wherever it was. Sometimes we packed a picnic supper, sat in the middle of the meadow, and chewing, looked up at the mountain.

"I love it here," I sighed, with my mouth full.

Ed nodded grimly. "So do I. But I'd love it more if there were a house on it. It can get durned cold around here in January and February."

About the tenth of August Ed called in a young builder named Barney Phillips. He pulled a piece of typing paper from the desk drawer, quickly sketched a house with three bedrooms, a living room, a bath and a kitchen. "Could you build that house for me, Barney?"

Barney squinted at the pencil scratchings, asked a few question. "Sure."

"When could you start?"

Barney flipped through a little notebook he carried in the pocket of his overalls. "Next Monday be all right?"

"The house we're in has been leased to someone else and we've got to move out on October first. That gives you six weeks. Can you do it?"

Barney grinned. "You just watch."

That was the answer Ed gave me when I asked him how we were going to finance this new project. The contract was for an unfinished house. Barney's price of $4,500 would have sounded like a bargain if we'd had even a tenth of it in the bank. "We'll make it somehow, you just watch," was Ed's reply to my tiresome question. We were to pay the sum a little at a time. So much when the foundation was poured, so much more when the walls and roof were up, another sum when the job was done and a final payment four weeks after we'd moved in. The longer Barney took to build the house, the more chance we had of raising the money to pay him, and that was the irony of it; we had hired him because he could do the job fast. We were working against ourselves.

During the first four weeks construction proceeded at a normal pace. Receipts were good at the shop, a check came in for a magazine article I had sold, and we were able to keep up. At that point the scene changed. With only two weeks to go before the October-first deadline, the building site began to look like the old vaudeville act of West and McGinty. Wiring, digging, welding, cutting, nailing, sawing, all went on at the same time. The wonder of it was that the men from the glass company did not arrive before the walls were up, the electricians did not install the fixtures before the ceiling was in, and thanks to these and other miracles the house hung together very nicely and always has. But speedy work meant speedy pay. We began to fall back on demand notes.

At the last Barney had five carpenters on the job at once. Perhaps we wouldn't be able to move on the first, but it wouldn't be long afterward and then another payment would be due. "Only a few hundred dollars" was the way Ed put it, but I refused to be comforted.

"Well?" I said gloomily. "Where's it going to come from? Got any ideas?"

"Sure," Ed retorted. "The morning mail should be sorted by now. Let's go pick it up."

In the mail was a letter from my agent saying a certain magazine had asked me to do an article for them but their usual payment was "only $200" and she was sure such an assignment wasn't worth my time.

I lit out for the telegraph office on a dead run and was nearly trampled to death by Ed.

"You little gold mine," Ed crooned to me after the message had been sent. "You beautiful, sweet, little gold mine."

"You didn't have to push!"

"Did I hurt you?" He was all concern. "Oh my, did I hurt your right hand?"

"What do you mean, my right hand?" I sniffed. "I type with both hands."

Ed patted me lovingly on the shoulder. "Ah, yes. But you don't need both hands to endorse a check. . . ."

We moved in before the carpenters had moved out. We had to shift a pair of sawhorses in order to plug in the electric range and for two weeks the finishing carpenter arrived at eight o'clock every morning. We had tried to postpone moving day, but the people who had leased the house we were in kept saying they had to have a place to live and the morning their furniture arrived we decided they meant business.

Books, chairs, organ, beds—our new house was smaller than the one we had been renting and it was running over with our possessions well before the Castagnos had carried the last article in. We found a place for everything, though we could scarcely walk between the living-room chairs without turning sideways. The house was a far cry from those pictures I had clipped out of the magazines. But it was our own, and it was in the right place. October—just one year

136

since we had assumed ownership of the *Record*. I sighed. "I never dreamed we'd have a home of our own so soon."

Ed had grown thoughtful, which I should have recognized as a bad sign. "The house is too small," he said, "and I know it isn't what you wanted. But we're better off here than to go on renting."

"I like the house!"

He didn't seem to hear me. "Just as soon as we can, we'll add another section about the same size as this."

"If we can, someday, fine. But darling, we've only been in the Valley a year. We're in debt. You can't do everything at once. Why, in a year's time, you've already . . ."

"It would be nice to have a bigger living room, with windows to the ceiling, looking right up at the mountain. And then this room would become the dining room. There would be another bedroom, down at the far end. . . ."

"Ed Groshell!"

He grinned. "Happy first anniversary, sweetheart!" he said, pulling me down into the chair beside him. I would have told him he was crazy. But right then, it slipped my mind.

vi

The first night we slept in our home at the foot of Mount Si, I lay in bed and reflected that there is no sound as beautiful as silence. It had been the same when we moved to our farm after four or five weeks in an apartment in Chicago. In Chicago there had been trolley cars, busses, squealing brakes and quarreling people. Our first night on the farm I had not slept for an hour, just listening to the wonderful absence of sound. In the Snoqualmie Valley our rented house was on the big transcontinental highway and then the nights were torn apart by the roar of Diesel trucks, the explosive pop of air brakes, the thunder of a transport shifting into a lower gear. None of that now, in our little house in the meadow. This was peace. In the still darkness, I thought— There is a side to the misfortune of being deaf that I have never understood before. The deaf assume there is always sound. They cannot experience utter tranquillity for only the hearing can *know* when there is nothing to be heard at all.

My reflections were shattered by what sounded like a woman—or a herd of women—crying in the distance.

"Coyotes," Ed murmured sleepily.

All along the country road, the dogs began answering them. "They sound awfully close," I said.

"They probably are," said Ed, by way of comfort. "Haven't you been reading those stories you write for the paper?"

It was true. I was the author of an article about a local man named Nate Greene, a trapper for the state game department. Cougar, bobcat, crows, skunks, coyotes—there were so many of them in our Valley that reducing their numbers was a full-time job. My own article pointed out that Mr. Greene had killed as many as 264 coyotes a year by trapping, and killed two or three times that many by poisoning, but I hadn't realized how close to home he could do it. What I remembered best about that feature story was the subsequent telephone call from the trapper's wife.

"You referred to my husband as a predatory trapper," she objected, "and I just want you to know, he isn't at all, he's a very nice man."

I began to think of some of the other news items we had carried in the *Record* concerning the wild life to be found in the back yard.

There were many deer, of course. We had arrived in the Valley during deer season, when we had received so many hunting stories that an item about a woman shooting a five-point buck got lost in the shuffle and appeared, without a headline, among the social notes about tea parties and potluck church dinners. When I asked the mayor of Snoqualmie what the regular date was for town council meetings, she replied, "The first Monday of every month, except for hunting season." The town clerk, also a woman, liked to hunt deer, and the mayor and all the councilmen were whole-heartedly in sympathy with the practice of postponing official business until she'd bagged her buck.

Bear? Yes, we'd printed many a story about them. In fact the first one had taught us that our readers take their wild animals seriously; when a pair fresh from the domesticated corn fields of Illinois made a reportorial error in this department it was not to be laughed off. We'd been in Snoqualmie about a month when a woman came into the office to tell me about a big father bear who had brought two cubs into her plum orchard and in plain sight of the house nearly stripped the trees of fruit. Having been accustomed to nothing wilder than a hungry pheasant, I was intrigued, and that week devoted my column, The Last Word Department, to the tale. Maybe I had misunderstood the lady, or maybe she was as near-sighted as I was ignorant. In any case the first mail brought a very downright letter from a subscriber who pointed out that father bears don't go in for child care and besides, at this time of year—November— little bears have grown at least to college age.

There had been a good many bear stories since. One, about a boy who went into his own back yard and not a hundred feet from his house shot a 140-pound bear. Another news item in the *Record* had told about the clerk in a North Bend grocery store who went home for lunch and had no more than dropped the crackers in his soup than he spotted a bear in the orchard behind the house. He jumped up, grabbed his gun, ran outside, shot a 250-pound bear, went back and finished his lunch.

The next week a young farm boy went into the barn used mostly during the winter. He stooped to tie a shoelace, and out of the corner of his eye he saw the feed box move. It shouldn't have, because the barn was supposedly empty. The boy straightened up to take a better look, and in so doing came nose to nose with a bear.

The boy ran out one door, the bear out another. Both were tearing at high speed, both raced around the barn, but in opposite directions. As a result, they met again. Two head-on collisions with a human were enough for the bear. He took to the woods. The boy finished tying his shoelace.

Our local bears were apparently no match for our local people, though in one instance a bear had emerged the winner. Two of our readers were driving along a main highway one summer evening when a large black bear jumped down the bank and landed on the car with a tremendous thud. The bear shook himself and limped off, but the front end of the car was demolished.

It was all right to put myself to sleep counting news stories about coyotes, deer and bear, but I began to recall that we had printed quite a few stories about cougar, too. One told about a local high-school boy who treed a six-foot cougar not 1,500 feet from the back door. The boy fired just as the cougar sprang and killed him with one shot.

"Don McFarlane Tracks and Shoots 200-lb. Cougar," had been another page-one story in the *Record,* though the event had not seemed to startle either our readers or Mr. McFarlane. I had been frankly incredulous. So was Ed, but for a different reason. The most elusive of the local critters is the cougar, who therefore brings the highest bounty; the man who bags a cougar earns seventy-five dollars in bounty and twenty-five dollars for the cat's skin.

"McFarlane was out three and a half hours," Ed had moaned, "and he made $100. Ever hear of a country editor making thirty dollars an hour?"

I nudged Ed. "How close in do you suppose cougars come?"

Ed lifted his head from the pillow. "Huh, what?"

"I was just wondering, the coyotes sounded so near. Do cougars usually come in that close too?"

His head dropped and he pulled the covers up to his ears. "Cougars," he muttered. "You wouldn't wake up for an earthquake. Cougars, ha! Go to sleep. . . ."

vii

It was our second Thanksgiving in the Valley, and this time we had something to be thankful for! We were going to eat turkey instead of pork chops. And rather than working at the shop until eight o'clock at night, we were going to go home at noon.

"Progress!" said the eternal optimist I had promised to love, honor and obey.

The side of the picture he chose to look at was truly a bright one. Our subscription list continued to grow. Just Plain Bill was still with us so we weren't worrying about finding a printer. With our new equipment we had almost forgotten about "mechanical difficulties." We were turning out more and better commercial printing. Yes, we had made progress, and in only fourteen months.

The picture had another side. The previous Thanksgiving we had owed $26,000, and some $12,000 worth of stocks were tucked away in our safe-deposit box. This Thanksgiving we still owed Nick $5,000, my father $3,000, the bank $2,500 on a demand note, and the former owner $17,000. Grand total, $27,500. After a year of progress we had a bigger debt than we'd begun with, and all our securities were gone.

Ed knew these figures better than I did. If he could grin and say, "Progress," I had better learn to grin back. I made a silent resolution, and progressed into the kitchen to stuff the turkey.

6

When we left Chicago, our downtrodden high-salaried friends knew we were the luckiest people in the world. Even those who found their way to the wilds of Washington and observed that we might be luckier if we had more sleep and more money still insisted, "Well, at least you're your own boss!"

The day a subscriber slammed the office door so hard she cracked the glass, we began to wonder. A week or two of such joyful encounters and the wonder flowered into awful certainty. The man in business for himself isn't working for "himself" at all—he's working for his customers. "You're your own boss," indeed. We had just as many bosses as we had subscribers, and when we bought the *Record* there were 1,800 of them.

The first thing we learned about our readers was that they were all editors. They knew what should be printed, how big the headline should be, and the page on which it should appear. If we had obeyed them, the eight or ten inside pages would have been blank but for a couple of reports about loggers injured on the job, without headlines and in the smallest type we had; everything else would be on the front page. On April first, we numbered every page of the paper "Page One," and Ed wrote a howlingly funny editorial saying now at last everyone should be satisfied. Nobody laughed.

We soon discovered that though our subscribers were sure we didn't know anything about the newspaper business, they thought we knew everything else.

We were racing against the clock one Thursday afternoon when the telephone rang. "Say, I saw a want ad in the *Record* a few months back," said the woman's voice at the other end of the line. "It was for a washing machine. I forgot to write it down so would you tell me what it said?"

"What was the date of the paper?"

"Oh, I thought you'd know *that*," the woman exclaimed. "Sometime in April, I think, or maybe it was March or May."

Once production stopped while I tried for seven minutes to convince a subscriber that I knew nothing about the care and feeding of carrier pigeons. "But the pigeon just landed here, and I don't know what to do," she repeated. "I was sure *you'd* know."

Among our subscribers were many servicemen. One, in a U.S. Army radio outfit in Germany, used to send us messages by way of a ham operator in Seattle. Another, stationed on Guam, wrote home that the one birthday present he wanted was a subscription to the *Record*. When his mother bought the subscription she insisted it go to him air mail.

"The postage will run high," I protested.

"That doesn't matter, I've got a job at the laundry now," she said. "And my son hates to wait to find out what's happening back home." For three years she air-mailed the *Record* across the Pacific—$3.50 a year for the paper, $9.36 a year for postage.

When war broke out in Korea we had many a subscriber near the front lines, and one of them, a sergeant by the name of Ambrose, had great confidence in the power of the local editor. Musical comedy star Martha Wright comes from Duvall, one of our Snoqualmie Valley towns. When she replaced Mary Martin as the lead in *South Pacific,* I interviewed her mother and grandfather and wrote a feature story about her for the *Valley Record*. With the story were several pictures I had obtained from her mother. One or two were poses to gratify any press agent but others of the star as a little girl reportedly made the lovely Martha wince. Shortly after the story appeared in the *Record* we got a letter from subscriber Ambrose. It was written in pencil, on paper that was none too clean, and in handwriting that was none too steady, for which he apologized; the spot he was in hadn't been designed for letter-writing. He begged us, please, to send him an autographed picture of Martha Wright, because it would do so much for his prestige in the outfit.

It seemed to me that the letter spoke for itself. I sent it to Martha's mother, Mrs. Fred Wiederrecht, and asked her to forward it. "Just tell her," I added, "that if she won't send him a picture of herself I *will*—and it will be one of those baby pictures." In no time the sergeant in Korea had received an autographed picture and a personal letter from Martha Wright as well.

Of course she would have done it anyway, with or without the bit of blackmail, but we were proud to have been an agency through which a soldier's wish was made known and granted. We were brand-new country editors, and we were already being of service to our subscribers. But when a subscriber came in and asked us to help him find a wife, it was a different matter.

He was a little man, about fifty years old, with sad eyes and a voice that shook with loneliness. There was so much sadness in him he couldn't find a place to put it. His wife had left him, his sons had joined the Army, he was all alone and he would like to find a new wife. Here was his seventy-five cents, and would the editor please write out something real nice?

Ed excused himself hastily and fled to the corner in the back room where I was wrapping a printing order. "What will I say?" he whispered. *"You* go talk to him."

I shook my head firmly. "Oh, no you don't. Marriage is not my department. I'm in charge of dancing partners, remember?"

Ed hissed, "I'd be glad to give you a promotion. . . ."

"I wouldn't *think* of reaching beyond my jurisdiction."

Reluctantly, Ed returned to his customer, who was now so very sad he was leaning on the counter for support. They conferred in stage whispers—no one, the little man said, was to know who had placed the ad—and at last the classified was composed and Romeo left, a little bit of sadness already dissolved by his conviction that the *Record* would find him a Juliet.

Proudly, Ed brought me the ad he had written. "IS RO-MANCE DEAD? Set a date and a time and a place and I'll be there. I want to meet a nice woman who is lonely for the companionship of a respectable middle-aged man. This is not a gag—I am lonely, too."

"Sounds to me like you've written quite a few of those before." I commented acidly. "Or is it spontaneous talent? Anyway, there is no name, address or phone number. How is Juliet to answer it?"

"Oh, yes, well . . ." Ed looked sheepish. "I told him I'd say in the ad, 'Address letters to Romeo, care of the *Valley Record.'* "

That advertisement appeared in four issues of our paper, and Ed had plenty of time to discover the role of marriage broker is a demanding one. Half our readers were convinced the ad was a gag, and they co-operated enthusiastically by writing gag letters and making gag telephone calls, the latter around two in the morning. The other half assumed that Romeo was one of the men at the print shop, probably the editor himself, and began eyeing the personnel (all of whom were married) in a disapproving way.

Ed's biggest problem, however, was Romeo himself. Complete secrecy had been promised and Ed maintained it loyally. Since no one, not even members of the *Record* staff, must know who had placed the ad, Romeo would not come in to pick up the replies unless Ed was alone in the office. But he could not control his eagerness, so he hovered around the street outside, gesturing violently whenever he spotted Ed through the window. He was not easily discouraged. There are two mail deliveries a day in Snoqualmie, one at about nine in the morning, the second about four in the afternoon, but if Ed shook his head at four—"No, no letters today . . ." Romeo was back at the window at five, and again at six.

By that time Ed's head was coming loose from shaking "No, no!" but the front office was usually empty so Romeo would slide in, lacking nothing but a long black cloak, and whisper, "Any letters for me today?" He looked so sad when he asked, it seemed impossible that he could look sadder when Ed said no. Somehow he did. Loneliness welled from his little black eyes and sadness would strike him so hard he trembled with it. But he would be back the next day.

Ed did not give him letters obviously written by practical jokers—it would have been cruel to do so. And at last, after four weeks, a serious reply came. At his tryst with Ed that evening, Romeo's sad face broke into joyous smiles. He took his wallet from his pocket and said, "Here, I owe you for the last two ads. Now you fixed up everything for me I want to pay. . . ." His debt cleared, the letter clutched in his hand, he went out into a world now suffused with the rosy glow of romance.

The next evening he was back in the office, sadder than ever. He had been so overjoyed at hearing from Juliet that he had gone out celebrating and lost the letter. "I got to put another ad in the paper," he whispered, hoarse with despair. "You write it for me, something real nice?"

This time the ad said: "WILL THE JULIET who answered Romeo's ad please send phone number; he lost it."

Perhaps Ed hadn't put his heart into the writing, for Juliet did not reply. After a few days Romeo lost all confidence in the newspaper and took his burden of sorrow elsewhere. Ed promised me that from then on he would let our readers find their own wives.

When a subscriber stomped into the office and issued an ultimatum of some kind, Ed and I consoled ourselves with the quip we'd heard another country publisher make—"You have to be read to be wrong." As receptionist, I faced subscribers day in and day out. When the office door opened, I stiffened instinctively, and until I saw the face or heard the tone of voice, I felt and acted like a chicken thief who has just stepped on a creaky board. If I saw the customer was frowning, I had to fight a desire to drop to the floor behind the counter and crawl out on my hands and knees. Smiling —I had to keep from sighing out loud. Friend or foe, the customers took our meetings far more casually than we did; after all, they had been telling the editor what to do for years, it was Ed and I who were green. That first year, the best we could do was stand our ground. I was routed only once, by the only customer we've ever had who registered a complaint by crying.

We hadn't put her news in the paper. Didn't we like her? And at this point she burst into tears. She leaned on the reception desk and gave herself up to crying. Tears fell on her coat and spotted the velvet collar, they ran down her nose and landed splat on the counter. As speechless as she, I simply handed her a box of Kleenex. In a few minutes mopping-up operations were complete and she departed quite cheerfully, saying, "Well, I got to get home now. Always have dinner on the table by 5:30." She took the Kleenex with her.

In those days our machinery was dilapidated and the printers we found to run it were even more so, so it was possible to find a good deal to complain about in the *Record*. But our subscribers weren't consistent. The man who laid us out one moment was the one who bought fifty copies of the paper when he left on vacation; he was going to visit friends all through the Middle West and he wanted to show them how much better *his* home-town paper was than *their* home-town paper. The woman who announced in the presence of six other customers that she had no interest in the paper had come into the office to pay her subscription two years in advance. Sometimes even a complaint was a compliment. A man stopped Ed on the street and said brusquely, "See here, I saw a picture of the Snoqualmie River in the Seattle paper. How come you didn't print it in the *Valley Record*?"

"It would have been old stuff," Ed explained. "Everybody saw that picture in the Seattle paper, just as you did yourself. You wouldn't be interested in seeing it again."

"Is that so?" the man bellowed. "I don't care how many Seattle papers it was in, it don't count unless we have it in our own paper, too."

The only demand our multitude of bosses seldom made was that we give them the paper free. Once we agreed to barter. A man came in and explained that he hated to give up the local paper but he just didn't have the three dollars. "I raise bees," he said. "Let me pay in honey, and I'll take the paper for two years" and we agreed because we had no idea until he carried the "payment" in from his car, how much honey you can get for six dollars.

A little old lady in a rocking chair was the first person to demand a free subscription. Her father had been one of the first white settlers in the Valley. I had begun to write feature stories for the *Record* about the history of the Valley and for this reason I interviewed her. The little lady was friendly until I got up to leave. "I don't think it's fair," she burst out. "I'm one of the oldest residents of this entire Valley. I think you ought to give me a free subscription."

"But you said you read the *Record* every week. . . ."

She nodded briskly. "Yes, I do. My neighbor next door, Mrs. Twisk, subscribes. I borrow it from her. But I think I should have one of my own."

"I'll see that you do . . ." and that week I put her name on the subscription list with the note that she was to receive the paper free for the rest of her life.

The next week Mrs. Twisk canceled her subscription. "No use me paying that money every year," she explained. "My next-door neighbor gets the paper now and she told me to come over and read hers."

"How many times do the customers get to sock you," Ed said wearily, "before you can sock them back?"

"This was a nice little old lady. . . ."

"I know, but I'd fight her fair, at least until she hit me over the head with her rocking chair."

We laughed, when the sound didn't stick in our throats, about our efforts to get new subscribers. When we bought the paper there were only 1,800 people to tell us what to do; then there were 1,900; soon after, 2,000; and the more successful we were the more customers who would always be right instead of us.

"Someday," Ed would say dreamily, "I'm going to forget all that, and be a fearless journalist."

That day came. Perhaps Ed was a little more tired than usual, or perhaps we'd received another of those letters from Chicago telling us how lucky we were to be our own boss. In any case the telephone call which took Ed from the dinner table that night had the same effect on him that you get by pouring lemon juice on baking soda.

"Are you going to print a story about my son's wedding?" a woman demanded.

Ed asked for names and places, recalled the story, and sure that what he was about to say would please our customer mightily, he answered, "Yes, his bride sent me the story this morning, and it will be in this week's issue. It's a very nice story, too. . . ."

"I don't want you to print it!"

Ed glanced at me, and down at the dinner cooling on his plate, and there was a funny strained look about his mouth. "I'm sorry, Mrs. Wolfe," he said carefully, "but I didn't catch what you said. . . ."

"You are not to print that wedding story! If you do, I will cancel my subscription!"

This was the direst threat of all. Ed moved cautiously, though I could see a storm gathering in his face. "Have you read the story your daughter-in-law sent us?"

"Yes."

"Are the facts in it correct?"

"Yes."

"Then why don't you want me to print it in the *Record?*"

"My reasons are my own affair. You don't have to worry about them. All you have to do is leave that story out of the paper."

Ed drew a deep breath. Fearless journalism was unleashed at last as he retorted, for the first time since we had "been our own boss," "In that case, Mrs. Wolfe, I am going to print that story!"

"And *I* am going to cancel my subscription!" The telephone lines quivered with the sound of receivers crashing into place.

Mrs. Wolfe's subscription would not run out for another three months. "She said to cancel it," Ed insisted. "And it sounded like she meant it."

"If she wants a refund, she can come in and get it," I said. "Until she does, she has the paper coming to her and she's going to get it."

At the proper time we sent Mrs. Wolfe a bill. She was in the office a few days later. "Here's three dollars for another year," she said, dropping the money as if it were verminous. "But I want you to change the name on the subscription from *Mrs.* Wolfe to *Mr.* Wolfe. This is *his* money."

The next year she took out a two-year subscription to the *Record*. The year after that she and her husband bought a little store and they became regular advertisers in the *Record*. And somewhere along the line, at a point none of us could positively identify, she became a good friend of the *Record*, too.

ii

The heart of the country newspaper is its correspondents. Not foreign correspondents, those men in trench coats who are best known at the home office for their genius at creating misleading categories in their expense accounts. A correspondent, to a country editor, is a woman who writes about the doings in her own community. She's a housewife. She gets her "scoops" over the telephone in the kitchen, she writes them in pencil on any kind of paper she can find, and she often has to wash the pie crust off her hands before she can get to work. Country newspapers cover large, sparsely populated areas, and these women who write their "locals" are as important to them as wires are to the power company.

The day we bought the *Record* we met everyone who worked in the shop, but for months our nine or ten correspondents were faceless by-lines. They had distinctive handwriting. In fact, their spelling was pretty distinctive, too.

But one day as Ed was correcting a sheaf of "locals" he reflected, "You know, these women are our only representatives in their particular communities, but we haven't had the time to call on them, much less teach them some of the things they ought to know. How many of them have even visited the plant? Yet if they don't know us and don't understand our problems, how are they going to be good salesmen for the *Record*?"

I agreed heartily.

"Fine," Ed said. "You should drive around and visit our reporters, even those who write no more than a couple of paragraphs a week. And from now on you're in charge of all our correspondents."

In some ways, our correspondents were all the same. They were all friendly, they all stuffed me with food, they all knew more about the Valley and the *Valley Record* than I did, and they all offered to quit because "You'll probably want to look for someone good—after all, you come from Chicago."

One of them had been writing for the paper for eighteen years. She had outlasted several publishers and was now composing wedding stories about young people whose birth announcements she had written. Her name, to people of all ages, was Flossie.

Flossie's area was a farm community, but no city-room genius in Chicago or New York ever covered his territory as thoroughly. She fretted about getting every single "doing"— every visitor, every pinochle party, every auto trip into Seattle. If the morning mail brought her news, the afternoon delivery was apt to contain a frantic note asking, "Did I write up Mrs. Sarno's news? She called me especially and you know how she is. And did I spell her cousin's name right?" She worried particularly about finishing her news before the rural mail carrier came by. Many a Monday her mother, Grandma Pickering, who was even then a good deal closer to eighty than she was to seventy, would phone her daughter and say, "Flossie, you just leave your chores go today. I'll come over and do them because I know you've got to finish up your news."

There was always some important bit telephoned in five minutes before the mailman was due. Again and again her envelope of news contained a scribbled note—"Hope you can read this. I'm writing it at the mailbox while Julius (the rural carrier) is waiting. Please forgive handwriting. . . ." Because of Flossie the word "correspondent" will forever evoke this picture—of a middle-aged woman in housedress and flour-bespattered apron, trying to steady a bit of lined notepaper against a wobbly tin mailbox, frowning as she wets the tip of her pencil against her tongue so she can "finish up her news."

Writing about Grange meetings and quilting parties and church suppers for a country weekly is not the way to earn even your first million. During her long service Flossie had written news when the rate was so low she received fifty-four cents if she filled an entire column. But Flossie kept on writing news, and Flossie paid the light bill, and bought a piano for her son, and paid for his music lessons. Old subscription files prove that for eighteen years, even when her earnings were only a dollar or two a month, she always paid for her own subscription.

As "Bureau Chief" of our country correspondents, I decided to make an innovation. I announced that *Record* correspondents would hereafter get their *Record* free. To my amazement Flossie was more defiant than pleased. "I *always* paid for my paper," she told me, and three times a letter from her contained three one-dollar bills and three times I sent them back before I won the point. Flossie, being British by descent, lost every one of our battles except the last one. She accepted the subscription, all right, but every year thereafter she gave in return a box of homemade jams and preserves. Wild blackberry jam, plum jelly, peach preserves, apple butter, pickled melon rind, mint jelly with the leaves right in it—I couldn't have bought them in a store for five times the price of a subscription.

I speak particularly of Flossie because she was the veteran, but her juniors on the staff, women who had written for the *Record* for only eight or ten years, were like her. Every business call ended at the kitchen table over a pot of fresh hot coffee and a plate of homemade cookies or cake. There was the glorious day I visited four different correspondents; when I got back to the shop I hadn't done a thing to improve our journalistic practices and a truthful account of what I'd been doing all day sounded like the menu for a Scandinavian smörgåsbord.

Theoretically I was supposed to be teaching our correspondents how and what to write. "Look at that!" Ed would say pointing to some item like the one which read, "Mrs. Buchmeister passed away June 30 and was buried Saturday, June 26." Even the Linotype operator had been startled by this one, for in capital letters he had written afterward, "No wonder she died???????" There were others, almost every week.

"John Riley and Sam Duncan left town this week," a correspondent once reported. "They are at Fort Lewis to be inducted into the Army." Another wrote an article about a local boy who had enrolled in a "lifeboat training course"; he is still training lifeboats, so far as I know. Still another sent us an item about a local boy who made a trip to Chicago and while there, telephoned a local girl enrolled at Northwestern University. The story read, "While in Chicago, John Winters had a nice visit with Margaret Mathews, daughter of Mr. and Mrs. Lloyd Mathews by telephone." Spelling was as casual as the grammar. We had stories about people from Sue City, Iowa, and soldiers at Sand Lois Obisko, California. One of our correspondents set a record of twenty-three mistakes in one paragraph, but spelled Swedish names, places and organizations without a single error.

During a rare spell of perfectionism, I once telephoned a man whose name I was certain our correspondent had misspelled.

"This is the *Valley Record*," I said crisply. "I'd like to check the spelling of your name, which appears in a news item this week."

"What's that?" the man asked.

"I wanted to know, what is the correct spelling of your name? We have it 'Frances' for your first name. F-R-A-N-C-*E*-S. Shouldn't it be *I*-S?"

There was a pause. "Well," he said at last, "maybe. Some spell it one way, some another. I don't know."

"But how do you write it yourself?" I insisted.

He chuckled. "*E*-S, mostly, because that's the way it's always been in the paper. But you go ahead, lady, suit yourself."

The simplest part of my job as boss man for the correspondents was hiring and firing. They never did anything to fire them for, and they did the hiring.

The first time it happened, I was nonplused. A correspondent I hadn't even met decided to move into Seattle, which of course meant she could no longer write for the *Record*. I heard about it from the woman she had selected to replace her. Another of our reporters had to give up her job because of poor health. Her note of resignation said, "My neighbor, Mrs. Turner, says to tell you she wants to write the news so she started this week." In time I got to like the arrangement. It saved me considerable worry, this editorial matriarchy. Except for the day I stood up on my own feet, hired a new correspondent, then found the retiring reporter had also hired a new correspondent and it wasn't the same woman. I took a leaf out of Solomon's book and solved the problem amicably by dividing the territory in two and giving one half to her choice, the other half to mine.

One afternoon a tall, angular, gray-haired woman strode

into the *Record* office, slapped three dollars down on the counter and said, "I'm subscribing to the *Record*." The transaction complete, she asked, "How much do you pay for news?"

I had stammered out, "Eight cents a column inch . . ." before I thought to ask her why she wanted to know.

"That's good pay," she said briskly. "Higher than they give at Issaquah or Monroe. So I'll go to work for you."

I tried to object. She waved me to silence. "You aren't getting news from the community where I live. You ought to." She turned to the friend who had come in with her. "Well, Nellie, meet the new *Record* reporter."

She turned back to me. "Eight cents an inch. That's not bad but what else do I get?"

I blinked but couldn't help grinning. "We'll give you a commission of one dollar on every new subscription you bring in."

Her hand came down on the counter, palm up. "Give me back a dollar."

"But you haven't . . ."

"I just this minute brought in a new subscription!" She smiled broadly. "Mine."

I didn't have anything to say about hiring that correspondent, but at least I had seen her. However, when our correspondent in the community of Cedar Falls took a full-time job and could not continue to write for us, I hired her replacement by telephone. As usual she had been selected by her predecessor, so the call was a formality which I performed out of sheer stubbornness. She mentioned she was still in school and we could pick up her news at the principal's office every Monday morning.

I covered the mouthpiece with my hand and whispered to Ed, "She's a high-school girl, apparently. Do you think we ought to hire someone that young?"

Ed shrugged. "Your department, dear . . ."

So I hired her, sight unseen. On the appointed day I went to the high school. No Cedar Falls news at the principal's office. I asked to talk to her. Her name was not on the enrollment list. Had I tried the junior high school?

"Oh, *no,*" I objected. "She can't be that young. She's writing for the paper." But I did drive to the junior high school. Uneasily I repeated her name several times. No, she wasn't a student there—how about the grade school? I didn't believe it, but it was true. Our correspondent, our only local representative in a community of several hundred people, was practicing penmanship in the back row of the sixth grade. (We found out she needed the practice.) But she turned out to be a pretty good correspondent. Her mother could spell, her father could type, and her sister knew what was going on. She's the only reporter I've known who blew her first pay check on bubble gum.

Eventually I had to fire someone. The hawk-faced reporter who had pinned me to the wall of the *Record* office and hired herself liked journalism so much she was selling everything she wrote for us (and paid her for) to another newspaper (which paid her a second time). This worked out so well that she went even farther. She began copying news items out of a third weekly and selling them to us both.

"Enterprising," Ed commented when I presented him with the evidence.

"We can't keep her," I said. "If we're going to steal news out of someone else's paper, we don't have to pay her to do it for us. We'll have to get rid of her."

Ed's eyes narrowed. "You keep saying 'we.'"

"Well, you're the boss, after all, the big boss. . . ." Ed was shaking his head in a disturbingly deliberate manner, but I continued my argument. "Besides you know how better than I do—for years you've done a lot of hiring and firing. . . ."

"Not of women," Ed said firmly.

"But this is just a housewife, a perfectly harmless woman. . . ."

"I'd sooner face up to Jumping Joe Savoldi than a perfectly harmless woman."

I wailed, "But I never fired anyone before!"

"How well I know," Ed murmured. "Remember Violet?"

Did I remember Violet! The corn flakes-fed housemaid, the one Ed fired for me at an almost inestimable risk to life and limb. I sighed. "All right, dear, I'll fire this correspondent. But if I'm not back in the shop by four o'clock, notify the next of kin."

Once I daydreamed about replacing three or four of our correspondents with one well-trained newspaper woman, who could theoretically do the work of ten housewives and (still theoretically) do it right. For a time we did have a journalism-school graduate on the staff. Her tenure of office will be forever remembered by Ed and me, as well as by the whole town of Carnation, for the day she telephoned the Carnation fire department to see if the volunteer firemen had been called out during the week.

She found two telephone numbers listed in the telephone book. One rings the fire department office, which in a town of 600 is located in the Town Hall. The other is a special hook-up ringing the telephone of every fireman in Carnation. She chose the latter. Volunteer firemen dropped whatever they were doing, grabbed their coats, and raced to the phone. One of them was lying sick a-bed with flu and fever, but barefoot and weak he got to the phone, too, and all twelve firemen heard simultaneously the businesslike voice of our journalism graduate: "Hello, this is the *Valley Record* calling. Have you any news for the paper this week?"

Despite this experience, one time we let our cry for help be heard in the various journalism schools in this state, and several bright, pretty girls came out to Snoqualmie to apply for a job. I have my own reasons for remembering one of them.

I thought it had been a good interview. I had questioned the girl thoroughly, and she had given answers that convinced me she was just right for the job. Our "help" problems, in the reporting line, were solved. "When can you start?"

Her interest dropped away visibly. "I'm sorry," she said, "but I wouldn't be interested in working in a place like this."

I blurted out, "What do you mean?"

She shrugged. "Well, this is out in the country. I plan on working on a big paper. There aren't any openings in Seattle right now but I'd prefer San Francisco, anyway. Or possibly Chicago, or St. Louis."

"May I ask why you came here and applied for the job?"

She looked through the window at Snoqualmie's sleepy street. "I didn't know it was like *this*," she said, "and anyway, I thought it would be good experience to be interviewed."

I said sharply, "Look here, this is a small town, of course. And this is a weekly newspaper, not the *San Francisco Chronicle* or the *New York Times* or the *St. Louis Post-Dispatch*. But a weekly can be just as good a newspaper in its own way as a big daily. And it's wonderful to live in the country. Working on a small-town newspaper is a wonderful experience, too, something you'll miss entirely in the city. I know what I'm talking about. I worked on a big Chicago daily. I . . ."

She asked politely, "Oh, did *you* graduate from journalism school?"

"I never went to journalism school."

"Well?"

It was a significant word, and it hung in the air for what seemed like a long time. Then she stood up. "Well, then I

suppose you have to be satisfied with . . . with this . . ."
and she gestured around this funny country shop and this
funny little town.

I don't remember who ushered her to the door. I sat
right where I had been, with my head in my hand, wondering if that girl would live long enough to be half as good as
Flossie.

7

When we moaned about help problems, we meant help in the mechanical end of the business—printers, apprentices, Linotype operators, pressmen. The frontshop, or editorial department, continued smoothly as it always had and as, we thought, it always would. There was Margie, the ninety-pound bookkeeper, who doubled in brass on Thursday afternoons as a one-girl mailing department; Hermia, the assistant editor; Ort, the advertising manager. Let the backshop toss on troubled seas, up front our course was steady.

And then Margie gave notice. Her husband had found a good job in a town thirty or forty miles away, and they would soon be moving.

"As if we hadn't had enough trouble in the back," Ed

moaned. "Now we've got to start looking for help in the front."

Ed had been learning various operations in the backshop. His answer to help problems now was— Do it yourself. If I were to be of any help to the business, that would have to be my philosophy, too. Besides, he had developed a habit of studying me silently and muttering, "If I had only known, I would have married a Linotype operator instead of a writer." Here was my opportunity to prove I wasn't useless.

"Don't worry about replacing Margie," I said airily. "I'll take over her job."

Ed looked skeptical. "Margie acts as receptionist."

"Huh! That's easy."

"She also addresses the papers."

"What's so hard about that?"

"And Margie does all the bookkeeping."

I winced. I got *A* in high-school algebra but at that point I apparently hit my peak as a mathematician. Even my handling of a checking account in Illinois had not been without incident. Just before Christmas I had figured out my balance by adding, rather than subtracting, $100 on a check stub. This resulted in one of the most lavish holidays we ever enjoyed, with lots of presents for everyone, though seven checks bounced on Christmas Eve and if our little white-haired housemaid had not had a savings account it might have been a very awkward situation indeed. But here was Ed, learning to do many a chore in the backshop which he had never done before. Surely I could do my part. "I'll do the bookkeeping, too," I said, though I didn't know a double-entry ledger from a double chocolate soda.

"I don't know. . . ." This last brave statement of mine made Ed more skeptical than ever. "I don't see how you can do your own writing and keep house and do so many different jobs at the shop, too."

"I haven't kept house since we came," I retorted, "as anyone can see with half an eye. As for the rest, all it takes is careful scheduling."

Ed agreed. The way to get things done was to make out a list of the jobs we had to do, and then arrange them sensibly in a schedule. Schedules make for efficiency. The circles under our eyes, the aches in our backs—all because we hadn't been efficient, we hadn't worked out enough schedules.

After that we lived by schedules and lists of jobs. If we didn't finish all the jobs on the list, it was because we hadn't scheduled them right. Nothing dull about it, though. The unexpected was a daily occurrence so yesterday's plan was never any good. In our first 365 days in business for ourselves we must have worked out 365 schedules without repeating ourselves once. It made for efficiency, of sorts, if doing every job at a dead run is efficient.

My basic schedule went something like this: Alarm clock at 6:30, breakfast, housework, and getting the boys off to school until 8:30, writing at home until 2 P.M., work at the newspaper from 2 to 6, drive home and get supper for the boys, run boys' bath at 7:30, supper for Ed and me at 8, then proofreading or bindery work or whatever chores we had brought home from the shop. Bedtime? When the work was done.

There were a few flaws in our method of planning. We ignored the irrefutable fact that it takes time to get from one place to another. I always figured I could stop work at our home outside North Bend at 2 P.M. and start work at the shop, five miles distant, at exactly 2 P.M. Anything untoward, like running out of gas (the schedule never listed "stop at gasoline station," so we didn't stop), threw us into a tailspin. If a friend from out of town dropped in for a chat he found himself talking to the tops of our heads; we were looking at our watches.

Scheduling also led to a certain businesslike approach to matters unbusinesslike. I remember the glad day when my schedule read, "Finish work, 1 P.M., 1 to 4 P.M. do whatever I want." This was after three years in the Valley, and I had never made a social call or stopped at a friend's house for a cup of coffee. So promptly at 1 P.M. I went to the telephone and called one of these long-neglected friends.

"Martha," I said crisply, "I have a list here of social calls I have been wanting to make for the past three years. The first on the list is to see my neighbor's new baby, but he's two years old now and undoubtedly taking an afternoon nap. Your name is second on the list. So if you're not asleep, I will be glad to call on you from 1:15 to 3:45."

When I took over Margie's job, Ed suspected that no schedule in the world would make a bookkeeper out of me. Luckily, he kept a sharp eye on my efforts, and within two weeks we were advertising for a bookkeeper.

The first applicant got the job. "I'll stay as long as you want me to," she stated, "unless I get pregnant."

I gulped. "Are you . . . I mean, do you . . ." I gave up. "The Falls Printing Company," I said austerely, "would not think of interfering with the wonderful course of Nature."

"Good," she said briskly. "Now, what would you like me to do first?"

It was time to pay the bills. I explained our system. Last month I had begun at the front of the file, and paid all the way through the *J's*. So this month, she should start at the back, with the *X's, Y's* and *Z's*.

She looked at me curiously. "I have never run into that system at any of the other places I've worked. If you'll tell me what your receipts will be between now and the fifteenth of the month, I'll pay the bills in the, uh, usual way."

"Receipts?" I repeated, with a hollow ring to my voice.

She nodded briskly. "Most business houses can anticipate pretty accurately what their income is going to be."

"They *can?*"

She cocked her head to one side, studied me, and suddenly smiled. "You don't know much about this sort of thing, do you?" she said, indicating the day sheets and ledgers and other dollars-and-cents paraphernalia I had presented her with.

"For the past year I could have done a good job of book-keeping," I told her, "just by knowing how to fill out a disbursement sheet."

Although I failed as a bookkeeper, I made good as a mailer, a line of work in which the necessary ratio of brains to muscle fit me like a glove. The old Wing mailer Margie had used was costly, since many hours of high-paid typesetter's time were needed to keep up to date the printed names and addresses which fed through it. So we shelved it and bought an addressing device which could be maintained by the cheapest help in the world—the publisher's wife.

Ed didn't quite trust me with anything that had a motor, so he bought a treadle-type addressing machine and *I* was the motor. "This thing is so simple," he said kindly, "I don't think you can possibly do something wrong."

The theory was that unlike other antique equipment in the shop, I was not subject to "mechanical difficulties." I pumped my machineless machine every week for three years. Insert the folded paper under the stencil, push down with the right foot, bring the right foot up, slide the addressed paper out and start over again. Addressing 2,000 papers a week for 156 weeks comes to 312,000 times that I pushed the treadle down and brought it back.

I was hard at it one day, pumping papers through at the rate of about 1,500 an hour, when one of our local practitioners or chiropractic walked into the shop. He watched for some time in silence. Then he asked, "Do you do that often?"

"Once a week."

"Once a week!" He shook his head. "My, my," he murmured, "that *is* too bad. My, my . . ." and still shaking his head, he went quietly out the door. He was a perfect gentleman and did not rub his hands together until he got outside.

I claimed, sometimes loudly, that the mailing department

never made a mistake and never had a breakdown. Lucky for me that no one noticed the day a stencil stuck while I kept pumping and pushing papers through. Lucky, too, the man named Lee Lewis, if he needed something to start fires; he received eighty-three copies of the *Valley Record* that week.

Three years later I was promoted from mailing to circulation department. A friend from Chicago who came out to visit us paled at the fact. "Circulation departments" in Chicago are peopled by men who don't care whom they hit, and during a circulation war, they don't care how hard. In blue jeans, sneakers, and an old plaid shirt, I put on a pretty good imitation every Thursday morning, though I didn't dare run over anyone for fear he might be a paid-up subscriber and the extent of my goon tactics was to cover up all the Seattle newspapers on our local newstands with copies of the *Valley Record*.

Filling Margie's shoes (which, incidentally, I could have done with one foot) as receptionist and telephone girl was a delightful job. I began to meet and talk with people. Our readers were not only the people of Snoqualmie, where the shop was located, but of all the other towns in the Snoqualmie Valley—North Bend, Snoqualmie Falls, Cedar Falls, Fall City, Preston, Carnation and Duvall. Some have eight or nine hundred population, others have signs at their "city limits" proudly claiming two or three hundred. There were farmers, loggers, ministers of nine different denominations, Indians, men who had found platinum in Alaska and others of the "rocking chair brigade" who live on relief, the irreproachable civic leaders and the people who get talked about and don't care, high-school kids, housewives, truck drivers, saloon-keepers, all-night waitresses. Our assistant editor, who had lived in the Valley for almost twenty years, was my tutor, and I studied names and faces and personal histories like a senior cramming for a last exam. Of all the mental gymnastics I attempted, none trickier than trying to remember how local people were related to each other.

"Now Hilda Svendsen is a Smith," Hermia would begin patiently, "and so is Marjorie Nelson. But then, you see, Marjorie's brother-in-law, Sam Nelson, married her first cousin, whose name was Smith originally but his father died and his mother remarried and the stepfather adopted him and changed his name. So that means . . ."

When a pretty girl named Martha Grafton ordered wedding invitations for her marriage to someone named Rance Grafton, I did not bat an eyelash. On the other hand mother and son often did *not* have the same last name, and I got used to that, too. I committed my only bad *faux pas* during those first few months at the desk the day a young woman came in and asked if I could cash her pay check.

It was for $200, far more cash than our till had seen since we bought the business. "I'm sorry . . ."

The young lady had a sweet face, but it looked worried. "I wonder what to do," she said. "I'm leaving on my vacation very early in the morning, before the bank opens. I must have the money. Have you any idea where I might be able to cash a check?"

It was almost seven o'clock. The bank had been closed for hours, of course, and now all the grocery stores were locked up, too. But it suddenly struck me that there was still one place in town that was open and probably well supplied with cash. "I have it!" I said, really pleased with myself. "Go over to the tavern. I bet they'd have $200 in cash."

The girl's face lost its worried look and a slow smile turned up the corners of her mouth. "I'm the teacher at the Seventh Day Adventist grade school," she said. "How do you think it would look to have a tavern's endorsement on my pay check?"

ii

Just Plain Bill was going to leave us. He had a sick cousin in Montana, he explained. "But I'll be back," he promised. "I was never in a shop I liked better." On payday he disappeared over the horizon via an eastbound Greyhound bus.

"Do you think he meant it," I asked Ed, "about coming back?"

Ed shook his head. "He was headed east. A guy like that doesn't turn around. He keeps going."

"Well, cheer up. If he keeps going long enough he's bound to come back."

"Sure," Ed grinned, "but will we still be here when he checks in from Vladivostok?"

The parade of printers which followed Just Plain Bill included men of every conceivable degree of skill and sobriety. One was an eighteen-year-old apprentice who preferred running the big newspaper press to joining the Army, another was a man seventy-eight years old who had got his first job in a print shop when he was ten years old. No applicant was sent away without a day's work and a chance to show what he could do; for a while it looked like the Chicago public library was sending us all the old men in their reading room, one at a time.

Many of our printers were the kind of men whose proper names sounded inadequate after you looked at them. Shaky, for example. He had a name like Jack Simons or Tom Smith, but he looked like a professional gambler on a Mississippi riverboat, or perhaps an itinerant ham actor with a strong preference for playing the villain. Wide-brimmed black hat, set at a rakish angle. Long coat, belted in tightly. Cigarette in a long holder. His build was sturdy, but his hands were slender, with long, sensitive fingers. Shaky had reformed too late. Those long fingers shook too badly to do good work. His sturdy body shook. Even his voice, which should have been as firm as that of a landlord foreclosing the mortgage, came out in tremulous gasps. We wanted help desperately. But poor Shaky proved what Ed was beginning to suspect—that some kinds of help are worse than none at all.

We dreamed of the day when our backshop would be

manned by competent men who liked to stay in one place. Meanwhile Ed fell back on his theory that if he couldn't find a man to do the job, the only way to get the paper out was to do the job himself.

When the Army drafted the apprentice who did the press work, Ed stepped up and said, "I'll run the press."

Feeding big sheets of newsprint into a forty-three-year-old press is not a difficult job, if you've done it before. A press run normally took about two hours. It was noon when Ed climbed up to the pressman's platform, flipped the switch, and slid the first sheet of paper into the big press. Instantly, there was trouble. The big sheet of paper had not rolled smoothly around the cylinder, across the bed of type and out onto the delivery board at the other end. Instead it had glued itself to the ink rollers.

Ed got down from his perch, lifted the heavy rollers, and bit by bit picked the sheet of paper off. The ink used on such a press is the consistency of honey, and Ed would have looked a lot better if it were the color of honey, too. It took him about fifteen minutes to clean up the mess and get ready to start again. He washed, as well as he could, climbed back to the pressman's platform, slid a fresh sheet of newsprint down the board. The same thing happened again.

Olga was at the Linotype that day, and Ralph, our pillar in the backshop, was preparing pages for the next press run. Olga winced when Ed turned off the press for the second time, once more climbed down, lifted the rollers, and crawled into the inky mess.

Ralph called, "Leave it, Ed. I'll run the press as soon as I've finished over here."

Ed said doggedly, "I've got to learn sometime."

Another fifteen minutes of clean-up work, another try, another mess. Not knowing the machine, Ed assumed the trouble was what he had to expect as a beginner. The apprentice had assured him, when he left the week before, that the press was in perfect running order.

About two o'clock, I said, "Stop for a while. You haven't eaten breakfast and you haven't had lunch."

Ed shook his head. "I'm not hungry."

"Can't you make him quit?" Olga whispered to me. "He looks sick."

But Ed would not give up. It might be a long fight, but he had sunk his teeth into the enemy and there was no shaking him off. At six o'clock I went out to the restaurant, bought a hamburger, and brought it back to the shop. He ate it because I climbed up on the pressman's platform beside him and held it under his nose.

A number of sheets would go through properly. Then came the tearing sound as the paper caught in the wrong place, and the clank of metal as Ed groped for the switch and turned off the motor. He hardly spoke. His mouth was set in a hard line and his face, despite the smears of ink, looked pale and haggard.

When Ralph was washing up to leave, Ed called him over to the press. "Am I as stupid as I look?" he asked wearily. "The press is supposedly in good running order. For eight hours, I've figured the trouble was me. But I'm beginning to wonder."

"Here, let me run a few sheets through. . . ." Ralph climbed up, flipped the switch, and with the easy motion of the expert fed a sheet of paper into the press. There was the sickening sound of paper tearing, the jarring clash of metal against metal, and then sudden quiet. "Good night," Ralph muttered, "no one could feed that press. It's way out of kilter."

Ed waited silently while Ralph made the adjustments. As silently he cleaned the press, washed his hands, climbed back on the pressman's platform. He finished the entire press run, just a few minutes before midnight.

He got down very slowly, as if every joint and muscle ached. He walked to the water faucet, drew a glass of water, and took the aspirin bottle down from the shelf. His hands trembled as he shook three tablets into his palm.

"Thank goodness that's over," I breathed. "Now you can go home."

Ed shook his head. "I've got to write the editorial."

I was worried, and hence exasperated. "You've got to get some sleep!" I said crossly. "You'll be sick!"

Ed grinned. "That's a fine way to congratulate me in my hour of triumph. I just learned to run the press."

"The hard way. How could that pressman have told you the machine was in 'perfect running order'? He must have known it wasn't. And he knew you were going to try and run it."

"Too bad he's already quit," Ed said dryly. "I can't fire him."

"Why must *you* run the press? You're doing too many jobs already."

"I'll tell you why. Pa Kennedy would know why. Because now I'll never have to count on some punk apprentice or drunken pressman to do that job. Now I can do it myself."

"You can't do everything. It worries me. . . ."

"I'm doing what I've got to do. Now I've got to write an editorial. Cheer up. You look gloomy."

I didn't say it, but it was on my tongue, that I would not look so gloomy if he did not look so ill.

iii

In December Ort told us he had been offered an opportunity that was too good to pass up, and would be leaving after he had finished his work for the big Christmas edition.

Ort was full of ideas and youthful energy. It was going to be hard to find another advertising salesman like him, and I said as much to Ed.

"I'm not going to replace him," Ed replied. "The last

publisher needed an ad salesman because he was a printer and spent all his time in the backshop. *This* publisher isn't worth his salt in the backshop, but advertising is right in his line. I'll sell the ads."

This was an amazing statement, for Ed had always claimed that he could not sell and would do any other work in the world rather than try. It was an aversion based on experience. During the blackest days of the depression, when the door-to-door salesman was the housewife's natural enemy, the manufacturer of a certain kind of fly spray conducted a campaign in Philadelphia. Ed signed up to sell on commission. He was given a long sales talk, and a can of the spray so small it fit into the inside pocket of his coat.

"Kind of a small can for a whole day's demonstrating," Ed commented.

"If we gave you a bigger one, they could see through the window that you're a salesman. Put it in the inside pocket of your coat, and don't take it out until you're through the door."

The manager did not explain how Ed was to make such a small amount of spray last all day. By the end of his first day, Ed had found out. He had covered the Germantown area thoroughly, and only one housewife had allowed him to demonstrate the product. Ed was so grateful, and so footsore, that he did a thorough job. The spray was noninjurious to any fabric, he explained, you could apply it to drapes, leather chairs, upholstered sofas, rugs, and with the friendly housewife egging him on, that's what he did. In fact he emptied the can. When he finally straightened up and returned the damp container to his coat pocket, there wasn't a drop inside.

"Well, now," he said eagerly, reaching for his order book. "How many cans would you like . . ."

"Oh, I won't need any for a long time," said the housewife. "You've done such a thorough job, and you said the effects last for weeks, didn't you? I'll pick some up at the store, sometime."

The end of the day brought the end of that effort in selling. Ed bore that housewife some malice until a week or two later, when for the first time he took out the same suit he had been wearing that day in Germantown. He put on the coat, slid his wallet into the inside pocket. There was a gentle thud as the wallet dropped through the bottom of the pocket and fell at his feet.

Ed took off the coat, stared at the lining. Two weeks earlier it had been dampened by the "noninjurious to any fabric" fly spray. He touched it gingerly, and it crumbled between his fingers. For a minute he cursed the manufacturer. And then he thought of the friendly housewife who had urged him on to give a demonstration and then refused to buy. He thought of her drapes, and upholstered chairs, and rugs—and he began to grin.

His second foray into the jungles of the advertising business ended even more abruptly. Men were needed to sell advertising in a college magazine. Ed was scientific this time. He listed the products college men use, and set out confident that there were hundreds of dollars in commissions to be made by selling ads to the manufacturers of these products.

His first call was to a hat factory. "You say I should advertise in a college magazine because college men buy my product," said the bright-eyed little man he talked with. "How come you know what college men wear?"

Ed had a truthful answer to that one. "I'm a college man myself."

"Ah . . ." The hat manufacturer cocked his head to the side, surveyed Ed with twinkling eyes. "You come in here to sell me some advertising, you ain't even wearing a hat?"

At that point Ed decided selling was not his line, and that he hated it, besides. A later success did not change his mind. When he was night news editor at the *Chicago Times,* his "slot man" and copyreader was deaf. Ed bet rewrite man Ray Brennan ten dollars that he could sell everyone in the city room on the idea of buying a blind Hearing Ear dog for the slot man. The dog would hear for the man, the man would see for the dog—a worth-while project, and Ed put it over so convincingly that he collected fourteen dollars at a dollar a head, as well as the ten-dollar bet from Ray. "I hate selling," Ed repeated even then. My guess is that he had always hated it because the right field had never opened up for him. Someone else had already thought of selling iceboxes to Eskimos.

As the *Record's* ad salesman, Ed set a new record in low pressure. He liked to call on businessmen, because he liked people and it was a blessed relief to escape, if only for a few hours, from the tasks that were his in the backshop. The only part of selling advertising which Ed disliked was mentioning anything about an ad.

"Call on Dan Thomasen?" I'd ask.

"Yes, had a swell talk," Ed would reply with real enthusiasm. "He's put in a new line. I looked all around."

"Is he advertising this week?"

At this point Ed always became evasive. "Well, I don't know. He might."

"But what did he *say?*"

"He didn't say."

"Ed, listen, didn't you ask him?"

Ed shook his head. "He knew what I was there for. If he wanted an ad, he would have told me."

The first day Ed covered the ad beat, he met a lot of people, he made a lot of friends, and when he got home that night the car was loaded like Santa's sleigh. He brought in armload after armload. A copper-bottom frying pan—he had called at the hardware store. A Nylon slip—he'd been in the dry goods store. Tools, a bicycle horn, groceries, phonograph records—I could have drawn a detailed map of his activities that day, for he hadn't made a single call without buying something. "Just doesn't seem right to leave a store," he explained sheepishly, "without throwing some business their way."

"You're supposed to sell, not buy!" I moaned, looking at two boxes of groceries which were eloquent proof of why a

174

man should not shop for food without a grocery list. Luckily most of it would keep and the rest we could freeze.

It was bad enough to shoulder a job he had to force himself to do, worse still to add it to the burdens he was carrying already. He leapt from reporting to editing to press work to advertising, and back again. "It must be wonderful to have so much variety in your work," a friend wrote from Chicago. "And how lucky you are to be your own boss." But by two o'clock in the morning Ed would have liked a boss who could send him home, and the only variety he was in condition to appreciate would have been that of going to bed on time.

Mornings I worked on my writing at home, afternoons I transferred operations to the shop. I was at work in the kitchen one morning in January when the telephone rang. "Now what," I thought irritably. "Wrong number? Someone wants me to come to a Stanley party?" I got up reluctantly and answered with a curt, "Hello?"

I recognized the voice instantly. Calm as it was, it brought a funny tight feeling to my throat. How many times had I called to ask what to do for the measles, or when should the boys come in for a checkup, or should I get a prescription for Hiram's sore eye? It was our family doctor.

"Please don't be alarmed," he said, "but we've got your husband here at the hospital. He's resting comfortably. Could you come over right away?"

"Resting comfortably . . ." I'd heard that expression before, and it always referred to a patient who was beyond hope and meant the doctors were giving him something to ease the pain. I felt my heart skip. "ED . . . What happened to him?" The wonder was I didn't shriek it.

"He got sick at the office."

"What's wrong?"

The doctor said gently, "I can't be sure without further examination. Don't be frightened. But come, as soon as you can."

I dropped the receiver. The month before Ed had bought

an old wreck of a car so that I would have transportation, of sorts, and not be stranded in a house two miles from the nearest town. Sometimes it ran, sometimes it didn't. "Please, God . . ." I heard myself say out loud as I stepped on the starter. The motor turned over, stopped, then responded with the roar that meant it would run. Luckily it was only a few miles to the hospital, for I drove as if I were taking my first driving lesson. At every turn, every stop street, I recited each move—slow down, now look to the left, now signal. "Keep your head," an inner voice pleaded with me. "It can't be as bad as it sounded. Ed's never had a sick day in his life. He's been working too hard, but he can take it. . . ."

And another inner voice cried, "But how long can he take it? He's forty-four years old. And when at last the work is too much and the strain is too great—then what?"

8

I must have presented anything but the picture of a woman "keeping her head" when I finally reached the hospital—running into the waiting room in a pair of faded blue jeans and an old T-shirt of Ed's, looking wild-eyed and maybe a little bit silly.

The doctor met me in the corridor. His voice was gentle, but it was disturbing to hear him choose his words so carefully. "He's all right, he's doing fine," he kept repeating as he told me what had happened. Two of the men from the shop had brought Ed to the hospital. They reported that he had complained several times that morning of a sharp pain around his heart. When they suggested he go home, he had flatly refused because they were in the midst of putting together the pages for the last press run.

"We can finish the job without you," they insisted.

"I can't relax until the paper's out," he answered. "No use trying."

And then suddenly he doubled up with pain and blacked out. He regained consciousness quickly, but he was gasping for breath. The two men half-carried, half-led him, to the car. He was clutching at his chest and could hardly speak, but he did manage to whisper, "Don't tell Charlotte. . . ."

"It could be one of three things," the doctor was saying. "A perforated ulcer, a coronary, or some other type of heart attack. But so far I haven't been able to find anything organically wrong. I suspect his real trouble is nervous exhaustion, producing symptoms of other more serious conditions."

"Where is he?"

"Right down the hall, in that little examining room. There wasn't a vacant bed any place else. Now remember, we've got him under sedation, to lessen the pain and let him sleep. Don't be disturbed if he doesn't sound natural. Be calm and cheerful, for his sake." And then he opened the door to Ed's room, and I went inside.

Ed was awake, or at least awake enough to hear and see me. He tried to smile. His face seemed strained, but his eyes had a dreamy look to them, with the pupils dilated and very black. I think I said something like, "Well, for gosh sakes, what're you doing here?" in that too-bright, too-cheerful voice I've always resented in nurses.

He said something, but his voice was so weak I couldn't hear him. I leaned over the bed, and he repeated his question. "Everything going all right at the shop?"

"Everything's fine."

"Are you sure they got the changes into that hardware ad?" I nodded emphatically.

"Don't let them put both grocery ads on the same page."

"I won't."

"I didn't finish the headlines for page one."

"I will. . . ."

And that's the way our conversation went. I thought my husband might be dying. He was as scared as I, because he thought so, too. But the two of us sat in that little back room of the hospital and talked about every finicky detail of this week's issue of the *Record*. "Let's get the paper out"—*that* was the life and death matter, not what might, in the process, have happened to him. I thought— Is this what is means to be in business for yourself?

Finally Ed whispered, "You better get down to the shop. And don't forget about the hardware ad. . . ." I was at the door when he signaled to me to come back. "As soon as the paper is out, will you come back to the hospital?"

"Darling, of course . . ." I leaned down to kiss him, and he murmured drowsily against my cheek, "Good, I want to see a copy of the paper."

It was one thing to be "calm and cheerful" in the presence of a man who is drugged into semiconsciousness, but Hiram and Johnny were going to be wide awake when I explained their father's absence, and I dreaded it. All afternoon at the shop I recited the half-lies I would tell them, but when I got home that evening after another trip to the hospital, I simply blurted out, "Daddy's not coming home tonight."

The two little boys were sitting in the middle of the living-room floor, reading comic books. Lunch pails, jackets, caps and library books were spread around them in a magic circle. They looked up. "Where'd he go?"

All the explanations I had concocted deserted me utterly, and I replied "He's in the hospital."

I needn't have worried. "Having his tonsils out?" Hi asked cheerfully, naming the only reason he knew of for going to the hospital.

"Has *he* got measles?" little Johnny asked incredulously, also measuring his father's illness by the yardstick of his own experience.

"Checkup," I mumbled, falling back on a half-truth.

"Oh." They knew all about that. You get weighed and

measured, the doctor looks down your throat with a stick, someone jabs you with a needle. They smiled at me, tactfully making sure I did not expect them to continue the conversation. I managed a passable grin. Released, they turned back to their comic books.

By nightfall Ed was telling doctors, nurses and orderlies that he was going to get out of bed and go home. Modesty alone deterred him from defying the lot of them and walking the five miles to the house; someone had thoughtfully locked up his clothes.

At noon the next day the doctor called me and said, "You'd better come and get him."

"But I thought he was to stay in the hospital for a week at least."

There was a smile in the doctor's voice. "The idea of hospitalization was to force him to rest. Believe me, he's not resting!"

The doctor had examined Ed thoroughly that morning, and when I got to the hospital he repeated his opinion that there was nothing physically wrong.

"Then how could he suffer so much pain?" I asked.

"Nervousness," the doctor said. "The nerves around his heart and stomach caused a tightening, or contraction, of the blood vessels, so that it was hard for his heart to pump blood through them. Result was severe pain. When he relaxes, the heart and blood vessels function normally and the pain ceases."

"What treatment is there?"

"Keep him in bed for at least two weeks. Don't let him go to the shop, or talk about the shop, or even think about the shop. What he needs is a good vacation."

Ed hadn't had a vacation for three years. To say the word seemed daring; to think about it, an extravagance.

"A vacation will help him right now," the doctor continued. "But of course it's not a permanent solution. There's one basic cause of his illness, and it's the thing you've got to correct. He's working too hard. Or I should say, he's worrying too much. Work itself may not hurt him, but the tension he feels over it will."

My face must have expressed my feeling of hopelessness. The doctor was silent for a moment and then he added, "Kind of a tough prescription to fill, is it?"

I nodded. We were still short-handed in the backshop. It still took a six-day week and a fourteen-hour day to "get the paper out." We still needed someone to sell the ads and run the press and make up the pages. These were the necessities by which we lived, sink or swim, from one week's paper to the next. They would not evaporate conveniently because the publisher was sick.

"Two weeks in bed," I repeated, as if saying something often enough and calmly enough made it come true. "And then a good vacation."

For a few days Ed was so shocked by being ill that he lay quietly in bed. I took over as advertising salesman and the men in the backshop divided his other work. But as Ed's pain lessened, so did his regard for doctor's orders.

"You make the calls," he instructed me, "and I'll draw up the ads you sell."

"You're supposed to be in bed!"

"All right, I'll draw up the ads in bed."

The moment I drove away he was out of bed, and he divided the day between working at the kitchen table and telephoning the shop to see what was going on. In the evening I tried to make him relax by discussing our vacation.

Ed shrugged. "Poor time of year for a vacation. Besides, I can't get away right now."

"The doctor said . . ."

"He said there was nothing wrong with me. Now, where are those page proofs you were going to bring home?"

And I was faced with the choice of making a scene, which

would be bad for him, or letting him ignore doctor's orders, which might be worse.

I was smart enough to realize that I couldn't make him relax by shaking a fist under his nose and shouting, "Stop being nervous!" I would be clever. I would offer suggestions so tempting that he would follow them without noticing that he was being pulled away from the shop. . . . When Sunday dawned clear and sunny, I suggested we take a day's auto trip to Mount Rainier.

Ed was still sick enough to listen to his wife, and even allowed me to drive the car while he stretched out on the back seat with a blanket pulled up under his chin. Hiram and Johnny climbed onto the front seat next to me and we set out.

In my enthusiasm for a change of scene, I had forgotten that January is not the best month in which to drive up the side of a 14,000-foot peak. Soon there were snowbanks at each side, and long stretches where the road glittered with a coating of ice. In time the last little settlement was well behind us. Not a house, not a car, for miles and miles.

When the snow got so deep chains were necessary, I stopped and turned the car around. We all piled out into a snowdrift, even Ed, and for an hour threw snowballs and laughed and played together. He was relaxing. My "cure" was working. I was triumphant.

The boys had no mittens, and their hands were cold; that was our reason for starting home. Ed got in the back seat, the boys vaulted into the front. We had gone a mile or two down the mountain when I realized something was wrong.

"Ed?"

He did not answer. The boys were singing a Cub Scout song at the top of their lungs. "Ed?" I repeated, a little louder. Still no reply. I cast a frantic glance over my shoulder. He was unconscious.

Thank God for whatever self-control it was that kept me from slamming my foot down hard on the brake, for we were going downhill on glare ice. I took my foot off the gas, waited helplessly for the car to roll to the bottom of the hill and stop.

I got into the back seat. "Ed . . ."

"It hurts . . ." He was conscious now, but his breathing was loud and irregular, as if he couldn't get enough air into his lungs.

"Where?"

He closed his eyes, his face contorted by a spasm of pain. But his hands answered. Weakly, they tapped at his chest.

Another heart attack . . .

That drive, with Ed half-conscious on the back seat and two merry boys chattering up front, must have taken less than an hour. But the ice seemed to stretch for miles and miles. Even a small skid might throw the children against the windshield and hurt them. Or the car might slide into a drift and get stuck, which would make our predicament even more desperate. There was nothing to do but hold the car to fifteen miles an hour, keep my eye on the road, hold tight, pray. And all that time, with the little boys' laughter ringing in my ears, I did not know but that Ed was dying.

At the first settlement, I slowed to stop.

"No, don't stop," Ed called in a strangled voice. "The worst is over. Keep on toward home."

The nearest doctor was still perhaps thirty miles away, somewhere in the direction we were going anyway. And what could he do for Ed, at the other end of a telephone line? I drove on. It was dark when we got home, and the longest, darkest Sunday I've ever known came to a close.

Our family doctor answered my call immediately. "It's another attack similar to the one he had two weeks ago," he told me after he had examined Ed and made him swallow a sleeping pill. "I recommend that you take him to a cardiac specialist in Seattle. I feel sure it's nervous fatigue, but you and Ed will feel better if you hear a specialist's opinion. And I could be wrong, too."

The specialist was as methodical and cold as a machine. For two hours he put Ed through tests and examinations while I sat in a pale-blue waiting room and tried to concentrate on a fashion magazine. Finally the nurse signaled to me to come into the doctor's office.

Ed and I sat side by side, facing the doctor. The verdict we heard was what our family doctor in Snoqualmie had told us two weeks before. "You've been living under tension too long. . . . Your nerves have finally rebelled. No disease— yet. But if these nervous attacks are repeated often enough, your heart will eventually be damaged, and then you will have 'real,' or organic, heart disease. . . ."

And his final words were, "What you need is a good vacation."

On the way home from Seattle, Ed agreed that the moment the Easter issue was off the press, we would leave on vacation. Thursday, March 21st—that was three weeks away.

"Promise we'll go, no matter what?"

Ed nodded solemnly. "No matter what."

ii

Mr. and Mrs. Charles Dwelley were nineteen and sixteen years old, respectively, when they married and bought the newspaper in Concrete, Washington. When their granddaughter was four years old, they went on their first vacation.

The owner of a small business who talks about vacation is a little odd, but he who adds the phrase "no matter what" is downright mad. We would leave in three weeks—Ed had promised. Forthwith he broke out with shingles.

Not shingles as I had ever known them, which confine themselves to an inflamed ring around the chest. Ed had shingles in the grand manner. All over his body, under his arms, at the backs of his knees, on his scalp. Sometimes shingles itch, sometimes they burn, but Ed had enough of them so that they could manage handily to burn and itch at the same time. Shingles kept him from sleeping, yet lack of sleep made the shingles worse.

At last he found that if he lay in a bathtub of warm water, the pain and the itching subsided. For ten days, that was our sleeping arrangement—Ed submerged in the bathtub, I tense and sleepless in the bedroom, wondering if his head might have slipped and was it time to charge in and drag him out of the water.

Ed's editorial that week was entitled "SCRATCHING THE BOTTOM of the barrel." In it he explained there was only one subject close to his heart, and that was his shingles. Only one question he had been able to ponder seriously, and that was how to get rid of them. The editorial brought instant and sympathetic response.

"Don't know what to do for the shingles," one reader wrote. "I've had more experience with the shakes." Another man appeared at the shop with a large jar of ointment and came back every afternoon on his way home from the lumber mill to see how Ed was feeling. A third phoned to say he didn't know of a cure, but he was working nights and would gladly scratch Ed days. A local music teacher sent a newspaper clipping about a gorilla in the St. Louis zoo who shared my husband's plight; he itched, though the cause of it was mosquito bites. The zoo keepers' wonderful cure was to pepper him with a B B gun whenever he tried to scratch. "How's this for a treatment?" said the music teacher's note. "If you can't get your wife to do it, call for volunteers." More of our readers had had hives, shingles and assorted itches than we had ever dreamed. They united valiantly behind their beleaguered editor.

Ed tried every cure suggested, except the B B gun. One sympathetic reader came to the house at night with a jar of homemade remedy, and knocking on the door awakened Ed from the first real sleep he'd had in a week. It took the contents of the jar, applied to his body like stucco to a wall, to put him back to sleep.

Ed was recovering from the shingles, and it was two weeks before our vacation was to begin, when Johnny came down with the mumps.

The doctor was reassuring. "He'll be over them by March twenty-first," he said.

I was so worried about Johnny's being well enough to travel that I scarcely noticed that Ed was now sporting a bad head cold. At the end of every day I sighed, "Only eleven more days . . . Only ten more days . . ." A week passed. Johnny, praises be, was almost well. A week to go. Then Hi got sick. Mumps.

"Will we be able to leave next week?" I begged the doctor, almost in tears.

"We'll see," he replied. "I'm not so sure that it is *mumps*."

In a day or two, Hi's face was back to normal. By that time the doctor was in the habit of stopping at the house once a day without even being called. "Just as I thought," he said. "It wasn't mumps at all. Send him back to school."

Two days to go. Johnny and Hiram were both back in school. But that night Hi went to bed without supper, and lay there listlessly, complaining of a bad headache.

"What's wrong, Hi?" I asked, hysteria tingling in the back of my throat.

"Oh, nothing."

"But why do you have a headache? Did you fall or get bumped at school today?"

He shrugged. "Oh, yes, *that*. We were playing a game during recess, and I hit my head on the concrete. . . ."

I raced to the telephone.

"A slight concussion," the doctor said. "Keep him in bed, and very quiet. Watch for exceptional drowsiness. If he should vomit or run a fever, call me immediately." That was the night of March 19.

The next day Ed's cold was worse but Hi was better. I got everything packed, cleaned out the refrigerator, took the house plants to the neighbor's, and made arrangements with the girl across the road to feed the cats. Tomorrow, tomorrow, we would leave on vacation. Surely we had already met and conquered all the "no matter whats."

I woke up the next morning with a funny tight feeling in my jaw. I rushed to the mirror. The left side of my face, from the back of my ear to the point of my chin, was swollen into a painful half-moon. I stumbled to the telephone. And literally stumbled. On the rug right below the telephone the big black mother cat was occupied in producing a new litter of big black kittens. That did it. I burst into loud sobs.

Somehow I managed to dial the doctor's number. "Doctor," I wailed into the mouthpiece, "doctor, come quick, our cat is having kittens!"

"Oh, I see," the doctor said, after a scarcely perceptible pause. "Anything else? Wasn't your vacation to start today?"

"Yes, and now we can't! Ed's got a bad cold, and Hiram has a concussion. Johnny's all right, but now *me!*"

The doctor asked me several questions, and listened patiently to my disjointed answers. "Doesn't sound like mumps," he concluded. "Sounds like glandular fever, not contagious. Look, is there any member of your family old enough and well enough to drive the car?"

"Ed could, maybe. . . ."

"Then for heaven's sakes put that fool cat outside, all the rest of you get into the car and leave. Don't wait another minute."

But we had to wait until the paper was out, so it wasn't until 4:30 that afternoon that the four of us got into the car and started out. Hi was stretched out on a pile of blankets in the back seat, nursing his concussion. Johnny was catching Ed's head cold. My face was so badly swollen I could scarcely open my mouth or swallow. Ed, our driver, was in relatively good health; all he could boast of was two heart attacks, a severe case of shingles, a head cold, and a sacroiliac that had slipped out of place that morning when he lifted a bundle of newsprint.

We stopped in North Bend to fill the tank with gas. Bake, the six-foot four-inch sergeant of the state patrol unit, saw us and called out, "Looks like you're going some place."

Actually we looked like a wholesale shipment for the county hospital. "Headed for California," said Ed, gay as a pallbearer.

"Through Snoqualmie Pass?"

Ed nodded.

Bake looked surprised. "Haven't heard about the snowstorm up there?"

"Don't believe I have." Ed sounded supremely indifferent. What's a March snowstorm, when all you have to do is drive 200 miles in the dark?

We crawled through the mountain pass, and found the roads clear and dry on the other side. Ed had been too tense to speak. Now he allowed himself a tremendous sigh. "Thank goodness, that's behind us. . . ." At that point, Hi sat up. "I'm going to be sick, Mama," he said, and threw up all over the car.

After fifteen minutes of clean-up work, we were ready to get back on the road. The doctor's warning came back to me with sickening impact. "If he should vomit, or run a fever . . ." I felt of Hiram's forehead. It was burning hot.

The nearest town was Yakima. "We'll go straight to a motel," Ed said between clenched teeth. "Put Hi to bed, and call a doctor."

There was no shopping for a good motel that night; we pulled into the first one we came to. Ed carried Hi inside and laid him gently on the bed. The little boy's skin felt tight, and his eyelids drooped.

"I'll find a doctor," Ed whispered, and hurried to the telephone in the manager's office. He was back a few minutes later. "Couldn't get anyone to come right away. But I reached two different doctors' wives and they both promised their husbands would call when they come in." He glanced anxiously at Hi. "What do you think—should I take him to the hospital?"

"He seems to be sleeping. Perhaps we'd better wait. . . ."

I had packed a box of food. Ed brought it in from the car, and I began to cook supper for Johnny. "Hungry?"

Ed shook his head. "You?"

"I couldn't swallow if I tried."

But Johnny had not lost his appetite. So I heated a frying pan, took a piece of steak from the box of supplies, and soon the room was filled with the smell of beef sizzling in butter.

Johnny was just sitting down to a steak sandwich and Ed and I were looking bleakly at each other, wondering what to do next, when Hi's voice split the unhappy silence. "Say, Mom," it said, and it was the heartiest, healthiest voice in the world. "I smell something good. What are you cooking?"

Ed and I tripped over each other to get to the bed. Hi was sitting up, bright-eyed, wide awake. I felt his forehead, his cheeks, his neck. The fever was gone.

"I feel just about starved," he said. "You got any steak?"

Ed and I looked at each other. "I'll cook it for him," said Ed, with a slaphappy grin.

"No, I will!"

"Let's both cook. And say, let's make enough for all of us."

Thus began our first vacation.

iii

The tired businessman's vacation is not very different from anyone else's. He arouses everyone in the family at six A.M. so that they can get out on the highway before the heavy traffic. He wants to see how many miles he can cover in a day so there's no stopping, or even slowing down, for sight-seeing and by the time he's ready to call it quits at night it's too dark to see anything, either. We weren't going any place, but we had to get there fast.

Ed was startled by my suggestion that we stop in a little town in Oregon to visit a college friend of mine. "But the new highway by-passes that town!"

"The town is only a mile off the road."

Ed shook his head. "Takes us out of the way. I figured on being in Roseburg by lunch time."

"Roseburg? Why? Who wants to drive way over to Rose-burg?"

Now Ed was really amazed. "For gosh sakes, honey, the man who bought our old Lee newspaper press has a print shop there, you know that. I wouldn't want to come only fifty miles from Roseburg and not drive over to see the Lee."

No, we didn't visit my college friend, but we did pay a call on a press.

Two weeks later we were back in the Snoqualmie Valley. We didn't have much of a sun tan, but you can't expect to if you don't get out of the car until after dark. We weren't exactly rested, either. But our vacation had been just what the doctor ordered, Ed felt. We had visited five weekly newspapers in Oregon and seven in California.

Vacation had been all-important to us, but until we stopped in North Bend on our way home we thought it was a matter of complete indifference to everyone else. We parked in front of a delicatessen and I went inside to buy a loaf of bread. North Bend's mayor was seated at the counter with a glass of Coke in his hand. At the sight of me he got off the stool and hurried across the store. "Just get back?"

I was immensely pleased that anyone had noticed we had been gone. "Why, yes," I replied happily. "Just pulled in this minute."

"Haven't, uh, talked with anyone?"

It was a puzzling question. "You're a one-man welcoming committee," I replied.

The mayor seemed to have something on his mind. He looked at me, then through the window at Ed and the boys in the car, then back again. "Well, I . . ." He squared his chin. "Haven't been home yet?"

I said uneasily, "No . . ."

There was a pause. "Well," the mayor said, "I guess you don't know your house has been robbed."

9

When the first issue of the *Record* under our ownership was about to come out, Ed decided to distribute sample copies to everyone who did not already subscribe.

"How many extra papers will you need so as to fill every box in the post office?" he asked Snoqualmie's postmaster, and after a moment of deliberation, Jerry replied, "Could you give me twenty, maybe twenty-five?"

That was readership to rouse envy in the heart of any big-city publisher. The advertisers, the subscribers, the publisher, all benefit from it; it's a wonderful thing for every one, except for the country editor who in his innocence writes an editorial telling everyone that he's leaving on vacation.

Ed had taken our readers into his confidence when he had the shingles, and been richly rewarded by their response. So in an editorial called "Operation Vacation" he confided, "By the time you read this paragraph we ought to be somewhere near San Francisco. . . ." That editorial appeared on March 21, and the rich reward followed on March 27, when a person or persons who apparently had absolute faith in whatever they read in the *Record,* broke into our house and made off with $400 worth of our belongings.

It was an unforgettable homecoming. Gone our contented smiles at being home at last, silent the children who had been bouncing excitedly in the back seat. We drove from the delicatessen to the house in tense and apprehensive silence. Before we left on vacation I had prepared a surprise for Ed, by arranging with a painter to finish work on the ceilings during our absence. Ed scarcely noticed, and I couldn't blame him; the surprise someone else had prepared was so much more spectacular.

The window over the kitchen sink had been broken. Glass lay in bits and pieces all over the sink, counters and floor. Our furniture had been shoved into piles in the middle of each room (that was the painter's handiwork) and a crazy maze of muddy footprints had hardened on the kitchen floor (these contributed by the sheriff's deputies). "It's fun to go some place, but it's great to be back home"—that's what you're supposed to say when a vacation ends. All we could think was, "Who did it?" and, "What did they take?"

The neighbor who had been feeding the cats in our absence saw our return and within seconds was sprinting up the driveway to tell us all about it. It was she who had discovered the open door, then noticed the broken window and the old stepladder braced against the wall underneath. It was she who had rounded up every branch of the law in this area—the town marshal of North Bend, the King County sheriff, and the Washington State Patrol. City, county, state

—they had all investigated, all asked the very questions we were now putting to ourselves—Who did it, and what did they take?

In the turmoil, nothing seemed to be missing. It was like Hiram's comment about the kindergarten roll call; you can't answer "Absent," you can only answer "Present." If "they" had stolen the coffee table against which I barked my shins every time I walked into the room, the absence of the table would have registered the first time I got through the living room without yelling Ouch. But it's hard to be conscious of things that aren't there. I didn't know my sterling silver candy dish was gone, until I reached for a bonbon. I studied the top of the desk for a long time before I realized it was the absence of my typewriter that made it look so bare. I didn't miss the satin comforter until a night turned cold. And so on. It was several days before the list of stolen property was complete and I turned it over to the deputies. Typewriter, silver, portable phonograph, records, comforter—it added up to $400 worth of property and such a big armload we felt sure one person could not have hauled it away.

Ed's last act before we departed on vacation had been to leave an address in California to which issues of the *Record* published in his absence were to be mailed. That was the reason that the biggest news of the week, the robbery of the editor's house, did not appear in the editor's paper. Ralph, our backshop foreman, and Marguerite, our new associate editor, agreed it was a bit of intelligence that would do nothing to help the weary publisher relax. The suppression of the truth about the robbery continued. In fact the more we knew, the less we printed, by order of the constabulary who wanted to work "in secrecy."

"We're hot on their trail," the sheriff's deputies told us, "but we don't want 'em to know it."

Since we live outside the limits of any incorporated town, police work in our neighborhood is in the hands of the county sheriff's department. Regulars on the beat are deputies Melvin Moe and John Anthony, who drive some 72,-000 miles a year in the process of chasing bad boys and locating stolen cars. About a month after the robbery, the team of Moe and Anthony marched triumphantly into the *Record* office.

"Ever seen this before?" Moe inquired, and held aloft the children's portable phonograph.

"The boys' phonograph!"

Moe grinned. "That's what I thought. We been lying out in the woods since nine o'clock this morning, listening to the kids that go in there to peel cascara bark. Four hours, lying behind a couple of logs. It was all of four hours, wasn't it, John?"

Anthony smiled wryly. "Longest time I ever knew you to keep quiet."

Moe's reddish eyebrows shot up. "I was listening!" He turned to Ed and me. "I had a pretty good idea who might of done it. Then I heard this one little kid telling about the new phonograph they had at home, and she kept talking about a bright green record. Your boys had a record like that?"

" 'The Arkansas Traveler!' " It was new, and it was their favorite.

Moe nodded sagely. "So we went to the kid's house, and there was this here phonograph."

"Then you know who the robbers were?"

Moe grinned. "Sure. But you just wait. We're going to find the rest of your stuff."

In a few days they were back with the satin comforter, a day or two later with the typewriter, until all the stolen articles were rounded up, identified, marked with tags saying "Case 93605" and deposited in the county building in Seattle. The sheriff's officers found everything "they" had taken. And then one evening, I discovered who "they" were.

I was cooking supper for Hiram and Johnny when the black-and-white patrol car wheeled into our yard and Officer Moe stepped out. "Wanted to make sure you were here," he said when I met him at the back door. He turned and whistled to his partner. "O.K., John, bring him in."

Anthony got out, opened the back door of the patrol car, and muttered, "All right, kid, come with me."

A boy stepped out. Anthony put a hand on his elbow and steered him into the kitchen. He stood near the door, hands in pockets, eyes on the floor, with one deputy on one side, one on the other. A teen-age boy, with blond hair and blue eyes.

"Well," said Moe, "here he is. Here's the guy we've been looking for."

Hi and Johnny stared at the boy, not saying a word. I was as silent as they. I didn't feel relieved, or grateful. I felt shocked, and a little bit sick at my stomach.

"How'd you get in?" Moe asked him.

"Broke that window over there. . . ."

"Who was with you?"

"I done it all alone."

"You couldn't of. Come on, kid, I heard this kind of answers before. You're just a punk to me."

"I done it all alone, I told you!"

The questioning lasted only a minute or two, but it seemed interminable. I didn't want to look at that sullen, unhappy boy any more than he wanted to look at me.

"Were you scared?" Moe asked him.

"Plenty scared . . ." the boy said, and then they took him back to the car and drove away.

The boy lived with a family whose name I had seen often, on our subscription list. Phonograph, comforter, silver, were found at that home. The typewriter was in a restaurant operated by a father-in-law. But no one in that family had realized any of the articles had been stolen. They told the police they thought the boy had bought everything—phonograph, records, silver, and $250 office typewriter. The boy never changed his story— "I done it all alone. . . ."

The next year property stolen during another robbery was traced to the same home. Once again the family had no idea the loot was stolen, once again the boy confessed and insisted he had done it all alone. But by then he had passed his eighteenth birthday. He was tried in a justice court along with thieves of all ages, and he went to county jail. A year later, he was dead, killed instantly when his hot rod crashed during a race with another teen-ager. Perhaps he had really done it all alone. It's certain he was very much alone when he went to jail, alone when he had to face the world afterward and ask for a job, alone when he died. For two years he had been the main character in many a news story and many an editorial we had written for the *Record*, but until the report of his death, he had never once been mentioned by name.

Shortly after his death the bookkeeper made a list of readers who were behind in paying for their subscriptions. One name stood out—the name of the family the boy had lived with. They had been *Record* subscribers for five years, the card showed, but now payment was six months overdue. I scrawled across the card, "Canceled for nonpayment." All afternoon the memory kept coming back to me of the evening Moe and Anthony had brought the boy into my kitchen.

One of their questions had been, "Did you know the Groshells were away on vacation?"

The boy had nodded, still staring at the toes of his boots. "How did you know?"

Surprise broke through the boy's sullen scowl. He looked up at Officer Moe as if he couldn't believe the man who had caught him could know so little. "Gosh!" he exclaimed, "I read about it in the *Valley Record!*"

We had lived through seventy-five Thursdays before we had
our first vacation. As a free-lance writer I had spent the
same number of weeks chasing the Muse around basements
and kitchens and other peoples' living rooms. About the
first of May Ed decided the time had come to provide me
with suitable working quarters.

He called in the men who had built our house in six
weeks and said, "Barney, my wife's birthday is on May
twenty-second. Her birthday present is going to be a little
house where she can write. About twelve by sixteen, with
a fireplace and some big windows facing the mountain.
O.K.?"

"O.K.," said Barney, who seems to share Ed's conviction
that anything worth doing is worth doing fast. "Cedar
board and batten?"

"Yup."

"Knotty cedar paneling, and a little fireplace?"

"Good. With a raised hearth about so high. . . ."

"You draw up what you want. I'll get the men lined up
for the first thing Monday morning."

By May twenty-second we had moved books into as beautiful a little studio as any writer, even a good one, has ever
deserved. It was built in the far corner of our meadow, next
to huge stumps of cedar trees that must have been 500
years old when they were cut a half century ago. Their
blunt tops are higher than the roof of the studio. They are
nineteen feet in diameter; five or six people could hide in
the hollow trunks. Fifty years of rain and wind have beaten
against them, and changed nothing but their color. Some
farmer of a few decades ago tried to burn them down, and
he had to give up, too. Huckleberry bushes and wild black-
cap vines grow in the dirt-filled ravines weather has etched

down their sides, and they are striped, here and there, by velvety-green moss.

"When are you going to blast those stumps out of there?" a neighbor asked. "You put up a real nice cottage and then leave those old things right next to it." I am silly, indeed, in this area where the "stump rancher" is the poor soul who can't afford cleared land and a truly prosperous farmer is the man who has finally got rid of every stump on the place.

Even Ed doubted my good sense. "It would look nicer without them," he said. "How about it?"

My protests were so violent he gave up. He tolerated the stumps, until a wealthy woman from Seattle paid us a call.

She admired the view, liked the house and approved of the writing studio. But the two cedar stumps brought rave notices. "How *fortunate* you are!" she exclaimed, as if she had just run onto a genuine Toulouse-Lautree in the sale bin at a second-hand store. "I've been having my entire garden landscaped in this new rustic manner, and the stumps they brought in and planted cost me $150 apiece!"

"How about it?" I asked Ed after the visitor had gone. "It really would look nicer without them. Let's blast them out."

"Don't you touch a splinter of those beautiful stumps!" said my now-aesthetic husband.

I'm sure Shakespeare wouldn't have done a better job on *Hamlet* if he had written it in a turret of Elsinore. But when I moved into my writing house at the foot of Mount Si, I was working on the historical novel about the Snoqualmie Valley later published as *Gold Mountain,* and I had the special pleasure the great writer missed of literally sitting on the spot I was writing about. Our acreage had once been part of the homestead owned by the man for whom the mountain in our front yard was named. My little writing house is not far from the spot where his cabin stood.

Every day I went out to write, I looked out on the prairie, the timber, the mountain and the river, which had awed the first immigrants from the dry plains of Kansas and Iowa when they made their way through the Snoqualmie Pass almost a hundred years ago. At my back were stumps of trees that had been cut down when lumber for houses hereabouts was fashioned with draw knife, froe and adz. My location may have done nothing for the book, but it did a lot for me.

A historical novel was actually a by-product of our attempt to make the *Record* a readable paper. As country publishers we were only three weeks old when a notice in the *Record* stated that the speaker for next Monday afternoon's meeting of the Snoqualmie Falls Woman's Club would be Mrs. Olive Quigley, the third white child to be born in the Snoqualmie Valley.

"You cover it," Ed told me. "Might be a nice feature for the paper."

"How can I spend a whole afternoon at a club meeting?" I protested. "We've got to get the paper out."

Ed burst out laughing. "Listen to that. The veteran Chicago newspaperwoman. Can't be out of the shop two hours on Monday because we've got to print a paper three days later. The pace out here too fast for you, kid?"

Mrs. Quigley was delightful. She had white hair, bright eyes, and the kind of genial philosophy and dry good humor that characterize people who look back over seventy or eighty hard years with affection because they know they aren't going to have to go through all that again. Mrs. Quigley spoke of going to school when daily routine included sending some agile pupil out to climb a tree to see if a war party of Yakima Indians was coming. The boy knew that if he reported "Yakimas are coming!" teacher would send everyone home. This had the effect of sharpening his eyesight to the point where he often saw Indians that weren't there, for the Yakimas never came. Mrs. Quigley told of the squatter who turned his pigs loose because he had so little cleared land he couldn't raise grain to feed them. The pigs, wild with hunger, terrorized the children; as a little girl Mrs. Quigley had seen them wade out into the river to feed on spawning salmon. Such reminiscences went into the story I wrote for our paper that week. But my notes covered pages and pages, and I could see that the little old lady with the twinkling eyes and warm chuckle had only just begun.

"I think I'll hold onto my notes," I told Ed that evening. "Someday, maybe, I'll have time to write a book."

Our readers said they liked that first story about pioneer days in the Valley. So whenever time permitted, I called on an old-timer, and his recollections of both the bad and the good of the good old days appeared in another feature story —"Meet Your Neighbor"—in the *Valley Record*. As the list of feature stories lengthened, my notebook of material for a book grew. There was no commercialism about these stories; they were about old-timers, not advertisers. They were a labor of love.

My ears are not infallible, and neither were the memories of the old people I interviewed, so there was hardly a feature free of at least one statement which was immediately challenged by at least one other old-timer. That particular schoolhouse stood on the north bank of the river, said an alumnus of the sixth-grade class of '86. No, it was on the south bank and I ought to know because my aunt taught there, someone else replied. Many a question was raised, but no matter how hot the controversy no one said we shouldn't have printed it. And the co-operation I received was enough to convince me that the nicest people in the world are at least seventy years old.

By and by it became generally known that the editor's wife was writing a book. This brought a shrewd comment from the wife of one of the Valley's early settlers. "You're going to get into hot water," she warned me. "Either you're going to change things around, and people hereabouts will say, 'Why, he didn't do that and I didn't do that.' Or else you'll write just what they did do, and then they *will* be mad!"

There are many Indians in our Valley. Their names are on our subscription list and in the news. So I was delighted when a young-hearted old-timer named Bill Stephenson offered to introduce me to Jerry Kanum, chief of the Snoqualmie tribe. Mr. Stephenson came to the Valley in 1884 and could talk the Chinook jargon from the moment he was old enough to talk at all. Chief Jerry was an old friend.

The old Indian was cordial. He recalled the days when the Snoqualmies had joined the Washington Territorial Volunteers to quell the warring Indians under Chief Leschi. To prove their loyalty, Snoqualmie braves tied six heads behind their canoe and paddled all the way to the capitol city of Olympia to show them to the governor. One came loose and floated out to sea, but they finished the trek with five. . . . He told of seeing Chief Seattle, when the city was so young there was "one big white building." Mr. Stephenson's questions opened up one memory after another.

Only once did the chief shake his head and refuse to answer. He spoke entirely in the present tense, so I interrupted to ask, "What year did that happen? How long ago was that?"

He shook his head. "We don't count that way," he said.

As we left, he said good-bye with the same cordiality he had shown when we came, and it wasn't until I received a letter from Mr. Stephenson some days later that I learned I had smilingly thrown the worst possible insult at the chief.

I did not understand the tribal organization of which the Snoqualmies are a part. The "Siwash Indians" were one group I'd heard of often and I asked the old chief what relation they were to the Snoqualmies. Perhaps I should have noticed that he ignored the question completely. Without any change of expression, without a second's hesitation, he went on talking. "Siwash," Mr. Stephenson's letter explained, simply meant "Indian," but the white man who said it was the kind to call a Negro a "dirty nigger." Mr. Stephenson wrote me because he was embarrassed by the thought of correcting me to my face.

I went back to visit Chief Jerry, and again he was perfectly courteous. The third time, he laughed and smiled. As for my *faux pas*—he ignored it, the finest courtesy of all.

With each interview there was a feature story in the *Record* and a new section of notes in my swelling notebook. Only once did I encounter resistance.

I tried to interview the white-haired town clerk of Carnation, Tom Bird. He was polite, but skeptical, at times downright bored. He told me there was no point in interviewing him because he'd never done anything interesting. My every question boomeranged and I found myself talking to fill in the long silences while he cocked his head to the side and appraised me.

"You see," he said after a while, "it's no use. Nothing about me worth writing about."

I had driven eleven miles for this talk, there would be eleven miles back, the precious hours were slipping by. This man obviously didn't like me but I wasn't going to spend an afternoon without getting a story. "Mr. Bird," I said snappishly, "I am going to write a story about you, one way or the other. One way is to write what other people have told me about you. The other is to write what you might like better—the things you wish to tell me yourself. Now then, which would you prefer?"

This was a pretty high-handed way of approaching a paid-up subscriber and the official who ordered the printing for the town of Carnation. But for the first time, he looked at me as if I were there. His eyes brightened, and I swear that his slow smile was one of admiration. After that I asked straight questions and he gave straight answers. This man who "never did anything worth writing about" had, among other things, helped to build the Panama Canal, played professional baseball with Ty Cobb, and worked his way through college and law school by ferrying cattle across the country in some of the first freight cars to cross the plains. We were the best of friends ever after, two devoted members of a mutual admiration society which held occasional meetings for almost six years. When, eventually, the first draft of *Gold Mountain* was finished, Tom was one of two men I asked to read and criticize it.

Tom made several keen observations, and saved me from committing several technical errors. I was writing of an era in which he had lived. He visualized scenes of the '8os against the background of his own memories, while I had to project them against settings before my eyes today. I wrote about a man's impressions as he stood in the wide Valley a couple of miles below the Falls and turned to gaze up at Mount Rainier. "Young lady," said Tom, "in those days a man standing in that spot couldn't see Mount Rainier. Scarcely a tree had been cut. You couldn't see any place, except straight up."

My second technical adviser was the late George Foster Kelley, who settled in the Snoqualmie Valley in 1898. Mr. and Mrs. Kelley came from Kansas. They had been married for five years before tales about the green, fertile state called Washington drew them west.

With $100 in his pocket, Mr. Kelley went to the depot agent and asked for two tickets to Seattle.

"Long way or the short way?" the agent asked.

"Might as well see the country," said Mr. Kelley.

So they took a "tourist sleeper," which had a cook stove at each end of the car, and traveled 200 miles east to Kansas City, 400 miles back through the state of Kansas, on through Colorado and New Mexico to Needles, California, where another line took them twelve hundred miles to Seattle. Their tickets cost $42 apiece, and they arrived in the Snoqualmie Valley with two trunks and $4.30 in cash. Fifty years later Mr. Kelley had the snappiest walk, the warmest chuckle, of any old-timer in the Valley, and he would have won any pie-baking contest he entered. His comment about my book was brief, but as rare and wonderful as he was himself.

He was nearly ninety when he read the book. It was a second carbon. No editor's blue pencil had been unleashed on it then and it was 650 pages long. I met him at the post office one morning, and said, "Sometime when you feel like it, I'll give you the manuscript of the book I just submitted to a publisher. If you'd be interested . . ."

"You got it at the *Record* office?" he asked.

"Yes, I'll keep it there. Someday when you happen to feel like it . . ."

Mr. Kelley walked with a cane, and there was fifty years difference in our ages, but he nearly beat me back to the *Record* office.

"This carbon is hard to read," I apologized. "So take your time. I don't intend to show it to anyone else. Three weeks, a month—keep it as long as you like."

Manuscript under his arm, Mr. Kelley nodded and headed for home. He was back in the office the next afternoon. "Here's your book," he said, laying the box on the counter in front of me.

I was astonished. "But Mr. Kelley," I said, "did you read it?"

"Sure I read it," he replied, "but if it had been any longer, I would of starved to death."

iii

September, 1951, the last lap of our first two years as country publishers, was a month to remember. Hiram advanced to the second grade, Johnny became of age and went from kindergarten into "real school." Hi began his first music lessons, and I began a long term of standing over him with a smile and a bull whip to make sure he did his practicing. These were landmarks to our life at home. At the shop, all was well. In January Ed had been carried to the hospital, in February our house had been robbed, but five months without a major catastrophe made us light-headed at our good fortune. "If we try hard enough, and stick with it long enough, things are bound to work out all right," Ed and I agreed. "But isn't it wonderful to have all that behind us. . . ."

There was nothing ominous in the fact that Hi celebrated his first three weeks in the second grade by coming down with something. After school that Friday afternoon he was pale and listless. Company was coming for dinner. I slowed my course from the stove to the dining-room table to the sink just long enough to ask if he felt all right.

"Just tired, Mama. And I've got a headache."

Tired—who wasn't? And for two years Ed and I had had so many headaches I didn't stop to think how odd the complaint sounded on the lips of a seven-year-old boy. I gave Hi an aspirin. Voluntarily he went to his room and lay down, which also would have struck me as strange if I hadn't been rushing to finish dinner preparations before the company arrived.

At bedtime, both boys came into the living room in their pajamas and said good night to our guests.

"Here, climb up on your Uncle Fred's lap, and how about a big kiss?" one guest said.

Silently, Hi obeyed.

The man laughed. "If it was spring," he said, "I'd advise you to give Hi a good dose of sulphur and molasses. He looks kind of peaked."

I put my hand on Hi's forehead. It was feverish. "Coming down with something," I said, in the ancient tradition of mothers who never cease feeling that if it isn't one thing, it's another. Remembering measles in the auto court, I added, "Thank goodness, it can't be measles. They've had 'em!" And I tucked the little boys into bed.

Our company, Fred and his wife Mary Louise, had three children of their own. After I'd put the children to bed I said, "It was your idea to kiss him. I trust it's something catching."

Fred grinned. "It's *always* catching. When kids are in high school, they bring home piles of homework. When they're in grade school, all they bring home is germs."

"Seriously, I hope you don't take Hi's germs home to your own youngsters."

Fred shook his head. "If I do, they won't be any different, or any stronger, than the ones they've brought home themselves."

"I suppose Johnny will get it, too, whatever it is. . . ."

Mary Louise said philosophically, "Don't you wish he would? Get it all over with at one time?"

When I went into Hi's room the next morning, Johnny was sitting at the foot of Hi's bed, soberly applying red crayon to a coloring book. Hi, always the early riser, was unnaturally still and his face was turned to the wall.

Johnny looked up. "Hi's sick," he said. "He threw up."

Mechanically I went through the routine. The thermometer—it read $103\frac{1}{2}$. A damp towel for his forehead. A pan; he had reached the bathroom once, but he looked too sick to attempt it again. The aspirin—but when he tried to swallow the tablet, he began vomiting.

One gains a feeling of security by going through these old, familiar measures. With each step accomplished, my uneasiness subsided. The last thing I thought to do was to ask him how he felt.

He gripped my hand with sudden intensity, and his voice was choked as he whispered, "Mama, my back aches, just terrible."

High fever, aching joints. I had had rheumatic fever as a

207

little girl, and the memory flooded back and with it, fear. Once again I ran to the telephone to call the family doctor.

At the time he was doing the work of four men. Two local doctors had left the Valley, a third had died. I knew how busy he was, how reluctant to make a house call unless he felt it was absolutely necessary. So when he said, "I'll be right out," I was convinced my fear was well founded. All I could hope was that Hi would come out of it as well as I had.

The doctor spoke of a "spinal," but he pointed out that the nearest laboratory was thirty miles away and that it was a painful ordeal to visit on a child and wouldn't cure or arrest his illness anyway. "Call me immediately if he shows any new symptoms or if his fever doesn't go down. Watch especially to see if he has any difficulty in swallowing. . . ."

And still I thought—rheumatic fever. At the door, I asked bluntly if that's what the boy had.

"It might be," the doctor said thoughtfully. "But it's too early to read the symptoms accurately." If he was evasive, I was too befuddled to notice it.

Ed stayed home all day Saturday, ironically, his first Saturday at home since we bought the newspaper. We hardly mentioned the bindery work stacked up for him at the shop, and his reason for leaving it undone we did not refer to at all. We both worked on long-neglected household chores with the zeal of Baltimore housewives scrubbing down their front stoops.

As the day progressed, it was clear that whatever Hi had "come down with," he was fast getting well. By nightfall his temperature was almost normal. He had eaten and enjoyed two meals; the boys were now using the pan beside his bed as a container for their color crayons. When both boys had fallen into peaceful sleep, Ed and I collapsed into the living-room chairs and admitted how worried we'd been.

"Thank goodness, *that's* over," I breathed.

Ed nodded, "I'll have to work at the shop tomorrow, to

do that bindery job. Five thousand booklets for Carnation Farm. They've got to be stapled, and the farm wants them first thing Monday morning." He leaned back, eyes closed, soaking up the healing silence. At last he said, more to himself than to me, "Only thing is, I wish I knew what Hi had had. . . ."

Monday Hiram was restless, Tuesday he had cabin fever in its advanced stages, so Wednesday, on the advice of the doctor, I sent him back to school. He seemed a little tired that evening, but nothing more. Thursday being Paper Day, I told him and Johnny to take the school bus that passed near the shop. They could help deliver newspapers to the post office and stores and we'd all go home together when the paper was out.

I remember the desk where I was sitting, even the direction I was facing, when I first noticed something was wrong. The paper was out, Hiram walked past to get his cap and jacket. He was limping.

"Hi?"

"Yes, Mama."

"Does your shoe hurt?"

He looked down at his feet. "Why, no," he said, genuinely surprised. "Nothing hurts."

"Maybe there's a nail sticking up, in your left shoe?"

He shook his head, and grinned at me. "I'd sure feel *that*," he said.

Ed came up behind me. He had been near enough to hear my questions— I could feel it.

Hi looked at me in a puzzled way. "What's the matter, Mama? Is there something wrong?"

"I . . . I thought you were limping . . ."

"Huh?" He laughed. "Gosh, no," and he turned and walked away from us toward the front door. He was limping, badly. With each step onto the left foot, his whole body went down hard. And he didn't know it.

Polio . . .

10

The county public health nurse knew how to be kind. She was matter-of-fact without being blunt, sympathetic without frightening me with too commiserative a tone or too sober a face. She asked questions, filled out her report, and then drew a large yellow sign from her brief case. "Everyone in the house, except the breadwinner, must remain in quarantine for three weeks after the day Hiram first ran a fever." And as she left she tacked the sign on the outside of the kitchen door.

I recalled how often, since we had moved into our own house, I had sighed, "Oh, if I could only spend a week at home!" When work on the newspaper seemed never ending, and some subscribers seemed to be developing too deadly an aim, I yearned to flee my post as co-publisher and co-target and hide behind the barricade of mending piling up at home. For 600 days, more or less, I had been out "meeting the public," sometimes head-on. Now, all of a sudden, I was to see no one, or even get near anyone.

Groceries would be delivered to the back door, but I was to wait until the deliveryman had gone before I opened the door and brought them in. There were to be no more glass milk bottles, washed and returned to the dairy; the milkman would leave paper cartons which I was to burn. Hiram, Johnny and I would be completely isolated from the world that had been too much with us. Our only contact would be the telephone, and Ed, the breadwinner, when he came home from work at night. I was locked up, he was free to go and come. But his was the harder role, by far.

I had the care of Hiram, it is true. He had four baths a day, in water so hot his skin turned red and sweat ran down his forehead into his eyes. He had to be amused, he had to be fed, and there was extra laundry and bed-making. I was shut off from the world; even the telephone proved to be an inadequate link. People mercifully did not phone me for fear of calling at the wrong time or saying the wrong thing, and when someone did telephone I could think of nothing to say. To me, the house was a blessed retreat, protected, not stigmatized, by the big yellow sign on the back door. Only once did I feel otherwise.

A good friend, all unknowing, drove into the yard. The back door was open, concealing the sign. She banged cheerily on the screen door. "Yoo hoo?" she called. "Where is everybody?"

From the middle of the kitchen, I said, "We're under quarantine."

She put her hand on the knob, began to open the screen door. "Oh, I'm not afraid of germs. I never catch anything. What've you got? Scarlet fever?"

Little Johnny was standing right behind me. We had never mentioned polio in front of the children, and I knew her light, gay voice would carry into Hiram's bedroom. I backed away from her and turning toward Johnny, said, "Go keep Hi company."

My friend was laughing. "My goodness, what *have* you got?"

Johnny was gone. In a second I heard the boys talking together. I turned toward my friend and whispered, "Hiram has polio."

The laughter dropped from her face. She retreated through the door, closing it with a bang. "I'm sorry," she said, "but I've got a couple of children of my own." She threw the words over her shoulder as she got into her car, and she drove off without saying, or even waving, good-bye.

For an instant, I felt unclean. But a moment later, I was busy running another tub of hot water and installing a radio in the bathroom so that the half-hour Hi had to soak would not be unbearable. Then there were fresh pajamas, sheets to be straightened, pillows to smooth, toys to put away. During that first week at home I baked dishes I had never had time to try, ironed clothing we had long since got used to wearing wrinkled, cleaned closets that could more easily have been sealed up, even wrote a column for the newspaper and an article for *Pageant* magazine.

During it all, it was Ed who suffered most. It was strange to live behind the barricade of the quarantine, but it was agony to pass back and forth across it. Ed had to meet people and answer questions, torn between gratitude for their sympathy and a wounded animal's instinctive desire to be left alone. It was he who had to keep his mind on his work, when it was filled with one question— How crippled will Hiram be? He who first, last and always, had to "get the paper out." Home offered no comfort, for there I was the busy one, running from chore to chore while Ed stood by and asked, "Isn't there *anything* I can do?" At night I

fell asleep quickly, exhausted by many necessary and unnecessary tasks. While Ed lay sleepless, and wondered, and
worried, and arose in the morning to cross over again into
the world outside.

It is no wonder that of the four of us, he was the only one
who cried. Not at home, where we could see him, but downtown, when someone asked him, "How's the boy today?"
There on the main street, with a friend's hand on his shoulder, the wondering and the worrying suddenly grew too big,
and he burst into deep and racking sobs. The man led him
around the corner and into a deserted alley. "Don't be
ashamed of crying, Ed," he said to him. "My God, man, don't
be ashamed. . . ."

Before Hiram's illness, we had heard of only one case of
polio in the Valley. The signs may have been before us a
hundred times—the twisted back, the leg brace, the useless
arm—but we had not had the eyes to see. We had printed
nothing about Hiram's illness, for fear of contributing to a
"polio panic," but the news traveled rapidly nevertheless.
Every day one of those who extended sympathy added,
"We've had polio in our family, too. . . ."

The woman whose tall, handsome son walked straight because he wore one built-up shoe, and we had never guessed
it. The woman who said, "Don't worry, Hi will get better.
My boy had polio . . ." and then began to cry. The clerk
in a local store who had waited on us for two years, without
ever mentioning the fact that his little sister was living in
an iron lung. It happened again and again; we discovered
the community of families stricken by polio, now that we
had joined it.

There was the community of sorrow and the community
of love for children. It was a memorable day when our good
friend Cece Thompson, who had three daughters of his own
and then adopted a fourth child—a girl!—came whistling up
to the back door with a five-pound box of chocolates for the
boys. It took something very close to brute strength to keep

him on the legal side of the quarantine sign; he wanted to see for himself how Hiram was doing. Another friend, whose only son was killed in action in the South Pacific, sent a present only a sensitive and patient man would have troubled to prepare. Ed came staggering into the kitchen one evening under a tremendous cardboard box. Every manner of stalk, leaf and vine was spilling over the top. He carried it into Hiram's room, and set it down on the floor by his bed. "Bill Hronek said he knew you fellows came from a farm in Illinois," he told the wide-eyed Hi and Johnny. "So he sent you a garden."

That's just what it was. From his own garden, Bill had taken corn, squash, carrots, pumpkins, tomatoes, beans, apples. But the corn was in its green sheath on a five-foot stalk. The squash and the pumpkins were "growing" on vines he had pulled up by the roots. The beans, the tomatoes, were tightly fastened to whole plants. Even the apples had to be picked, off limbs Bill had cut from his apple tree.

At the first word that the editor's son was ill, Bill had scratched the name "HI" on the dark-green surface of a growing squash. As the squash grew, the letters had swollen and hardened. When Hi looked at the "garden," he found a squash with his own name embossed on the side. He stared at it in wonder. "How did he do it?" he asked again and again. "Just how in the world did he do it?" It was unfair to Bill, whose own son had once been that young and that wondering, that he could not see the expression on the little boy's face.

Many a person who had never seemed to care if the local editor lived or died was a friend to the editor in trouble. The sympathy was so general that Ed was stunned the day he met a man who expressed none at all. And it was someone he liked particularly; it had been friendship at first sight. They met on the street, but the man made no reference to Hiram's illness. Ed dreaded, yet yearned, to tell

214

him about it. Finally he blurted out, "My older boy has polio. . . ."

The man frowned. "That so?" he said, turned on his heel and walked away.

Ed was so shaken that later he mentioned the incident to our associate editor.

"Perhaps you didn't know," she said. "His daughter had polio, too. She died. . . ."

Other than the public health nurse, our only visitor that first week was the school superintendent. He, too, knew the right balance of cheerfulness and sympathy, and it was only my own state of self-induced numbness and busy-busyness that made one of his remarks hit me so hard. "Dr. Templeton's children were about the ages of your two when one of them got polio. But the other one didn't catch it. So I wouldn't worry if I were you."

I nodded stupidly, indicating No, I wasn't worried, but the truth was it had never occurred to me that Johnny might contract polio, too. Yet Johnny had been on Hi's bed the morning he was sickest, Johnny had hardly been out of Hiram's room since. Two cases of polio? That was a catastrophe so monstrous I had not even thought of it.

When Ed came home that night I discovered another reason why his burden had been heavier than mine. He had been aware of the possibility from the first, and had already talked to the doctor about it. "No use separating them now," the doctor had said, "but watch Johnny carefully. If he has contracted polio, we will know a week to ten days after Hiram had fever. At the end of that time, we can consider Johnny safe."

Ed and I needed no calendar to tell us how many days had passed, but puppetlike, we turned toward it anyway.

"Three more days," Ed murmured, speaking what was in the minds of both of us, "and then the time will be up."

That's when I began counting time by hours, not days.

On the eighth day after Hi's first fever, Johnny complained of a headache. There was nothing to do. No serum, no preventive measure, nothing but to give him an aspirin, put him to bed, and wait. By nightfall he had a little fever. The next morning it had gone up to 102 degrees.

Half-numb, half-desperate, I kept asking Johnny if his neck hurt, or his back ached. I asked him until I was afraid to ask any more.

"Can you swallow, Johnny?" I must have said two dozen times. "Does it feel funny to swallow?"

But he always answered, "Nothing hurts, Mama, except my head. I got an awful headache."

Another report to the county health department, another notice to the school superintendent's office. And another week of waiting. If Johnny was to be crippled, it would show up in a week's time.

A traveling salesman from the Linotype company came through Snoqualmie that week. He was everything a salesman should be. Cheerful, self-confident, aggressive. He found Ed in the dark corner which served as a private office. The light from a single bare bulb shone on the stack of unpaid bills on the table before him.

"This is the day!" the salesman began as he rounded the corner. "Yes, sir, this is the day I'm going to see that you get the one thing you need more than anything else in the world!"

Ed looked up. He had been staring at the bills without seeing them, and the salesman's face seemed just as hard to focus on as the bills had been. "What is that?" he asked mechanically.

"A new Linotype!"

Ed looked at him, then back at the papers under his hand. One bulb hardly pierced the gloom but he had a feeling that the light was too bright for his eyes. "What I need," he said, "is courage."

"Ha! What kind of talk is that?" The salesman laughed

heartily. "You're the fellow has so much courage all the other weekly publishers think you're nuts. New job press in less than three months, new building inside six months, new newspaper press in seven months, and new equipment all the time. You're expanding. Don't let that stack of bills scare you. You're going places. That's why you need a new Linotype, a machine that will fit your way of doing things."

Ed said simply, "Jim, I have two boys. They both have polio. Expansion and new equipment? I won't care whether I succeed or fail, if something happens to the boys."

The salesman froze. The next hearty laugh, already rising in his throat, ended as abruptly as if it had been caught in flight and locked into a box. "Sorry," he said at last, and his voice was husky. "I talk so much I never know when to shut up. I'll come back another time."

Ed said, "Jim, I didn't mean to be rude."

"Why shouldn't you be?" The salesman walked away, but at the corner he turned back. "It's true about your having courage. You always had it. Don't let go of it now."

On Sunday afternoon a car turned into the driveway and a man we knew by sight jumped out. The door was closed, the quarantine sign clearly visible, but before we could protest he was inside the kitchen.

"Quarantine," Ed explained. "Our boys have polio. You shouldn't even come in."

"Why not?" the man asked. "My boy's got polio, too."

He had come to talk it out. His boy had complained about a headache, that had been the start of it. How had it been with Hi and John? Then a high fever—same with ours? And so on. He had a hundred friends and more, but for this brief and terrible moment we were closer to him than any of them. Before he left, he said, "You haven't put anything about this in the paper. How come?"

Ed explained that we had been afraid of creating a panic. "People would be scared stiff if they knew there were three cases of polio right here in the community."

The man shook his head. "You know what they're saying now? That there are ten, twelve cases. They're talking about an epidemic. Maybe someone hears about my boy, Jerry. They pass the news along. The next day someone else tells them about a case of polio they heard about—it's still Jerry, but they don't know the names, so that makes two. Every time someone whispers 'polio' it sounds like a new case. Scared? I'll say they're scared, because what they're whispering around and around in circles is so much worse than the truth."

The next day Ed heard rumors that corroborated what the man had said. In suppressing news, we had contributed to a panic rather than quieting it. So that week the *Record* reported that there was polio in the Valley, giving the actual number of cases and the seriousness of them, suppressing nothing but the names of the three boys. The story punctured the balloon of gossip which had blown three cases into an "epidemic." The panic stopped.

The long week of waiting passed, and when the doctor examined Johnny he found no stiffness, no limp of any kind. Ed and I breathed sighs of relief. And then, that same night, Hiram suddenly ran a temperature of 103.

The doctor was out on a house call. He came at midnight, having eaten nothing since noon. He looked tired, white.

"Why a second fever?" I asked. "Is it a relapse? What does it mean?"

"I don't know," he said quietly. "I really don't know. I advise you to take him to the Children's Orthopedic Hospital in Seattle." At the door, he turned back. "I want you to know one thing," he said earnestly. "You have done everything, everything, that you could have done."

Hi and Johnny had heard a good deal about the Children's Orthopedic Hospital. It is partially supported by donations from all over the state and everyone in our Valley, from the well-to-do down through the grade-school youngsters who bring pennies to school during the "Penny Drive," contributes to it. We had always thought it was wonderful that the children saved pennies for the hospital, and that they talked so sympathetically about the sick and crippled children their money would help. But now we saw the publicity through different eyes. Neither Hi nor Johnny knew they had had polio. "Orthopedic Hospital" meant "sick and crippled children." What would Hi's reaction be?

He was curious, and that helped. But he said defensively, "I'm not crippled!" When Ed and I drove him to the hospital, he made us promise we wouldn't tell anyone at school where he was.

We felt like parents who have put off telling their child he is adopted and suddenly find they have waited too long. At the hospital Hi was placed in a little waiting room while Ed went to the business office. Hi was cheerful, and amused by the angel robe the nurse instructed him to get into. It was evening, and the entrance hall was deserted except for two nurses at the reception desk. All at once the voice of one of them cut through the stillness. "Wouldn't you know it! They're bringing in another polio from Olympia. And I thought I'd go home on time for a change!"

My heart sank. I glanced quickly at the little figure in the white robe, sitting so patiently on a wooden stool. I could not tell whether he had heard. He grinned at me. "I'm sure glad none of the kids at school can see me," he said, "wearing this funny dress."

For eight days Hi was a patient at the hospital. His playmates were the worst of all polio cases. Hi joked with the little girl who had to lie face down in a kind of metal hammock. His "good friend," he explained to me, was the boy who could not move except in a cart pulled by someone else.

219

Visiting hours were for two hours a week, on Sunday afternoon. Ed and I found Hi in bed on an outside porch. By standing up, Hi could see over the brick wall and wave at Johnny, whom we had left in the front seat of the car parked in the street below. All around Hi's bed were his friends—the boy in the cart, another whose head was held up by an elaborate metal brace, another with great scars to show that his throat had literally been cut to save his life. Hi pulled me down over the bed and whispered. "Mama, those other kids had polio."

Hi was getting well. The second fever had not come from a "relapse," but from an infection in his ear. He was cheerful all through our visit. But he was too talkative, and his eyes were too sober for the laughter which came so often. When it was time for us to leave, he began swallowing hard, and looked the other way. We handed him a new comic book. Still swallowing, he flicked through the book, so quickly he could not have seen the pictures at all. That's what he was doing when we stepped into the elevator to go down.

In the entrance hall we met the specialist who had been caring for Hi since his admission to the hospital.

"Should we have told him he had polio?" Ed asked. "We didn't, because we were afraid of scaring him. But if he found out, and felt we had been hiding something from him, he'd lose confidence in us. What shall we do?"

"I wouldn't tell him, if I were you," the doctor said. "Later, perhaps, or perhaps never. I've known cases where the child never learned what he had had."

We were worried, until Hiram himself reassured us. The day we took him home, he referred so freely to his leg and the hot baths he'd taken that Ed asked, "Hi, did they find out what kind of sickness you had?"

"Oh, yes . . ." Hi did not look at us as he answered. "I had polio. But it was a *slight* case, Daddy, a very *slight* case." There was still defensiveness there. Illness had taken him far away from the healthy world he had always known. I thought to myself— It's going to be a hard road back.

Johnny returned to school, but for weeks Hiram stayed at home. There were exercises three times a day, long hours of bed rest, and twice a week trips to a therapist in Seattle. Gradually the injured leg grew stronger. By Thanksgiving we could see that we would not have to settle for a "slight limp," but that Hiram could play football, after all. Years later I asked Hi if he could remember which leg had been hurt by polio. He looked surprised. "I sure ought to, Mama," he said, chuckling, "because that's the way I learned left from right." And I remembered—it was his left leg, and every time he lay on the bedroom carpet, exercising the damaged muscles, pulling and stretching until the pain made him say, "Can I stop a minute now?"— every time the knowledge burned deeper into the little boy's mind of which was left, and which was right.

Finally the day came when Hiram was strong enough to go back to school part time. I talked to his teacher beforehand. "He has said over and over again that he doesn't want any of the kids to know where he's been," I told her. "He made me promise not to tell anyone he had polio. Yet I'm sure most of the children know all about it. What can we do?"

The teacher said, "Don't worry. I'll talk to the children. You can be sure no one will mention polio to Hiram, or even refer to the Orthopedic Hospital. You have no idea how understanding seven- and eight-year-old children can be."

When Hi went back to school, he still walked with a limp. He went down the corridor leading to his classroom with a determined stride as he tried desperately to control it. Seeing his approach, the boys and girls spilled out of the room, in a body moved forward to meet him.

"Hi, Hiram!" they sang out. "Hi, Hi!" and they closed in around him.

Hi blurted out, loud and clear, "I had polio but I bet you wouldn't even know it because I'm not crippled at all. See?"

The teacher smiled at me over the children's heads. I left quickly, knowing I could not be as calm as she was, nor as brave as Hi.

Now, after weeks away from the *Record* office, it was time for me to go back to work. The children were in school, the quarantine had long since been lifted. It was time to face the world, and I didn't want to do it.

Ed said, "Look, you don't need to work at the shop all day. In fact, I don't want you to. But you must get out. No one has met or talked to you for weeks and weeks. No one has even seen you. Hi is making his adjustment, he's facing the world. Now you've got to make yours."

"I can't! I'd like to work at home, just for a little while longer. I don't want to meet anyone, or talk about Hi and Johnny, and if anyone came up and started to be sympathetic I'd scream."

Ed took my hand. "You're running away."

"Maybe so. But I want to stay home."

Ed hesitated. After a moment he asked, "What's troubling you? There's something more than your dread of talking about the boys. What is it?"

I reminded Ed of that Sunday morning when Hiram was coming down with polio and one of our friends had stopped at the shop to see him. The man seemed to have something on his mind.

"We know why you two left Chicago. You came here because it was a good place for your wife to write. You don't give a hang about us as people."

Angry as he was, Ed tried to defend us both against such unfair charges. Our critic remained unconvinced and one word led to a harsher one. After an hour they parted acrimoniously, and Ed returned home gloomy and depressed.

Though he didn't want me to know, I ferreted the truth from him.

"What he said isn't true," I repeated endlessly. "No one else believes it. Why should he?"

"Because he wants to believe it," Ed replied wearily.

For weeks thereafter Hiram's illness kept me busy. Yet there were many times when I recalled Ed's conversation. I was locked up with the thought of it. Somehow, I couldn't help thinking that other Valley people, less vocal than our critic, shared his opinions. This anxiety, coupled with the obvious emotional one occasioned by Hiram's illness, only intensified my desire to insulate myself against the outside world.

"Please—don't let's talk about it! I'm going to stay home!"

Ed looked at me for a long time, and then without a word he walked away.

That night Hiram's teacher telephoned. "I thought you should know what happened in class today," she said. "You remember you asked that no one refer to the Orthopedic Hospital, or to Hiram's being there?"

"Yes . . . Oh, Mrs. Urdahl, don't tell me someone did?"

She laughed. "Someone did, all right. It was Hiram himself. First thing this morning he asked permission to make a short speech to the class. I said, Fine. We often ask someone to make a 'speech,' about a vacation trip, or some interesting experience. Hiram is a good speaker, too. He got up in front of the class, and stood up perfectly straight, and in a loud, firm voice he talked for at least ten minutes—about having polio and going to the Orthopedic Hospital!"

"Oh, my goodness . . ."

I hung up the receiver hurriedly. Thank God for a teacher like you, I had wanted to say. Thank you from my heart . . . But I scarcely said good-bye.

Ed watched me curiously. "Who was that?"

"Mrs. Urdahl."

"Something wrong?"

I shook my head. "No. Something very good . . ." and in a voice that was as much like Boris Karloff's as it was like mine, I repeated what she had said.

"That's wonderful! Why the long face?"

I replied with a mute diagonal nod.

Ed came to me and put his arm around me. "You see, Hi had a kind of battle to fight. He was afraid of sympathy, and he had a lot more reason to shy away from it than you have. If a seven-year-old boy can put his fears behind him, can't you?"

I squeaked, "Yes . . ."

"Good." Ed thumped me convivially, like a football coach who is sending a new man in to save the game in the fourth quarter. "Starting at nine o'clock tomorrow morning, you are going to run the front office. Answer the telephone, talk to everyone who comes in."

He took my chin between thumb and forefinger, turned my face around to look at me squarely. "Mother," he said softly, "you have never cried. Not when Hiram got sick, or Johnny got sick, or when Hiram went to the hospital. I cried lots of times, more than you ever saw or I ever told you about. It's all over now. How about it? How about right now?"

My husband should have been a rainmaker. I cried, and I cried, and I cried.

11

"Money isn't everything," a not very original friend on the old *Chicago Times* once remarked, to which Tom Howard, then chief photographer, retorted, "You're absolutely right. Health is one percent." But when we approached our third Thanksgiving as small businessmen, it was health for which we were most thankful.

Hi's injured leg was filling out and his walk was improving so rapidly we knew that by Christmas he would not limp at all. He tired easily, and he was gay one moment, tearful the next, but the doctors had warned us that such emotional aftereffects were to be expected. Ed and I were experiencing some aftereffects all our own, for the wounds of fear are slow to heal. I still met all major crises, such as finding the milkman had left four quarts instead of three, by bawling like a frightened bull calf. Ed's reaction was different. When he hadn't seen the boys for a few hours he greeted them with almost incoherent joy. Luckily they put it down to fatherly love, but it was more than that; all day he had been tense with apprehension lest they get sick again and he nearly drowned in relief when he saw with his own eyes that they were well.

On Thanksgiving morning the four of us lingered at the breakfast table and Ed called to order one of our periodic family meetings. "I'd like to have a discussion," he said, "about what we have to be thankful for. Let's start with the youngest member of the family. Johnny?"

Six-year-old Johnny rolled his eyes to the ceiling, wrinkled his forehead, finally intoned solemnly, "I'm thankful Mrs. Gallanar never makes me stay after school."

"Hiram?"

"Can I be thankful for two things?"

Johnny burst out, "Hi, that isn't fair! I was only thankful once!"

Ed raised a hand. "Order!" The boys turned to him, though Johnny was still mumbling rebelliously. "If you had a hundred things to be thankful for, what would be wrong with that? Well, Hi?"

"It seems to me," Hi began carefully, "that what all us kids have to be thankful for is Thanksgiving itself. You get a special big dinner and you don't have to go to school." He turned to address his little brother. "Look, John, you have that thankful as much as I do, so it shouldn't count for mine."

"Oh, all right," but Johnny's voice indicated he wasn't at all sure he hadn't been tricked. "Take another thankful, then, Hiram."

"I'm thankful I didn't have that bad kind of polio," Hi said in a small, small voice, "the kind my friend at Orthopedic Hospital had, and they had to cut his neck open so he could breathe."

For a moment none of us said anything. Then Ed cleared his throat loudly. *"I'm* thankful for something. Anyone know what it is?"

While the boys bombarded their father with guesses, I fell into reverie of Thanksgivings past. Two years and two months before, we had set out to prove that it's not too late to go into business on a shoestring. Our first Thanksgiving we had put up a rather weak argument for private enterprise by working at the shop until eight o'clock at night. By our second Thanksgiving it was hard to tell which was going down the drain faster—our illusions or our money. True, we had managed to disappoint those townspeople who predicted the former owner would have the business back in a year. "Last one year, and there's hope for you, last five and you're here to stay"—if our friend who had made that prophesy was right, we had only four years to go. However he hadn't predicted that after a year and more of hard work, we'd owe more money than we had the year before. Now it was our third Thanksgiving. Obviously we were making progress. We had reduced our debt to about the same amount it had been when we went into business two years and two months before. But it was hard to be thankful. The day before we had had to sign a demand note for $500 just to meet Friday's payroll. How can a small businessman enjoy Thanksgiving as long as it falls on Thursday?

"Give up?"

Hi and Johnny nodded, and Ed said, "All right, I'll tell you the answer. I'm thankful for the fact that I can spend all day Thanksgiving thinking about what I have to be thankful for."

"You're not going to work at the shop at all?"

Ed grinned. "I could. There's plenty to do. But I won't."

Hi said soberly, "Dad, does that mean things are better than they used to be?"

Ed looked thoughtfully at our eight-year-old son. "Yes," he said, "it does. Do you worry about the shop?"

Hi nodded.

"Tell me what you worry about."

"Sometimes about the workers," the little boy said, "sometimes about if the press will keep running. . . ."

Ed smiled. "That's all behind us, now. We've got good workers and we've got a big new press and it's sure to keep running. Not a reason in the world to worry any more. Now, you two run along and play."

The boys jumped up and headed for their rooms. "I'm still thankful," Johnny was saying as they rounded the corner, "about Mrs. Gallanar not making me stay after school."

I gave Ed a rueful smile. "Do you mean what you said? Our printers are all here to stay, our equipment is guaranteed to hold together, we haven't a worry in the world?"

"Sure, I mean it! Every month we have more subscribers and fewer creditors."

"Remember Ote Sloan? He said it took five years to prove you were here to stay."

Ed shrugged. "No law against doing it in three. We're in debt, I know. Someday we'll finish rebuilding the shop and someday we'll add onto this house. That will mean borrowing more money. But we *are* paying everything off, little by little. As long as business comes in, and we have the men and equipment to do the job, we're bound to come out all right, in time."

"But if . . ." I stopped short, ashamed of myself for beating the drums of gloom on the first Thanksgiving day Ed could spend at home. What if there were a strike at the lumber mill? my frightened little mind whispered. What if our printers went the way of Mr. Toski and Shaky and Just Plain Bill?

"If, nothing," Ed retorted. "You know what we ought to do, we ought to take a vacation."

Ed's mother and father lived in San Bernardino, California. Sensible at last, Ed and I held a leisurely discussion as to whether we could afford a trip south, and five minutes later decided to leave for San Bernardino the moment the Christmas edition was out. The boys had never spent Christmas with their paternal grandparents. More important, San Bernardino lies in a valley of perpetual sunshine, and we felt nothing could do more for two little boys recently recovered from polio than to remove them for a couple of weeks from our perpetual rain.

"But our bank account is overdrawn," I said, "and one mortgage payment is due on the first and the other on the fifteenth. Then there's the withholding tax, and you know we've had to spend it. . . ."

"We can use our credit cards and charge the gasoline," Ed said cheerfully, as if that answered everything.

Having airily ignored our big problems, we now concentrated fiercely on our little ones. First, it would be obvious that we were on vacation, even if Ed restrained himself from crowing about it in an editorial. During our last vacation a subscriber had broken in and made off with enough loot to pay for his subscription 150 years in advance. Would that happen again? And then, there was Caledonia.

Caledonia was a dachshund, whom we wouldn't have owned if my husband had confined his worrying to mortgages and let stray dogs figure things out for themselves. First he brought home a female springer spaniel with a spavined walk and bloodshot eyes. "She's hungry," Ed said, lifting her out of the car. "She needs a home." She was an old dog, so deaf she heard nothing but messcall, so nearly blind she saw nothing but our cats. She was too weary to wag her tail, but after a week of my loving care she had collected sufficient strength to kill my favorite tabby. We had twelve cats at the time and should have been grateful. But the mother cat was nursing four tiny kittens so I spent an hour and a half a day keeping them alive with driblets of warm milk forced down their throats with an eye dropper. I took the killer spaniel to the Humane Society in Seattle.

I thought it was odd, some weeks later, when Ed came home late from the shop and instead of bounding into the house he sat in the car and waved at me sheepishly through the windshield. I went outside. The front seat was faintly illuminated by light from the kitchen window. There on the seat, as confident as Ed was apologetic, sat a slender, aristocratic brown dachshund. She wagged her tail cheerfully. "This is my car," she seemed to say, "but I'm a liberal sort of gink. Hop in and sit down."

"All I did was open the door," Ed explained, "and she got right in. She was on the big highway. I had to save her from being killed."

"I know, I know," I said, sweet and sour. "She's hungry, she needs a home. Well, bring her in. We've got quite a few cats left."

But I was determined not to be saddled with this problem. I ran a classified ad in the *Record* asking if anyone had lost a dog and describing our dachshund. Her rightful owner responded immediately—by offering to give me the dog. He lived near the highway; she had taken to straying in and out of heavy traffic and for her sake he would be glad to give her to people who lived out of town on a quiet country lane. She was ours, and, oh, yes, her name was Caledonia.

In those days the road past our house was narrow and graveled. Sometimes no car would go by for an hour at a time. Caledonia had lived on a national highway for six years without getting a bruise, but at the end of her first week with us I had to stop work to rush her to the veterinary hospital. It seems she had taken an instant dislike to a truck, and in her efforts to tree it she had tangled with a wheel. Ironically the longest part of her stayed clear, while the part so small it was ridiculous, her right hind leg, was hit. After a week in the hospital, we brought her home. Still wearing what was probably the shortest leg cast in the world, she sallied out across the neighbor's pasture, took a dislike to their Irish setter, and came home with such a gaping hole in her hide that I had to rush her back to the veterinarian for some stitches.

I telephoned her former owner.

"Oh, she'll be all right after she gets used to the place," he said. "The thing is, she needs lots of love. Just stay home with her all the time and she won't get into trouble."

The problems— Do we dare leave the house vacant? What shall we do with Caledonia? Ed solved both with one masterly stroke. He gave both the house and the dog to someone we had never seen before.

A new doctor came to town, and the report was that he and his wife were living in the back room of the clinic with which he was associated. Two days before we were to leave for California, Ed met the doctor for the first time. It wasn't a long conversation.

"You the new doctor?" said Ed.

"Yes, I am."

"Living in that little room in the clinic?"

"Yes . . ."

"Poor place to spend Christmas. . . ." Ed explored his trousers' pocket with an inky hand, pulled out his key to our house. "Here, you and your wife move into our place Thursday afternoon. We'll be out of there by three o'clock. Well, so long, I've got to go run the press. . . ."

Two days later we rounded up sun suits and gasoline credit cards and headed south.

We made many New Year's resolutions that January in California, one of which was not to believe what they say about California weather. It rained in San Bernardino, gray skies and fog enshrouded sunny Riverside, and when we fled to Palm Springs we found our friends there swathed in fleecy stoles and huddling around their fireplaces. But we did relax.

The circles under Ed's eyes disappeared. He slept peacefully through the night, rather than jumping out of bed after three or four hours to stew over a pile of bookwork. He talked without drumming on the table with his fingers and he could sit in a chair without beating a rhythm on the floor with his heels. He acted like a fellow who is working for somebody else.

I noted these things with vast relief, for less than a year had passed since he had been half-carried, half-dragged, to the hospital, and it had been a hard year. Nervousness had caused the first heart attack, nervousness could bring another and still another. He said we had no reason to worry any more, and with 1,500 miles between himself and the shop, he was acting as if he believed it.

But when we got back?

"Let's resolve," I said on New Year's Eve, "that we won't work so hard any more. Let's resolve that you never go to the shop on Sundays, and you come home for dinner not later than nine o'clock at night, and that you never bring all those stacks of work home with you."

Ed grinned sleepily. "Sounds like a good set of resolutions."

"Then will you *promise?*"

"Promise?" Ed shrugged. "Sure, why not?"

As he had done when we went on vacation the first time, Ed left forwarding addresses so that important mail could be sent to us along the way. He was puzzled when letters arrived, but no copy of the *Record*. "Maybe the wrapper came off, and it was lost in the mail," I offered. "After all, newspapers don't get first-class handling."

But what we both remembered was that the year before the staff had kept us from knowing about the robbery of our house so as not to spoil our vacation. What was it this time? Luckily most of our vacation was behind us and Ed had had a good rest when we found out.

On the way north we stopped at my sister's home in Palo Alto. She had been on the subscription list ever since we bought the paper and there on her living-room table was the edition we had been kept from seeing. "OUR PRESS IS BUSTED!" the bold-face headline screamed at us from the middle of the front page. "If your paper is late this week, bear with us. We're as unhappy as you are. . . ." and the article went on to explain what had happened. The main gear of the big newspaper press, our beautiful big black $3,000 baby, had snapped while they were printing the first four pages of the edition. With the thermometer reading six above zero, and all roads covered with glare ice, they had driven twelve miles to the town of Issaquah where the neighborly owner of another weekly had let them print the next four pages on Thursday morning. Thursday evening they had driven twenty miles to the town of Redmond, where another weekly publisher with his heart in the right place had let them print the rest of the *Record* on his big press. The paper came out a day late, but the miracle was that they had been able to get it out at all.

Ed muttered, "The main gear . . ." I was about to say, "Don't worry, darling, they'll know what to do," but Ed was gone. He was at the telephone in the hall, jittering the bar up and down with a nervous forefinger and demanding, "Operator? Operator? I want long distance!"

Thus ended our restful vacation. There may be some family that has made the trip from Palo Alto to Seattle in less time but I wouldn't want to ride with them. Through the rolling Siskiyous, past snow-capped Mount Shasta, along the wide Columbia, Ed saw nothing but that big press. No beauties of nature could distract him from the question of how, in 1952, to replace the main gear for a machine made in 1897. By the time we pulled up in front of the plant in Snoqualmie, he was every inch the country publisher. Every muscle ached, every nerve was quivering, every brain cell was crying, "We've got to get the paper out. . . ."

The only balm was at home. The doctor and his wife had left everything in better shape than they had found it. The house sparkled, the potted plants were bursting with new growth, the cats were fat. And Caledonia, at last, had had all the love she needed. She hadn't left home for a minute and had even accompanied the doctor on house calls. "Now I know," the doctor said, "what they mean by a doc's hund." Homecoming was wonderful, except for the latest outbreak of mechanical difficulties.

It had been years since parts for the big press had been manufactured, and the main gear was not something that could be ingeniously reproduced with spit and baling wire. Yet here it was Monday morning, the press was no more functional than it would have been upside down, and on Tuesday morning we had to start printing the paper.

"We could arrange to print it on someone else's press," our foreman suggested. "That's what we've been doing."

Ed said grimly, "We'll print it on our own."

Sheer stubbornness supported him for the next twenty-four hours. He called an expert repairman, who assured him that the part was obsolete but he'd come out and see what could be done, in a few weeks.

"I've got to get her running by tomorrow!"

"Are you crazy?" was the repairman's helpful reply.

Ed called local garages and mechanics until he learned where he could borrow a wheel-puller. Paul Pieper, head man at the U. S. ranger station, saved our lives by lending the gadget Ed needed to pull the gear off the press. Once off the press, he carried it out to the car and raced thirty miles to a gear works in Seattle.

Yes, they could make one just like it. First, we'd have to take it to a patternmaker. In two weeks, they'd have a pattern, in another two the gear works would complete the job. . . .

"But I've got to use the press tomorrow!"

The foreman shook his head. Ed went to a second gear works.

There two men worked for three hours (the pair at nineteen dollars an hour) getting the three pieces of the broken gear back together again. They encased the whole thing in brass. Now it was a solid chunk. "Take it to your local welder," they said. "He can cut teeth into it. We can't do that here."

That was about seven o'clock Monday evening. The men wrapped the gear in asbestos sheeting, loaded it into the back of our Chevvy, and Ed drove the thirty miles back to the Valley with the trunk of the car hotter than a Bessemer oven.

The local welder shook his head. "I'd like to, Ed, but that's no job for me."

"Where can I have it done?"

"Take it into a gear works in Seattle," the man replied, and gave the nearly speechless Ed the address of a shop that could do it.

So it was load the gear once again, and back to Seattle and a third gear works. It was almost ten o'clock by then. "But you've got to do it," Ed pleaded, and they agreed to try. They worked on it all night. Ed was home about midnight, and back in Seattle at the gear works by eight o'clock in the morning.

The foreman looked at him curiously. "You're knocking yourself out over this. Who do you work for, anyway?"

"Myself," Ed replied tersely.

Ed was back in the shop at Snoqualmie at nine and by ten o'clock the press was running as usual. In twenty-four hours he had driven 240 miles to get back where he started. The gear was in one piece but I doubted if *he* was. But he was happy. The last gear works had given him a printing order!

Once the crisis was past, I began to drop hints that it was time to remember what we had said on New Year's Eve. But every one I dropped seemed to land with a loud crash. When I asked Ed not to bring home armloads of work, not to pace the floor, and please to come home for dinner at a reasonable hour, my anxiety showed through and I was as subtle as a fast right to the jaw. I always started out "suggesting" and ended up nagging.

"Remember what you said at New Year's?"

"I wish I could keep those resolutions."

"But you promised!" Having flung this irrelevancy at him, I would back into another corner. "Remember what the doctor said last year? He said you *had* to cut down. You are deliberately ignoring doctor's orders. . . ."

"He didn't explain how I was to get the work done in less time. Besides, he didn't know what he was talking about. I'm healthy as a horse."

Naturally these discussions, as I insisted on calling them, contributed less than nothing to Ed's peace of mind. "You must keep him from getting nervous," the doctor had told me after Ed's heart attack the year before, and yet the more nervous Ed became, the more I worried and the louder I shouted, "Stop being nervous!"

With envy I observed the way a friend of mine handled an almost identical situation. Chris, her husband, also owned a small business, and like Ed, he carried it with him every minute of the day and night. He, too, had had a heart attack and he was ignoring doctor's orders because, as he explained often, "I never did do what the doctor told me, and look, I've never been healthier in my life. I might as well live the way I want to. . . ."

I knew Chris's wife was as worried about him as I was about Ed. But where I was argumentative, she was serene. Where I kept bringing the tablets of "doctor's orders" down from the mountain and waving them angrily in my husband's face, she said simply, "You're the boss, dear. Whatever you want to do is all right with me." As a result her husband lauded her far and wide as a "good sport." I decided I had better pattern myself after her, for though Ed worked more than was good for him and came home late, the way I was helping him back to health would soon discourage him from coming home at all.

Sweetness and light did not come naturally. When Ed left to work at the shop on Sunday my gentle, "Good-bye, dear," was apt to be drowned out by the furious gnashing of my teeth. But I persisted, sure that I must be a model wife at last, because it was so difficult.

ii

We were gaining new readers every month. In one three-month period eighty-six new subscriptions had come in, all unsolicited since we never held any kind of campaign. Almost every week advertising revenue was higher than it had been the corresponding month of the previous year. In short, business was good. We hired a regular bookkeeper and for the first time in three and a half years we could ask loftily, "Have you paid the bills this month, Mrs. McNeely?" without bracing ourselves for her reply—"Ha! With what?"

Once a mad redhead had slammed the office door so hard she cracked the glass. Now she was a fast friend, and many another subscriber who had given us what-for during those first grim months had forgotten what it was they had been mad about. Best of all, we weren't the "new editors" any more, a fact which dawned on us the first time someone asked, "Say, what was the name of that fellow you bought the paper from?"

Now that they knew us better our readers sometimes disdained both mail service and telephone as a means of getting at the editor and came right to the house. They were always friendly calls; mad subscribers have always shown considerable delicacy about knocking the publisher's block off outside of business hours. Most of our house calls evenings and Sunday afternoons have been from people bearing seventy-five cents for a classified ad, and it was this errand which brought subscriber Verne Roberts.

Verne Roberts was born in North Bend almost sixty years ago and in that time has become well established as the town's best fisherman. He has been a prize fighter (A "canvas inspector," he says), a logger and a prospector; he can still put in a hard day's work and often does. But of most things, Verne takes an unconventional view. For years he had some of the outer attributes of a family man, such as a house and a wife. "I may not have the best lawn in North Bend," he admitted, "but it's the tallest." The house rose unpainted and untended out of a sea of slug-infested weeds, but when a neighbor complained that the creatures Verne was harboring were now moving over into his garden, Verne replied, "If you don't like my slugs, you'd better get some of your own." Mice were crowding them out of the house but when Verne's wife complained, "You'll have to get something for the mice," Verne retorted, "If they don't like the food we're eating, they can leave." She persisted. "Also, I haven't a stick of wood for the cook stove!" Verne gestured toward the piano. "Go in and knock off a chord." It's not surprising, least of all to Verne, that he no longer has the wife, the house or the piano.

I had never seen Verne until the night he came to the house, just as I was drying the supper dishes. An old sedan rattled up the driveway, gave one last sickly cough and died at the back door. Verne disentangled himself from the steering wheel, got out, and called, "This the editor's house? I want to put an ad in the paper."

Ed brought him into the house and gave him paper and pencil. For fifteen minutes Verne composed, revised and rewrote that classified ad. Finally the job was done to his satisfaction.

"WANTED," he had written. "Will buy or rent a team of Percheron horses to drag 1938 model car formerly owned by Ray Curnutt (short hauls). Or will hire traveling mechanic. If interested, call Verne Roberts, North Bend, P.O. Box 214, or call any tavern."

He pulled a five-dollar bill from his pocket. "Here, this cover it?"

Ed grinned. "Seventy-five cents."

Verne stared. "Is that all an ad costs?"

"That's all. . . ."

Verne found the change, Ed wrote out a receipt, and Verne

was about to leave when he caught sight of the old oak piano in the corner. He stopped so quickly he nearly fell over backward. "You got a piano!" he burst out. "Mind if I try a couple tunes?"

So Verne began to play. Shades of Virginia City and nineteenth century nickelodeons—all he needed was sawdust on the floor. He used every key on the keyboard and he sang every tune he played, verse and chorus. Hi and Johnny came out of their bedrooms and began dancing around the kitchen table while Ed and I leaned against the sink, enraptured.

After a few minutes, Verne moved from the Nineties into "Nobody's Sweetheart Now," and that was too much for me. I sat down at the little reed organ, hit stray notes until I found the key, and took a running dive into some fast accompaniment. After we had walloped out the final chord, Verne called, "Hey, come over here, we'll do a duo."

We divided the piano at middle C, agreed on the name of the tune and the key, and after that it was every man for himself. We played "Tiger Rag," "Mean to Me," "Indianola," and other compositions reflecting the advance culture of the times. Verne beat out the rhythm with his right foot, I thumped the floor with my left. "I know ten thousand songs," Verne stated, and if the boys had not turned the radio on for a heavyweight bout we probably would have found out if it was true. Two hours after he had arrived to place a seventy-five-cent ad, our subscriber departed. It was one of the most enjoyable meetings with a *Record* reader I've ever had.

"I still can't get over it," Verne said as he climbed back into the old sedan, "how cheap an ad is in the *Valley Record*. You guys can't make any money that way," and grinning and waving, he rode the bucking Buick down the drive.

iii

In April, Chris died. Only a few months had passed since I first determined to be as serene and sweet as Chris's wife, and his death meant more than the loss of a friend. It filled me with cold fear. What was I doing, trying to be a "good sport," too, but standing by cheerfully while Ed dug his own grave? Of course Ed claimed there was nothing wrong with him and hence no reason to follow doctor's orders. Chris had said that, too. For the first time I looked at the situation squarely: Unless Ed changed his pattern of day-to-day living, he would surely suffer a second heart attack, and if that didn't kill him, then the third or the fourth one would. It wasn't a matter of being a "good sport." It was a question of saving my husband's life.

It was a bitter question, because it was the first one in almost ten years of marriage that I had had to answer alone. It was with me all day and it followed me into sleep at night. Ed's nervous gestures, the dark circles under his eyes, were signs of fatigue I had once dismissed with, "Things will get better soon and he won't have to work so hard. . . ." Now they frightened me. We had been in business for ourselves for well over three years. We were still deeply in debt and Ed was still working too hard. But what if "things didn't get better" in time?

Slowly two alternatives formed in my mind. There was the "hands off" technique of the woman like Chris's wife, who wants, above all else, to make her husband's life pleasant. Or there was the "mother knows best" philosophy of the wife who knows what her husband should do and is right there to see that he does it. I wanted Ed to be happy, but I decided at last that much more than that, I wanted him to live. If he wouldn't follow doctor's orders, I would force him to.

I began in low gear by "suggesting" that we hire an extra printer, and what moment did I choose but the very day one of our largest logging companies was hit by a strike.

Ed stared at me in disbelief. "Honey, don't you know what happened? The strike at Mountain Tree?"

"That may be, but you're working too hard. I think we should hire another man."

240

"There's a *strike* in our Valley. Don't you realize what that can do to the newspaper? The men aren't earning any money, they aren't buying in local stores, the store owners say, 'What's the use of advertising in the paper, no business will come in anyway. . . .'" Ed began tapping the floor with his heel.

"See? You're jittery and nervous. It isn't good for you. You've got to cut down!"

Ed jumped to his feet. "If I'm nervous it's because there is reason to be. And we don't need another man. We've got three men in the backshop right now, besides Olga at the Linotype. Even if we needed more help, we couldn't afford it."

"We could borrow more money."

Ed looked at me long and silently. My face must have been stern because a stubborn look crept into his own. "We owe $22,500," he said, "and when we borrow more, *if* we can borrow more, it will be for a darned good reason." He walked out of the room, and thus ended my first effort to tell him what to do for his own sake.

For a month I stuck with it. If Ed was late for supper, I telephoned the shop and insisted he come right home. I threw so many phrases at him like "For my sake . . ." or "If you won't think of yourself, then do it for the kids . . ." that I managed to extract several promises from him: He would not go to the shop on Sunday. He would not get up and work during the night, no matter how long he lay sleepless in bed. He would not bring ledgers and other bookwork home with him. He would not . . . Proof of my success as a helpmeet was not long in coming. Ed broke out in his second all-consuming case of shingles.

Once more, the vicious circle. The pain and the itching distracted him during the day and kept him awake at night, and every sleepless night made the next day more intolerable. I tried to convince myself that the anxiety which lay behind the ailment was groundless, that Ed would not be sick now if he had listened to me. But it didn't sound quite right, even in my own mind. If the laissez-faire attitude was a poor way to keep your husband alive, subjecting him to a constant fire of Don'ts and Doctor's Orders was surely worse. What then? What *could* I do?

Shingles or no, Ed was at the shop day and night, because, of course, "We've got to get the paper out." But the next day he came home early. The moment he turned into the driveway I was marshaling arguments about why he shouldn't bring work home with him and why he should lie down to rest. He came into the house quietly, and his hands were empty. He threw me a weak grin and a quick hello, and went right past me to the bedroom. He was lying down when I came in, and he was flat on his back, staring at the ceiling.

"Are you all right?" I asked anxiously.

He nodded. "Just tired."

His face was gray. How much had he slept the past week— three hours, four hours a night, perhaps, and that broken by the torment of shingles.

"Hungry?"

"No."

"Shall I run a bath for you?"

"No, please, I just want to lie here for a while."

I turned to go. Ed's voice, with a funny restrained sound to it, called me back. "I probably ought to tell you. We don't have a Linotype operator any more."

"What!"

"Today was Olga's last day at the shop."

Olga, the Linotype operator in the pretty flowered apron, the first member of the staff I met and our unchanged and unchangeable mainstay ever since. The Linotype is the heart of the print shop, and Olga had been the heart of the Linotype. Ralph was an operator, but he had too much backshop work of other kinds to absorb Olga's job. Yet if the Linotype stood idle, we were no more in business than a baker would be without an oven.

Ed explained. For years Olga's husband had been hoping

she would give up her job. He wanted a wife who was more concerned about setting out his house slippers than she was about setting type, who worried about only one deadline and that was 5:50 P.M. when he got home for supper. We couldn't blame him—the newspaper had made a widower out of him on many a lonely night. Then there was Olga's little boy. With school out, he'd be home all day and his mother ought to be home with him. So today, the last day of school, was Olga's last day at the shop.

"Any idea who we can get to replace her?"

Ed said wearily, "I've tried. I don't think there's an unemployed Linotype operator in the state of Washington."

I wanted to comfort him but I couldn't face Ed and say the empty Pollyanna phrases that came to mind. It was a beautiful, sunny afternoon. The children were making happy sounds in the front yard and though the clucking of chickens was missing, it was very much like that afternoon in August when Ed and I had sat in the living room of our farmhouse and talked about the future. Since then we had raced against bankruptcy, and won. We had battled outdated equipment, miserable living conditions, and the worst weather in twenty-four years. Flood waters had risen to the back door of the shop, our house had been robbed, our children had contracted polio. Slowly, slowly, we had pulled ourselves forward, keeping up payments, improving the business, facing our critics and winning them over. We had even taken to guessing when the great day would be, the day when all our debts would be paid off. October, 1959, or could we beat that traditional ten-years-to-pay-it-off and make it by our eighth anniversary in 1957? It was fun to dare thinking about it, as long as Ed carried the spark of daring. Ed must have strength for two. I might cry, "Oh, I'm so tired!" but Ed was indestructible. And Ed must have courage, so much courage he would have it to spare when I lost mine. Being without a Linotype operator was far from the worst crisis we had ever met— it was Ed's reaction that frightened me. Ed without spirit, Ed heartsick and ill—what was the use of all we'd done, if to win the fight we were losing something so much bigger?

"Olga should have given notice. . . ."

Ed said quickly, "Oh, she did. She told me weeks ago."

"You knew! You've known all this time. Why didn't you tell me?"

Ed said quietly, "You've been working hard to finish your book. I didn't want to worry you."

So I'd been helping him, had I, telling him when to eat and when to come home and how much to work. I couldn't say anything but "I'm sorry, darling . . ." and pray he knew what I meant.

His hands were shading his eyes, and he lay so still I thought he might have fallen asleep. I tiptoed to the window and reached up to pull the curtain.

"No," Ed said. "I don't want to sleep. Come and sit here beside me. I want to talk to you. . . .

"About the shop. There's a lot about running a small business which you don't know, because I've taken care of it. The ordering of supplies, for example. Or the way to figure an estimate on a printing job. You should begin studying these things carefully, so that you could run the business without me if you had to."

"There's no need to discuss any such thing!" I cried it like a scared child.

"We never know. I'm older than you are."

"But it will be years and years before . . ." My voice trailed off, caught somewhere behind the lump of fear tightening in my throat. Years and years before you die, that was the rest of it.

Ed said gently, "There's a big scratchpad and pencil in that drawer there. There are some things I'd like you to write down."

"I don't want to!" I was determined not to cry but my voice was sharp with fear.

"Please, darling . . ."

I groped for the pad and pencil. "I wouldn't want to keep the business, I wouldn't want to have anything to do with it . . ." and added, choking on it, "without you."

"Think," Ed said. "Remember what we used to say, that it was a family business, that all four of us were in it together? Haven't we told the children— This is your business as much as ours, and therefore you must do your part to keep it going? Didn't we mean what we said?"

"Yes, yes . . ."

Ed touched my hand. "Then it would be up to you to keep the paper going until the boys were old enough to take over."

He hesitated a moment, but I could not speak. He patted my hand, and began matter-of-factly, "First, the matter of insurance . . ."

Slowly, forming each letter with care, I began to write. I kept my eyes on the paper. I didn't want Ed to see in them what I was thinking, that when we launched our brave venture the most terrible failure we could imagine was not half so big as this.

12

Surely Heaven's board of directors includes a vice-president in charge of fools who say a fig for high taxes and labor shortages and Big Business competition, we'll buy a little business all our own. About June 1, 1952, this worthy looked down and mused, "There's that silly couple in Snoqualmie again. Better let them come up for air." And so he took his celestial foot off our necks and things got better.

Ed had scarcely immortalized his second case of shingles with the briefest editorial of his career—six lines in which the word "scratch" appeared six times—when the red spots began to fade. And by the end of the week, we had found a Linotype operator.

We got his name from a man who knew a man he had once worked for. We didn't ask how good he was, or why he had left his last job. We grabbed name and phone number like dogs stealing a bone and ran for the telephone. He had moved, and he had no telephone, but after several long distance calls we reached his next-door neighbor and she agreed to "go get that printer fellow."

The man's name was Jim Halleran, but it was Mrs. Halleran who came to the telephone. Ed explained what we wanted.

"I'll have to go talk to Jim," she said. "You call me back tomorrow."

At that point a loss of twenty-four hours would have meant we would not get the paper out. "Look," Ed said, "I can't wait until tomorrow. Let me talk to Mr. Halleran himself."

"Oh, you can't do that," she said flatly. "All the way from our place to this place. It's too hard on him. Anyway, it would take him too long."

We had had one printer with a wooden leg (and goodness knows how many with heads to match) so Ed was quick to understand that this man Jim Halleran had some difficulty in walking. He hesitated to ask about it bluntly and besides, the only important question was, When can he start?

"I'm in a bad situation, Mrs. Halleran," Ed explained, trying not to sound downright desperate. "So would you go and talk to your husband right now, and call me back in a half-hour?"

"Long distance?"

"Yes, it's a long distance call."

"Can I call collect?"

"Certainly."

"Well, I don't know. . . ." She said good-bye. For forty-five minutes Ed sat at the telephone, eyeing it greedily. At last the call came.

"Jim can't come to work," Mrs. Halleran's high childish voice informed us, "because he don't have the money for a haircut." And neither Ed's reasonable arguments nor muffled sobs could persuade her.

Ed replaced the receiver with a bang. "I've got his address," he said. "I'm going to drive down this afternoon and look this guy over. Get your coat."

"I wouldn't know a good Linotype operator from a sabermaker. Why should I go?"

"I'll look the guy over." Ed shook his head ruefully. "You're coming along to look over his wife."

We found Jim and Bessie Halleran in a one-room cabin furnished with a double bed, a kitchen sink, a table and two straight chairs. Jim lay on the bed. Later we learned he had had polio as a baby, but physical therapy and other treatment which nowadays restore the bodies of polio victims weren't even on the horizon for a poor farm family forty years ago. Jim would have been a big man, had he been whole. He had tremendous shoulders, long muscular arms, big hands. But it looked as if his body had been broken in a dozen places and carelessly thrown back together again. Hunchbacked, twisted spine, limp, useless legs—he was crippled beyond imagination. His face was pale, framed by thick brown hair which had grown so long he had combed it behind his ears Hindu-fashion.

"Don't you worry about Jim being crippled," his wife assured us the moment we came in. "He can set two and a half galleys an hour."

I turned to smile at her. She had a lighted cigarette in one hand. Her other hand was feeling over the surface of the kitchen table. It touched the ash tray. She lifted it carefully and snubbed out her cigarette. Again her free hand felt for the center of the table and she set the ash tray down. The truth hit me like a fist. She was blind.

We stayed for a half-hour or more, and in that time Ed and I did not look at each other.

It was agreed that Jim would come to work for us. He had a friend who owned a taxi and would drive him to Snoqualmie early in the morning. As we left, Ed dropped a ten-dollar bill on the kitchen table. "Just to help you get squared away," he said vaguely—but I knew what he was thinking—because you didn't want to come without a haircut.

"Do you think he'll show up?" I asked on the way home.

Ed replied without hesitation. "I'm sure of it."

Remembering the weakness of some of our former employees, I asked, "You don't suppose he drinks, do you?"

"How could he?" Ed replied, just as positively. "They've been living off relief for almost a year. He hasn't had enough money for it."

Jim appeared right on time, in faded but spotlessly clean work clothes and with a haircut that exposed a two-inch strip of white skin around the back of his neck. He moved on crutches, his tremendous shoulders swinging the weight of his twisted body. He didn't break any records that first week at the shop, but we did get the paper out, and before long he was doing the best job at the Linotype anyone had ever done for us. Not only that—soon he was driving his own car.

"During the depression, I made a living as an auto mechanic," he told us, to our utter amazement. "I can fix up any car with hand controls so I can drive it myself. I saw an old Packard in a used-car lot that I kind of liked the looks of."

"How much do you need?" Ed asked, with considerable magnanimity for a man whose only remaining collateral were the fillings in his teeth.

"Hundred dollars," said Jim, and so we bought him a car.

He and Bessie rented a little cottage in Snoqualmie. They needed a load of stove wood, for the big black stove in the center of the room was not only for cooking but for heating as well. Ed ordered and paid for a truckload of wood. The cottage had not been occupied for some time and the grass in the front lawn grew to the knees; I hauled our mower from North Bend to Snoqualmie and cut the grass. Our mother cat also did her part to make them welcome. She had kittens, and I took the cutest of them to Bessie so she would have something to keep her company.

Bessie was a furious housekeeper. She scrubbed, polished

and waxed, until she had beaten that little house into sub-mission. It was she who split big chunks of slab wood into fine kindling; the only aspect of the job that ever irritated her was keeping the hatchet as razor-sharp as she thought it ought to be. It was she who did the shopping. Jim would drive her to the store and sit in the car while Bessie felt her way along the shelves. Months later, Bessie asked to borrow a typewriter. With a few packages of colored papers, scissors, paste, and a greeting she composed herself, she made a hundred Christmas cards and sent them to all her friends.

"One thing about a guy like Jim," Ed remarked, "it's so difficult for him to get around he isn't apt to be a drifter. I bet he'll be with us for ten years."

"He does seem happy here," I admitted uneasily, because I was accustomed to almost everything but having things work out for the best.

"The way things are going," Ed said with a grin, "I may have to give up my annual case of shingles next year."

I laughed, but I said a little silent prayer, too, that Ed would truly relax and stay well and that I would cease being such a darned fool about the way I tried to help him do it. If we have ever hit the very bottom of despair, it was surely the afternoon Ed talked to me about how to run the business without him.

After that talk I thought of going to the doctor, but I didn't because it wasn't a physical problem. It was a personal, al-most a spiritual, problem, mine and Ed's. How must my im-pulsive, hyperkinetic husband live from day to day so as to succeed in this family project that meant so much to him, and yet not be destroyed by the struggle? Once I had thought I could save his life, but now I knew the most I could do was help him save it himself. But how?

Help came, most unexpectedly, not from the doctor, or from a minister or a psychiatrist, though I thought of con-sulting them, too. I was in the grocery store, contemplating a shelf of canned goods but frowning mightily because I had just been thinking about Ed. The doctor's wife came by, pushed her shopping cart next to mine, and exclaimed, "My, what a worried look. Did you leave your grocery list at home?"

There are moments when one's private mind is so full the gentlest tap brings the contents flooding out, and that was one of them. The doctor's wife had six children, and I hope she wasn't in a hurry to get home to them, because her greeting and her sweet face made me want to tell her things, and praises be, I told them all! My worries about Ed's health, my efforts to keep hands off and my reason for going to the other extreme—for about fifteen minutes she had no more chance to get a word in than did the tuna fish on sale for twenty-eight cents a can.

When I finally came to a breathless halt, she was smiling sympathetically. "I understand very well. There must be hundreds of thousands of wives in the same spot you're in. Right in our own little clinic, we see so many men who have nervous heart attacks or ulcers or high blood pressure, or some other ailment which comes from driving themselves too hard. I've often thought— Every one of these men has a wife, and what is she doing to help him?

"I don't think you were 'all wrong' when you were concentrating on making Ed's life pleasant. An overtired, nervous man needs a peaceful home. You weren't 'all wrong,' either, when you changed your tactics and tried to force him to follow doctor's orders. You would be foolish to pretend, as Ed is pretending, that he doesn't need to.

"But you can't force a man to give up one way of day-to-day living. However, you can offer another way of living and make it so attractive he'll adopt it voluntarily."

"How?" I exclaimed. "It sounds fine, but it also sounds impossible."

She smiled. "A wife has to be clever," she said softly.

For days my head throbbed with good intentions. Slowly these truths emerged. First of all, I had been talking about Ed's "way of life" as if it were entirely separate from my own, and unaffected by my "way of life" or that of the children. I had been demanding that he change the hours he kept and the things he did, but hadn't for a moment asked myself if the hours *I* kept and the things *I* did were helping him to make a change.

I had been demanding that he spend more time at home. "You've got to learn to relax," was the order I handed him twice daily, like a pill. But how "relaxed" was the atmosphere I created at home? Ironing, vacuuming, cleaning the closets, doing the washing—since I worked in my writing house or at the newspaper shop during the day, I saved all these chores for Sundays and evenings and I went at them like a slaphappy prize fighter rushing into a free-for-all with his eyes closed. I enjoyed it. It was a change from the sedentary "thinking" kind of job I had all day. But what was I contributing to my worried, tense husband's peace of mind by filling his quiet moments at home with the swish, roar, clatter, kerthump and bang of every electrical appliance in the house?

The worst of it was that I had been so proud of myself. Flattered and nurtured by the exclamations of friends, "My, I don't see how you get so much done, and you write books, *too!*" I had failed to see that anyone can "get so much done" if simply getting something done is more important than the wear and tear on the family.

The sight of the laundry basket brimming with unironed clothes made me quiver, and my left hand had to keep my right hand from reaching for the dust mop when I spotted the little cottony rolls of dust under the bed, but the Sunday following my talk with the doctor's wife I resolved not to do a single bit of housework. More important, not even to think about the housework I wasn't doing. As a perfect example of what not to do, last week's "day of relaxation" sufficed. During Sunday breakfast there had been little conversation because I had been busy drawing up a list of jobs to be accomplished that day. The moment I downed eggs and bacon and one cup of coffee, I jumped up from the table and began to do the dishes. At that Ed went into the living room and sat down to a pile of office work. "Why, you didn't even finish your coffee!" I scolded, partly because I knew I should urge him to relax but more particularly because I wanted to wash the cup. Thus had ended abruptly the day's first opportunity for relaxation. And who had been deaf to its knock, but I.

Six times a week Ed began the day with two cups of black coffee, the first consumed alone at the kitchen table (I didn't take time to sit down with him), the second while standing at the door, his eye on the clock. The day of rest would henceforth start off with a leisurely, old-fashioned breakfast, and this first Sunday of my resolve began that way. No lists, no jumping up from the table. It was a peaceful meal; I had almost forgotten how pleasant conversation can be if you don't have to shout above the whirr of the washing machine. Long after the food was gone, we talked. I reheated the coffee, filled our cups, and we talked some more. Suddenly Ed burst out, "Great guns, we've been sitting here for an hour and a half!" He looked at me apologetically. "Don't you have something you want to do—I mean, have I been keeping you . . ."

"No, no," I said quickly, repressing the old urge to begin tidying up in all directions. "There's always plenty to do but nothing I have to get to right this minute." It was the truth, the utter truth. We hadn't run out of clean clothes or clean dishes, and why was a little dust under the bed suddenly insupportable on Sunday when it hadn't been hurting us all week?

"Good," Ed said contentedly. "We seem to have so little chance to talk. . . ."

Later that day Ed brought out the forbidden office work, and the word "Don't!" rose in my throat automatically. "Don't work on Sunday" and "You promised you wouldn't bring work home from the office . . ." and "The doctor said . . ."—somehow I managed to swallow them whole. Now that I was looking more closely at my methods of "helping" my husband I could see I had been taking a negative approach to everything. It was a gray, rainy afternoon. Why shouldn't he work at home for an hour or two, unless I had something better to suggest? So I tried to think of something. I couldn't. My imagination was rusty from disuse.

That was just it—I had been busy reminding him of what he shouldn't do and hadn't spent one thoughtful moment on what he might do instead. For imagination (and wasn't that what the doctor's wife had meant by "being clever"?) I had substituted rules. "Let's make a rule you never go to the shop on Sunday," was one I had set up so dogmatically. But there was many a bleak Sunday afternoon when he wouldn't have missed much by working at the shop. And no matter how bright and sunny Friday afternoon might be, it had never occurred to me to drop whatever I was doing and say, "Come on, let's quit work and go for a hike." Why? Because to me Friday had always been a work day. Two errors in one. I had tried to force Ed into the conventional living pattern of the man who works for someone else. It doesn't always fit the man who owns his own business. Ed wasn't automatically through work in forty hours, but if he must work fifty or sixty, surely he should have been allowed to schedule them as he pleased. The reason I had never seen that occasional weekday holidays might fit in nicely with Ed's plans was that they would have forced me to change mine. To the error of conventionality I had added the sin of selfishness. Not a helpful combination. I would have to do better.

It was a warm July afternoon when I sent this particular resolution on its solo flight. Work on my novel was going top speed but about mid-afternoon I pushed back the smoking typewriter, threw Chapter Fifteen into a box and drove to the shop. Ed was at his desk, frowning over a stack of invoices. "What are you doing down here?" he asked, a bit more surprised than pleased. It wasn't a good moment for a wife with psychology shining in her eyes to try to Be Clever for the first time.

"Would you take me out to the golf course and teach me how to play golf?" There, it was out.

Ed looked astonished. "Why, I . . . Well, of course I've always wished you would take up golf."

That was the truth—he had spoken about it again and again, but I'd always shrugged off the suggestion. In the pursuit of greater interests I had not seen how rare and wonderful was the husband who actually wanted his wife with him even on the golf course.

"Besides," Ed mused, "I haven't played enough golf myself to know how to teach anyone else."

And how true that was! He had played twice during our seven years on the farm, once in our two and a half years as country publishers. My conscience stirred uncomfortably. How much golf would he have played if I had been willing to go along with him, instead of being a "good wife" by telling him to run along and play with someone else?

Ed looked at the work on his desk and shook his head. "I can't play golf. I've got to finish this stuff today."

"Throw it in the car and we'll take it home with us," I said, though the old, worried wife was reeling at what the new, clever wife was saying. "I'll help you tonight after supper and we'll have it finished in an hour."

"Well, I don't know . . ." but he followed me to the car and soon we were on the first tee and I was holding one of Ed's clubs and wondering if I'd ever learn to knock the ball as far as I could throw it. Ed was saying, "No, hands a little closer together, that's it. Now, here, get the feel of that club, it's like a pendulum. . . ."

He wasn't frowning over a pile of invoices, or sweating it out in a dark corner of a thirty-five-year-old building, or arguing with printers or placating subscribers. He was out in the fresh air, he was about to get some exercise, he looked as happy as a kid at Christmas and he was following doctor's orders! I hardly heard what he was telling me, but I think it was something like, "Look, honey, the important thing is, you got to relax!"

One or two successful attempts at being "clever" weren't enough to save my husband's life, but they did give me confidence that I was learning how to help in the right way. Needless to say I enjoyed the golf games and the Sunday breakfasts as much as he did. I was startled, then amused, by the discovery that he had been worrying about how to get *me* to relax. What a treadmill we'd been spinning! Two jitter cases trying to catch up with each other in order to say, "Here, now, you've got to slow down." Tension is contagious, we'd proved that. But it looked as if peace of mind might be, too.

I found that every day contained potential moments of relaxation, if we slowed down enough to see them. In the course of making business calls, Ed and I sometimes passed the grade school during recess. One day I said boldly, "Let's stop and watch the baseball game. That's Johnny at second base, and Hi is fielding . . ."

Ed looked at me oddly. "We've got to get back to the shop. We're late already."

"That's silly! The entire recess lasts only fifteen minutes."

Ed grinned. "I know it's silly. I was just repeating word for word what you said to me a few months ago when *I* suggested we stop."

"Oh." It was a small "Oh," too.

"Look at the arm on that kid!" Ed burst out. "Say, that was a nice catch Hi made, too. I think I'll start practicing with the boys. Evenings, for a half an hour. Sunday afternoons . . ."

It's a cinch Ed and I got more out of that recess than the youngsters did. Fifteen minutes thinking about our children and baseball, instead of a difficult printing order or an overdue bill. Fifteen minutes of sitting still, hands idle and weight off the feet. It was as good as an hour's nap or a shower and change of clothes. "Let's do this again," Ed said as we drove away, and we have, many times.

Somehow it is possible to be well and happy even if you own your own business—I believed that, but until that first "recess" in the yard of the North Bend grade school I was trying to decipher the riddle without the key word. I had already discovered a good deal about getting Ed to relax away from the shop, and that was a good start. But the cold facts of life cannot be denied. Even if we were out of debt (oh joyous thought!) and were financially able to take long week ends and two vacations a year, we would still work eight hours for every three we played, and at least forty-eight out of every fifty-two weeks would be dominated by work, not by leisure. Therefore the answer, not only for Ed but for every other breadwinner who is the "worrying kind," could not lie in getting away from it all but in learning to go through the common, ordinary workday without twitching nerves or pounding heart.

I had often heard, "You're such a wonderful help to your husband in his work. . . ." But how did that compliment hold up under close inspection?

Not too well, I discovered. I had my list of jobs, Ed had his. Our lists were interminable, but we compiled them independently, as if each of us were in business for himself. Ed never got to the bottom of his list, and that worried him, I knew. But I never got to the bottom of mine, either, so it never had occurred to me that relieving him of a chore or two might be more important than finishing my own. We were in business together, but somehow in the struggle to survive, the "together" had been lost.

In his office one morning I found Ed making out his list for the day. He was frowning and tapping the floor with the toe of his shoe. Glancing at the list I saw an item "Telephone calls to . . ." plus a string of names and companies. It was underlined, circled, and now Ed was nervously ornamenting the letters with doodles. I had always known how much he dreaded telephoning. Forcing himself to make calls was a strain. Putting them off created even greater tension. Following an impulse, I said, "My goodness, I have already written most of those calls on *my* list. You might as well cross them off yours. . . ." He looked so relieved, so grateful, I knew the impulse was good. With a flourish he crossed off "Telephone calls," but fortunately with a light pencil so it was easy to copy the names after he'd left the room.

Women take to the telephone like small boys to a junk pile. Making a few calls seemed a small contribution indeed until I measured it by the peace of mind my doing it brought to Ed. I found there were other items on his work list which were my meat and his poison. They were all trivial, it is true. But I couldn't help him with the big jobs. I couldn't run the press or make up the front page or estimate commercial printing jobs. Big jobs like these didn't bother him, anyway. They exhilarated him in the doing, once done left him with a sense of accomplishment. It was the little jobs, always at the bottom of his list, always at the back of his mind, that bit in and festered. Phone calls, business letters, thank-you notes, a personal appearance at some club meeting where the local paper should be represented. Like most men Ed could work long and hard when he felt he had "something to show for it." Like most women, I had spent a not inconsiderable part of every day washing dishes that were soon to be dirty and making beds that were soon to be torn apart. It was I who had been indoctrinated to handle those pesky odds-and-ends jobs; they didn't make my heart pound or my nerves jump.

Combining lists made for efficiency, too. Ten telephone calls at one sitting do not take twice as much time as five phone calls today and five tomorrow. If you're set up to write business letters—desk clear, fresh carbon on hand, stamps and envelopes out—that's the time to write all, not part, of them. So actually I didn't increase my own burden of work by an ounce.

And what wonderful doses of appreciation my grateful husband administered in return! The first time I answered a couple of his long-unanswered letters he treated me as if I were a Linotype operator.

ii

Even in the backshop, once an area where the owner took his life in his hands when he asked, "Is that your right name?" we seemed to have a firm grip on our problems at last.

True, when we ran into our new Linotype operator's former boss, he asked, "Jim still with you?" and we reflected that he shouldn't sound quite so surprised, since it was then only two months since we had hired Jim. But the paper was coming out on time, the subscription list was growing, and we were slowly chipping away at the mammoth debt incurred by our policy of expanding in all directions at once. The mere absence of catastrophe was too much for Ed. He began making plans.

"I'd like to add onto the house," he would muse, "but that would take all the money we could borrow, and it would be years before we could pay it off and borrow again to add onto the shop. It would be more sensible to build the shop first. After all, it's productive; a home is just an extravagance. But then it would be years before we could have a larger house, and now when the kids are at home is the time we need it most. Hmmm . . ."

All it took was one ray of economic sunshine to bring Ed out of the dilemma. The strike at Mountain Tree Farm came to an end. "One hundred and fifty men are back to work," Ed sang out as he came through the kitchen door. "One hundred and fifty pay checks at the end of the week, 150 spenders back in town. The stores will do better and so will we."

"Oh, by the way," he called, now that he was in the living room and out of range, "I went over to the bank today and borrowed $10,000."

I knew our contract with the former publisher kept us from borrowing on the shop. We owned ten shares of investment-fund stock of such little value we had not bothered to sell it during the purge of our assets two years before. We owned two Chevrolets, one three years old and one a year old. There was the emerald ring I got from my great-aunt Sarah, but I thought I had kept pretty quiet about it. In short, if we had anything that was worth anything, how come we still had it?

"Borrowed $10,000?" I asked. "On what?"

Ed sounded surprised. "On this house, and the property, and"—he had the grace to hesitate here—"your writing house."

It was my turn to be surprised, for oddly enough I had not realized that our home was the most desirable kind of possession in the world, the kind you can borrow on. The basic costs—$1,500 for the property; $4,500 for the shell of the house; $5,500 for plumbing, wiring, fixtures, heating plant, and for finishing and furnishing; $1,500 for my writing studio—had been met with a writing check here, a demand note there. My ear had been attuned to the heavy footfall of our creditors and I had been blind to the fact that these scattered payments, no matter how small or how painful to meet, would in two years' time make us the owners of something against which we could borrow $10,000.

"I'm glad our credit is good," I said. "But since we still owe so much, why borrow more?"

"Why?" Ed exclaimed, all too brightly. "For our new building program. I couldn't make up my mind whether to start on the house or start on the shop, so there's only one solution: we'll build them both at once."

"No! Darling, on $10,000?"

Ed's expression took on a protective vagueness. "W-e-e-lll . . . that probably won't do it, no, but then . . ." He brightened up. "We'll start out and see how far we can go."

Before my mind's eye a view sprang to life of half a house, with the bathtub, for example, protruding beyond the wall the carpenters had stopped building when the money gave out. "See here, it's all very well to be a visionary, but I . . ."

Ed interrupted, "You finished your novel, didn't you? You've sent it off to New York, haven't you?"

"Writing a book is one thing," I said gloomily. "Selling it is another. May I remind you that I have written seven books and sold one?"

"Hmmph," Ed exploded. "This one is good. If they don't take it, they're darned fools."

"Try depositing that in our bank account." I gave the gravy a vicious stir and took another tack. "It is now the very middle of the building season. Even if you went ahead with this crazy notion, you couldn't find anyone free to take on a job, much less two jobs."

Ed smirked. "Elmer Brown is going to build the shop. Mr. Dubuis is going to build the house."

"Huh!" I retorted intelligently. "Wait till you ask them."

"I did," Ed replied, ducking around the corner, "weeks ago. . . ."

In August, work on the shop began. The existing shop was made up of two parts—the old frame building and the somewhat larger addition which two years earlier we had built at the rear. The plan was to construct a wing at the side of the old frame section, then raze the old building and, by erecting a third section, fill in the corner between the new wing and the two-year-old addition. The beauty of the plan was that we would go right on working while the building was going on.

The contractor, Elmer Brown, with bulldozer and bulldozer operator, arrived appropriately on press day to begin the excavation. It was a typical press day. The equipment had developed undiagnosable ailments. The Linotype operator was having trouble setting type, due, he explained, to the fact that he needed glasses. We all had deadline jitters and Ed's selling price for the works was going down by the minute when Elmer Brown ran into the shop and shouted, "Anyone know where your water pipes connect up with the town water system? The bulldozer just cut through a pipe and she's rising pretty fast."

Since I couldn't do anything but write, I was expendable, so it was my job to find someone who knew where the cut-off was. No one I could find had any idea where the blueprint was or even if one existed. No one could remember when the water mains had been laid. "A long time back," people said, indicating it had probably been done the day before God made Adam. My task became clear. I had to find someone so old he had been a sidewalk engineer when the pipes were laid.

I began the search. The street corner near the post office was a daily trysting place for all the grand old men of Snoqualmie. Ironically, not a one was there that day. The town garbage truck came down the street, driven by a man who had grandchildren and had himself been born in the Valley. I hailed the driver and asked, "Do you remember when they laid the water pipes on this street?"

"I'm not that old!" he replied, grinning. "Better try old man Bennett."

I ran down the street to Mr. Bennett's house. He had gone fishing, but his wife gave me two likely names. I raced back to the shop, jumped into the car, and out of the corner of my eye caught a glimpse of Elmer Brown, up to his ankles in muddy water and holding his hands over the pipe like the little Dutch boy with his finger in the dike. I drove to one house, then to another; one man was in the hospital and another was out fishing. In less than an hour I knew the names of the twenty oldest men in Snoqualmie but I still hadn't caught up with one of them. I went back to the shop. The crisis had passed. The lot was a sea of mud, Elmer was soaked head to toe, but he had capped the pipe and saved the day.

About that time one of the men I had been seeking showed up on the street corner. He had come to the Valley in 1890 and for half a century owned the general store opposite the newspaper shop. He had a quick mind and an amazing memory, and the memory showed through now as he surveyed the receding flood.

"I remember what happened right here, forty-three years ago today," Otto Reinig mused. "There was a hotel, standing where your newspaper shop is now, run by a fellow named Howard Johnson, a relative of the McClouds. He called it the Snoqualmie Hotel. Six o'clock in the morning, August 7th, 1909, the hotel caught fire and she burned to the ground." He chuckled. "All that water you have there would have been useful. Too bad it came forty-three years too late."

"Do you know where the cut-off is?"

"Sure," said Otto. "They put the line down, so . . ." He squinted up and down the street, surveyed the distance between curb and sidewalk, pointed to a spot and said, "Dig here." Elmer Brown dug, and in two minutes we found the cut-off.

"Thank goodness for your memory, Mr. Reinig," I breathed.

"No trick to remembering about that fire," he said, smiling. "Both the fire in 1909, and now this flood of yours, they happened on my birthday."

There was just time to do it. I ran inside, and the front page of that week's *Record* carried the message, "Happy Birthday, Otto!"

The first week of our new building program was also the week that a thief or thieves unknown broke into our shop.

When Ed and I went to work Saturday morning we found a pane of glass had been neatly removed from the front door and the cash drawer behind the counter lay upside down on the floor. As we reconstructed it, the thief had removed the pane, thrust his hand through the opening to turn the doorknob on the inside, and gone immediately to the cash drawer. He had emptied it, but when he pulled it out all the way to see what treasure might lie in the back, it had tricked him by falling out onto the floor. It must have made a merry noise. Paper clips, thumbtacks, pencils, streetcar tokens and old meat-ration coins were lying all over the floor. No doubt it had been enough to frighten him away.

I had to repress a groan. Things had been getting better. Ed had been more relaxed. And now, to get him nervous and worried all over again, a robbery.

But Ed was actually grinning. "Poor simp," he said, "trying to make a haul by robbing the local newspaper."

"How much did he get?"

Ed laughed. "Darling, he got all we had. Two dollars and fifteen cents, when I counted it last night." He looked at the hole in the front door. "But I can't forgive him for making off with that windowpane. That's going to cost some dough."

iii

Hiram was eight that summer, and he had never been to camp. Ed and I decided it was an experience he should have, and we told him about the Y.M.C.A. camp on Orcas Island, one of the San Juan Islands off the coast of Washington. Hi lost his heart to the idea and it was decided he would go for a week in August.

But we didn't want Hi to get the idea that good things come easy, especially if he was to own his own business some day, so I said, "The week at Camp Orkila will cost twenty-five dollars. I'll pay half of that, but if you really want to go you'll earn the other half."

We had never paid the boys for working at the shop; that was their obligation and we didn't want to put helping mother and father on a cash basis. There are not a great many ways in which an eight-year-old can earn $12.50, and we didn't suggest any. It was Hi who heard that the berry farm down the road needed pickers and it was Hi alone, without any physical or moral support from his elders, who walked to the farm and applied for the job.

"You're two years below the age limit," the owner said, "but I'll try you for one day. If you can pick clean as the grownups and don't fool around, you can come back again."

At the end of three days, Hi had earned $2.50. The next day it rained. "They don't pick in the rain," the little boy cried. "How am I going to get enough money for camp?"

Ed said jokingly, "Why don't you go out and sell subscriptions to the *Record*?" It was a job he expected the child to recoil from. It meant ringing doorbells, walking miles, meeting strangers, not to mention strange dogs. He would have to range far and wide because our coverage was already so complete.

Hi's response was an eye opener. "Oh, could I, Dad, honest? Would you let me, Dad, honest?"

Reversing our previous stand about not paying the boys for work in the shop Ed said, "I'll pay you seventy-five cents commission for every new subscription you get."

So the next morning Hi set out. He had a receipt book and a pencil in one overalls pocket, a big scratchpad in the other, and an armload of *Records*. In his head was a sales pitch he had worked out himself. Ring the doorbell. You don't take the paper? Here, let me show you one, because if you see it you'll want to subscribe. You do take the paper? Then how about sending a gift subscription to someone else? And finally, out with the scratchpad, and ask the client to write down a news item.

I never saw my small son in action, because every morning I took him to the end of some country road miles from home, and drove away. He walked all day. When the big round aluminum watch he carried said five o'clock, he asked at the nearest house to use the telephone. He called the *Record* office, giving me the latest directional findings, and I'd drive out and pick him up. He was always miles from his starting point.

In the morning, he cut quite a figure as a salesman. There was a brown paper sack containing his lunch. It hung from his belt, secured by a big safety pin. Pencils protruded from the pockets of his jeans. His step was firm and his smile, over the top of his armload of papers, was confident. By five o'clock he was a tired, dusty little boy. His sample papers were gone. The scratchpad was rumpled and the receipt book smudged. He had walked from one house to the next; some people had fed him cookies, other had slammed the door in his face. But he never came home without at least one new subscription and soon he was asking, "You said I had to earn half of the money for camp. But if I earn more than half, do I have to pay more than half?"

Once Hi apparently ran into some stiff sales resistance. Back against the wall, he decided the clincher might be to offer a premium. The man signed up, but shortly afterward appeared at the *Record* office. "I came to see you," he explained to Ed, "so as to collect my cigar."

"Cigar?"

Our new subscriber grinned. "Yeah, I took out a subscription from your son. He said if I would, his dad would give me a cigar—all I had to do was to come down to the *Record* office."

Ed burst out laughing. "Well, by George, if he said that, I'll make good. What kind do you like?"

The man's grin widened. "I just come down to tell you about it. You see, I don't smoke!"

Johnny and I took Hiram into Seattle to catch the bus for camp. He was fully equipped. Blanket roll, suitcase, and an old Girl Scout mess kit which he tried to hold upside down so no one would see the insignia. He had five dollars spending money in his jeans, and he had earned every penny of it. Until the very moment when the bus driver started up the motor, he talked of nothing but camp. But just at the last, his face appeared at an open window and he called down to little Johnny, "You do my work for me at the shop," he said—and was there a bit of wistfulness in his voice?—"And I'll use half my spending money to buy something at camp for you."

His head disappeared into the boyful, joyful interior, and the bus pulled away.

13

As a palliative for the small businessman's jangled nerves, I cannot recommend remodeling his home and adding onto his shop at the same time. At night Ed brought home a nervous system that had been jolted all day by the whine of power tools and the banging of hammers, and on entering his place of refuge was apt to trip over a sawhorse. At the shop there was cement dust in the type metal, at home it was in the coffee. Our tools of living, both at the shop and at home, had to be stacked in piles. If a minor adjustment on the Linotype called for a screwdriver, production stopped while everyone in the backshop looked for it. Life was no more orderly at home. When Ed fell exhausted into bed, he looked first to make sure the bed was still there.

Directing operations at our home-building site was Henri Dubuis, a Swiss. Mr. Dubuis is the elder of our local Seventh Day Adventist church and a devout man, stringently honest and conscientious. His crew consisted of two other members of his church, one a missionary recently returned from forty-five years of service in Africa. Mr. Dubuis was the architect, the contractor, the head carpenter. He did everything we would let him do and he worried over what we wouldn't let him do, as he showed the day he asked gently, "May I inquire what type of draperies you plan to use at these front windows?"

I said none whatsoever. When we asked for a span of windows twenty-five feet long, rising fourteen feet off the ground, it was to enjoy the view of the mountain they framed, not to cover it up. This pleased him, and so did our choice of materials, all natural, all indigenous: big fir beams supporting a ceiling of unvarnished hemlock decking; untreated knotty cedar for the living-room walls and Eastern Washington pine in the bedrooms. Only the floors made us traitor to the Pacific Northwest. Those in the living room and the new bath were of Vermont slate, and the bedroom floors were covered with grass mats from Haiti. But we made up for our disaffection when it came to the big corner fireplace. No manmade brick or Arizona sandstone for us. We were living on land once owned by the homesteader for whom Mount Si was named, and Mount Si literally filled the view out of every window. We would bring the mountain right into the house by building the fireplace out of it.

"Just be sure you get big enough pieces," the two masons who were to build the fireplace warned us. So every Sunday afternoon for a month we drove our two Chevrolets up a logging road to a point where a tremendous rock slide had poured down the mountain's side. Straining muscle and innard Ed loaded the trunks of the cars with hunks of gray-green basalt three feet in diameter, while the boys and I climbed up and down the slope selecting stones about the size of, and no harder than, our heads. It took hours to find pieces as weathered as we wanted them (my prizes were those on which moss was growing) and more hours and dollars at the osteopath's before Ed could again walk in something approximating an upright position. But we had a nice rock pile when we got through.

"Hope you got enough," the masons commented cheerily when they arrived to begin work. "Rocks are kind of dirty and mossy but a good scrubbing with muriatic acid and they'll brighten up."

"Don't you touch that moss, unless it's to water it!"

They looked puzzled, but they agreed and soon were hard at it with hammers and chisels. I uttered silent thanks that Ed wasn't home to see what they were doing. Whistling happily, they were splitting all the biggest rocks in two.

At home we sat around and shivered because a wall had been knocked out between the old house and the new unheated part, but we didn't sit around very much because all but the kitchen chairs were buried under the mountainous pile of furniture in the living room. As Ed constantly reminded me, home life is an extravagance anyway since it does nothing to pay off the mortgage. It was what the building program did to production at the shop that really mattered.

While the wing was going up beside the old frame building, carpenters and masons were separated from the editorial office by the wall of the old shop. Not a particularly soundproof wall, but it did keep the carpenters out of the big press and the printers from charging into the power saw. Once this three-sided section was complete, the next step was to raze the venerable Falls Printing Company erected "temporarily" in 1917. This was a blow terrible to none but the growing colony of English sparrows under the eaves, and it was a blow that never fell. A man in Snoqualmie who wanted to add onto his house came into the office and offered to buy it for $500 and move it off the lot, sparrows and all.

We transferred everything from the frame building into

the new three-sided shell, and uncovered lost items that publishers of twenty years before must have died looking for. Among them was a printed sign advertising HAIRCUTS, 50¢, SHAVE, 25¢, and a good supply of posters extolling the beauties of the Valley to passengers on a railroad line which had not run passenger cars through this area for twenty-two years. We piled everything, old and new, into the new wing, and the housemovers came to take the building away.

For three days they assaulted her with saws, house jacks, and tremendous square timbers. The old building creaked and groaned but she was solid as Mount Si and at noon one Sunday they had her high and dry on the bed of an old Army truck and were ready to roll down the street. We went home for an hour and so missed her departure, but on our return we could detect traces. There a telephone wire ripped loose, there a limb broken off a tree. These were the signs that marked her course from the corner of Falls Avenue and River Street to Bert Roselair's back yard.

Of course this left our editorial office without an east wall, and for a few breathless hours the front end of the *Record* looked like an exhibit at a housing show. It was now October, a month in which more rain falls hereabouts than some states see in a year. Ed and I tried to think good thoughts while Elmer Brown tussled with sheets of waterproof—we hoped—building board. Soon a temporary wall was put up. Now all we needed was dry weather until the last section, two walls and a roof, could be erected to fill the vacant corner. All we needed, other than a rich relative or another loan from the bank.

For it all took money, and between the house and the shop that $10,000 we had borrowed so hopefully was dwindling away with frightening speed. Being the pre-Christmas season, business was good, but those columns entitled "Accounts Receivable" were not something we could parcel out at the end of the week in lieu of pay checks.

There was my writing—but as a vein of gold, I chose this

critical moment to pinch out. For two years I had been spending most of my writing time on the historical novel about the Valley, thus neglecting other free-lance work. Three magazine pieces sold in the spring brought in a thousand dollars but the Falls Printing Company had swallowed that whole long before we began to talk building program. The last half of the year, when we were attempting to support all the building trades single-handed, my total contribution was $90.70, not enough to pay one of the carpenter's wages for one week. Daily I hoped for word that the novel had sold, but on this subject a great hush seemed to have fallen over New York.

In this new financial crisis Ed effected what proved to be a great saving: He made all his election bets on a cash or subscription basis; that is, he'd get cash if he won, we would pay off in *Record* subscriptions if he lost. He bet on everything. Daylight-saving time, oleomargarine—and, oh yes, Stevenson vs. Eisenhower.

"I'll clear $100 in a day," he bragged. "More than you've made in six months, you little ex-gold mine. I'll make us rich!" I should have known that a fellow who voted for Hoover in 1932 was not one to make a killing on a presidential election. Had I wanted some really accurate predictions I would have done better with a ouija board. For weeks after November 2nd the *Record* office was visited by one perfect stranger after another, each demanding a free subscription. It was no use wondering where Ed had met them, because they all were able to produce a penciled note in Ed's handwriting, saying something like "Good for one year's free subscription to the *Record* if the Republicans take Ohio . . ." or ". . . if Texas swings to Ike . . ." and so on. The notes were on paper napkins, café checks, old envelopes, the backs of counter checks, and other forms of legal tender—at least in the *Record* office in November of 1952.

By that time various executives of the bank across the street were dropping in at the shop "just to see how things are going," "things" meaning the bank's money. First the cashier, who watched construction silently, hands in pockets and an unreadable expression in his eyes. Then the office manager, a few days later the vice-president, and finally the man who owned us if anyone ever could, the president and chairman of the board of directors.

Mr. Hall had started his career some forty years before in a little bank located in a town with 250 population. Now he was the head of seven banks, and it was my guess he didn't get there betting on presidential elections. He went back into the shop, and surveyed the machinery and what the men were doing with it. He walked into the new wing and observed, "Concrete blocks, eh, cement floor, fireproof . . . Mmm . . ." Then he returned to the sidewalk and watched Elmer Brown and his crew setting blocks for the final section of the building. Ed had stayed by his side and answered all his questions, but the bank's solicitude had been preying on him and he finally quipped, "Well, Beadon, when do you foreclose?"

Mr. Hall's blue eyes twinkled but his voice was solemn. "Nothing like that, Eddie," he said. "I came over to tell you not to worry." He cocked his head sideways, indicating the unfinished building, the carpenters, bricklayers, plumbers, electricians. "I know what you already owe, and I know how much cash you've got left of that last ten thousand. But I don't know what's ahead of you. I can see you've got a program worked out in your own mind, and it's a good program, good for the whole Valley. So you sit down and figure out how much money you're going to need to carry it out, and then you come over and see us. We'll have it for you."

He looked thoughtfully at the dumbstruck local editor. "Now let's see, you've been here three years, haven't you? Only three years." He shook his head, and then this man, who had built one little country bank into a system of seven, added, "I never would have done what you've done, in only three years."

As newcomers to the Valley, back in the days when we still

owned some stock, we had turned over $10,000's worth of gilt-edged certificates as collateral on a fast loan of $3,000. Here was the same bank offering us unlimited backing when we hadn't dared ask for it because we couldn't think of anything we could borrow on. Why? They knew us now. Three years ago, we had been that couple from Chicago. Today, well, there was Mr. Hall, grinning and waving as he walked back to the bank, and his last words to Ed were, "Now remember, Eddie, we don't want you to worry."

From then on, Ed relaxed visibly, and within a week of his talk with the bank president he was listing a $3,000 inventory for a retail stationery and typewriter store. "We'll put it in the corner office," he said, "and whoever is working at the front desk can double as a sales clerk. Typewriters, stationery, envelopes, school supplies, paints, adding machines. We'll put in a good stock. Well . . ." he slapped his thigh briskly and stood up, "better go over and see Beadon."

In mid-November we decided we would hold Open House in the new building on December 21, the last week end before the Christmas holiday. Construction must be finished, walls painted, woodwork varnished, stationery store fully stocked —it seemed like an impossible goal. Meanwhile nothing must interfere with getting the paper out, so we worked on Saturdays and Sundays and what we laughingly referred to as our "free evenings" during the week. Mr. Dubuis thought he could have the house finished by Christmas, too, so the hammering and sawing and painting at both ends of the line became more frantic than ever.

Other families were taking Christmas-tree decorations out of the attic, starching the lace curtains, filling the kitchen with the sweet spice odors of fruit cake. Our home was in chaos and our preparations for the holiday consisted of marking prices on boxes of thumbtacks, figuring out the mark-up on pencil sharpeners, and the like. Several times the little boys said wistfully, "Christmas is coming"—a fact they would never have discovered if they had stayed at home.

273

Finally little Johnny whispered, "Mama, aren't you even going to take us to see Santa Claus?"

"How can I drive all the way into Seattle, with all the work I have to do?" At that my conscience let out a fearful holler. Hadn't we been into Seattle three times that week to get supplies for the stationery store? I hadn't baked a cooky for the boys but I had been very efficient about ordering several square yards of sheet cake for the Open House. I hadn't bought a single Christmas present, but we had spent $1,200 on stationery and office supplies and $600 on portable typewriters. And when little John had asked if I couldn't give him a box of color crayons, what had I answered but "Heavens, no! That's *for sale!*"

"Johnny, darling," I said, gentle now because I was ashamed of myself, "You'll see Santa Claus. . . ."

Heaven should have made it hard for me to keep my promise, but Heaven let me off easy. Santa came to the Snoqualmie Valley. In fact he appeared in North Bend, Snoqualmie, Meadowbrook and Snoqualmie Falls. Sometimes he was short, sometimes tall. His weight varied, too, and even Johnny noted that he changed both his suit and his voice from week to week. There was the day Santa sounded like Jim North, the high-school football coach, and another day when he sounded like Ed Opstad, the superintendent of schools, but no matter, Johnny saw Santa four times and it was going to be Christmas, after all.

The week before the Open House was hardly the time to test the camel's back with one more straw. That was the moment one of our printers chose to announce that he was leaving as soon as the Christmas edition was out. The day before the Open House we heard by way of the weekly publishers' grapevine that our other printer had been dickering to buy a newspaper of his own. He would be leaving, too; he had just forgotten to mention it.

That left Jim, a nearly helpless cripple, and Bob, an apprentice who had never seen the inside of a print shop until he started with us two years before. I cried, as I had so often before, "*Now* what will we do?"

Ed shrugged. "Nothing we can do right now, except get ready for the Open House. Now, where did you put that case of stamp-pad ink?" Perhaps it was fortunate that we were too weary that night even to talk about it. By two in the morning, the building was ready for inspection. We went home, waded through sawdust, fell into bed. When we got up the next morning, our future without printers was still a subject we couldn't face. This was the big day, the day of triumph over three years of trouble. We were going to keep the smiles on our faces if we had to hook the ends of them over our ears.

It was a day to remember, tired and worried as we were. Some 350 people came: officers of the big union local, who shook Ed's hand and said, "We want to thank you for building up our town"; executives from the big lumber mill, who said, "You have shown you have faith in the Valley"; a young red-headed mother with five of her seven red-headed children, the eldest seven years old; they sat down politely, ate their cake, and all said "Thank you" before they left. Tycoon or laborer, dowager or schoolgirl, curiosity shone in their faces as they walked through the plant and laid gentle inquiring fingers on the mysteries within it.

There was a dignity to the occasion created not by Ed and me but by the attitude of our guests. A dozen men who had had reason to visit the plant on business during the previous weeks had already seen everything there was to see at the Open House. But they came anyway, for visiting unofficially could not be substituted for paying their respects at the proper and official time. The prize was Neil Jarrett, town councilman and a man who remembers Snoqualmie when all the buildings had false fronts. Neil had been working in his yard all morning. When he went to the post office for his mail he crossed the street to make his first visit.

"I just want to tell you that I can't get to the Open House until about five o'clock," he said, though the Open House was going on all around him. "I've got to go home and change my clothes."

He was back soon in double-breasted business suit, white shirt, necktie and neatly creased hat. He signed the guest book, inspected the entire plant as if he'd never seen it before, chatted with Ed and a dozen others. On the way out, he asked, "How long are you going to be down here?"

"Nine, ten o'clock tonight . . ."

"Good," said Neil, nodding briskly. "I've got to do some errands, and go home for dinner, but I'll be back later. After I change my clothes." And he was back later in appropriate clothes to help us clean up the place.

Every now and then I thought about the two printers leaving, and the congratulations echoing all around us suddenly had a hollow ring. Ed seemed unperturbed. The one time my worries rose to the surface and I threw him a look that said, "How in the world are we going to get the paper out?" he grinned and whispered, "Cheer up, kid. Maybe we're in a bad spot. But think of that goofy printer of ours who's about to go into business for himself."

My biggest worry was about Ed, and what this new crisis in the backshop might do to him. If he worked too hard— but I must be clever about this, I reminded myself, I must not burden him with my worry. And then suddenly it struck me funny. We were both so tired—only frequent doses of scalding black coffee were keeping us going, for nothing wakes you up faster than burning the skin off the roof of your mouth. Yet here I was, all set to worry about whether Ed would notice I was worrying about his worrying. . . . I grinned weakly. "We've lasted three years and three months. Twenty-one months to go to reach that magic five-year mark. Think we'll make it?"

"Sure," Ed replied, with the greatest confidence in the world. "You wait and see, something good always happens when you need it most."

Ed had been no seer concerning the election but this prediction of his checked in right on time. A man had just handed me a dollar bill in payment for fifty cents' worth of air-mail envelopes when the station agent at the Snoqualmie depot, a man who doubles as Western Union operator, walked in and handed me a telegram. It was from my literary agent in New York, and said:

RANDOM HOUSE HAS BOUGHT YOUR NOVEL CONTRACT COMING AIRMAIL CONGRATULATIONS—YOU'RE ON YOUR WAY LOVE—BARBIE.

I had the telegram in one hand, the customer's dollar bill in the other, and for what seemed like hours I looked senselessly from one to the other. Fifty cents out of a dollar—it might as well have been a problem in advanced calculus. Luckily Gloria, our bookkeeper, was nearby. "Would you mind figuring out the change?" I asked in a hollow voice. "Here's the money he gave me . . ." and I handed Gloria the telegram.

"Other hand," Gloria said gently.

It was a good Open House, after all.

ii

Christmas Day came on Thursday that year, so we had to get the paper out by Wednesday afternoon. That allowed three workdays between the furor of Open House and the pandemonium of getting out one of the biggest issues of the year. By five o'clock the papers were distributed, everyone had gone home, and the only visible signs of the struggle were the circles under our eyes. I sighed, "We made it. . . ."

A puzzled look came across Ed's face. "Good heavens, it's Christmas Eve. Have you done your Christmas shopping?"

"Christmas shopping?" I repeated, stricken.

"The stores stay open until eight," Ed said. "You take one car, I'll take the other, we'll meet at home. Here, I'll call the kids and tell them we'll be a little late."

"I'll get a baby sitter. . . ."

Ed shook his head. "Don't need to. They've got two already. The electrician and the plumber are there."

No questions about "buying locally" that year, because Ed and I did all our shopping in less time than it takes to drive into Seattle and back. Thanks to Paul Pieper, chief of the U.S. forest rangers in this area, we even had a Christmas tree.

Paul was in the drug store making a last-minute purchase of a box of candy when I coursed by, dragging the salesgirl by the arm and issuing rapid bulletins, "I'll take that. Wrap up one of those. Give me two of that. . . ."

"Charlotte, what in the world are you doing?" Paul asked. "You should be home with the kids, singing carols around the Christmas tree."

"The kids are at home with the plumber and the electrician. As for the tree. . . ." I gulped. "The tree. Oh, Paul!"

Paul helped me into my car, and I followed him to his house. He found a perfect Christmas tree, went into the basement and built a good sturdy stand for it, and loaded it all into the back of the car. "Merry Christmas, Charlotte," he said, "And if you can't find your lights, give me a call."

It was eight when Ed and I arrived for Christmas Eve at home. One baby sitter was connecting the furnace with the new heating system and the other was putting electric outlets into the new living room. The little boys sang out, "We hid the presents we've got for you. Don't you try and find them." We agreed solemnly, though it had been months since we could find anything smaller than a baby grand. We surveyed the holiday scene. Rugs in rolls, furniture in piles, and rolls, floors, windowsills coated with a thick layer of sticky white cement dust. We fed the boys, put them to bed, and then Ed and I got out the broom and the mop and the vacuum cleaner. The plumber finished at nine, the electrician by ten, and by one o'clock Christmas morning Ed and I had cleaned the house and moved furniture into the new living room. At that point Ed began to decorate the Christmas tree and I wrapped the presents.

We had about three hours sleep before the boys were at the door calling, "Can we begin now?" When viewed in the unkind light of day the tree seemed to be decorated on one side only and not very high up even there, and it was obvious the Christmas packages had been wrapped by someone who couldn't tie her own shoes. But the boys were ecstatic, and in our own weary way, so were we. We lay back in easy chairs, and first we looked through the huge windows at the mountain, and next we watched the fire blazing in the big stone fireplace. We owed about $18,000, and we were fresh out of printers, but we'd reached an important goal: Our building program was complete. Even Ed said so.

We began the New Year with a beautiful new shop, a beautiful new home, and no problems which could not have been solved by a couple of competent printers who wanted to take their pay out in grateful smiles. We didn't need two men, Ed decided. If he worked in the backshop with Jim the Linotype operator and Bob the apprentice printer, we could get by nicely with one good man. After several weeks of looking for One Good Man, I began thinking of him in capital letters. But he didn't show up. There weren't even any tramp printers, who apparently don't circulate quite as freely during cold weather. We took consolation where we could find it: We were broke again, and couldn't have paid One Good Man if we found him. So Jim set the type, Bob and Ed put it into the pages, Ed ran the press.

They got the paper out on time, too, and did a nice amount of commercial printing every week as well. In fact Ed developed a superior attitude, frequently echoing Pa Kennedy, by asking me, "And what can *you* do? Write? Ha!" Only the advance on my novel, and payment from a magazine article which came in that January, kept the love-light in his eyes.

Happy as the situation seemed, I was uneasy because I knew it couldn't last. During the winter months business is slack. But could the trio of Bob, Jim and Ed keep up as volume increased in the spring? I was convinced, too, that it wasn't "good business" for the owner to drop from sight as Ed had been forced to do. The old-time printer-publisher couldn't leave his shop and the customers had to come to him. But ours was no longer an old-time operation and local businessmen were already asking me, "Where's Ed? Why doesn't he come around any more?"

I was uneasy for another reason. Jim's work at the all-important Linotype was not improving, it was getting worse. Some time before he had explained that he needed glasses. We insisted he get some, but his work afterward was worse than ever. He had more and more head colds, always contracted over week ends and holidays. Giving him more time off was no solution, either; the longer he stayed home to rest, the less he was able to do when he came back to work. And Jim held the whole shop in his hand, for he was the only one who knew how to run the Linotype. If anything happened to Jim . . .

If I noticed these things, surely Ed had, too, and yet he said nothing to me. I was worried about Jim, but even more worried about increasing tension for Ed, so I kept silent, too.

One evening Ed brought home a manual of instructions for the Linotype, and a big chart of the Linotype keyboard. He spread them out on the dining-room table and began studying them. "I think I'll try to learn a little bit about the machine," he said, a little too casually to suit me. "Just in case . . ."

The situation must be far worse than I had believed, for Ed had often remarked that he would sell out if the only

way to keep the business was to chain himself to the Linotype. "Something happen?"

Ed nodded. "Guess so. You know when we were gone last
Thursday and Friday for the publishers' convention? Jim
was drunk the whole time. It wasn't until Saturday that Bob
got him sober enough to come in and set some type. Bob
didn't like to tell. I found out from someone outside the
shop."

"I had been noticing . . ."

"I was afraid you might. I hoped you wouldn't, so you
wouldn't worry."

This startled me. Who were we trying to protect from
heart attacks and shingles, anyway?

"I just can't fire a guy like that," Ed continued. "A cripple, with a wife who can scarcely see."

"Then what are you going to do?"

Ed grinned. "Pray constantly," he said, "and shave once
a day."

iii

Hiram was nine years old that January. One evening
shortly before his birthday he was bubbling over with an
incident that day at school. His teacher had been locked in
her classroom, and Hi and one or two other muscle men of
the third grade had been called upon to get her out.

"Couldn't we put something about it in the paper?" Hi
asked his father. "My teacher would sure be surprised."

Ed delivered a lecture to the effect that no one, not
even the owner's son, could use the *Record* as a tool for a
practical joke, and that we must never think of a newspaper
as a plaything, but a responsibility which we all four shared,
and that anyone who wrote for the paper . . . He stopped
abruptly, or almost as abruptly as we had stopped listening,
and an idea came to him which proved to be pure inspira-

281

tion. "Hi, I wonder . . ." He studied the little boy's solemn face and big brown eyes. "Would you like to write for the paper if you had to do it every single week?"

The brown eyes widened. "Gee," Hi exclaimed softly, "do you mean I could?"

"You'd have to think up your own subject. You'd have to sit down with Mama or me, and dictate the things you want to say and we'd write them down. You couldn't be silly, you couldn't skip a week just because you didn't feel like writing . . ."

Hi nodded eagerly as every qualification was listed.

Ed grinned. "All right," he said, "let's sit down and have a family discussion."

So the four of us took places at the kitchen table. We decided on a title. Because of the column of birth announcements called The Tri-Corner, it was unanimously decided to name Hi's column The Hi-Corner and place it on the opposite side of page one. Monday night would be dictating night, we further agreed. As for subject matter, that would be up to Hi. It might be some special event at school, or his comments on events outside of school, or simply his opinions on some subject. Johnny would be his leg-man, keeping his ear to the ground for newsworthy items.

Ed wound up the discussion by outlining the fundamentals of journalism, as they affected a nine-year-old: Be brief (he explained at length); include as many names as possible; choose subjects of interest to the greatest number of readers; and remember, space in the paper is precious, so use it well or we'll have to turn it over to someone else.

"How about me?" little Johnny piped up.

There was a wistful note in his voice. "Do you want me to write for the paper, too?"

"Would you like to?"

Johnny shook his head. "Not until I'm old, like in the third or fourth," he said solemnly.

282

Hiram said quickly, "John, someday you'll write a column, too."

"But what will we call it, Hi?" Johnny asked.

Looking down on his little brother, Hi said, "How about the Low Corner?"

Johnny nodded. But his blue eyes were round and sad. "It just seems," he said softly, "like I don't do enough work for the paper."

"Johnny darling, you sort out leads and slugs, and you sweep out from under the Linotype, and you stamp the dates onto the cuts. . . ."

He brightened. "Does that count as much as writing?"

I threw Ed a pointed look and then turned back to Johnny. "My dear fellow," I said, trying hard to match the little boy's solemnity, "you are a printer, like your father. He's been needing One Good Man. Hi and I are only writers, not half as important as you."

"Really, Mama?" Now he was plain delighted. He threw himself into his father's arms, and the printers left the room while the writers got together for the first Hi-Corner ever composed.

"While walking from lunch at the North Bend grade school last Friday," Hi began, "I saw Kathleen Grina running to Mr. Rachor's room. She pounded on the door to the janitor's office and she looked frightened. When she saw me she asked where Mr. Rachor was and I said it looks like he's out. . . ."

After the columnist and his leg-man brushed their teeth and went to bed, Ed and I confessed to each other that we were worried. "I can hear someone saying— That item about my cousin coming out from Seattle didn't get in the paper this week but the editor found room for his kid's stuff.' "

I nodded. "The fact that it will appear on the front page may cause trouble, too. 'My club news never gets on the front page. But that Hi-Corner is on the front page every week, because the editor's son writes it.' "

After the paper came out that week, we received three phone calls about The Hi-Corner, all expressing undiluted approval.

"Everyone who has talked to me about The Hi-Corner has liked it very much," I said, trying to reassure the author's worried father.

"Sure. But it's what others say that we don't hear that bothers me. After all, no feature, Hi's column or any other, has a place in the paper if the majority of our readers don't want to read it."

The next week Hi wrote about one of our community centers, outlining some of the activities it offered to kids hereabouts. The week after that, he editorialized in favor of the March of Dimes. The following week, The Hi-Corner covered a high-school basketball game. By the end of four weeks Hi had raked in more fan mail that Ed and I had received in four years. His detractors, if there were any, kept silent and always have. The incident that smoothed the last worry line from Ed's brow occurred a few weeks before there was to be an election in the town of Snoqualmie. One of the councilmen telephoned. "I'm a candidate for re-election," he explained, "and I'd like to put my views before the public. Could I be interviewed for an article in the *Record?*"

"Why, sure," Ed replied. "I'll be glad to talk with you and work out something for my editorial."

"Who said I wanted to talk to *you?*" the city father retorted. "I want Hi to interview me for his column. Then I know everyone will read it."

Monday night remained Hi-Corner night, and those of Hi's fans who had asked, "Now tell me, just between us, does Hi really write that stuff himself?" should have witnessed the routine. Hi usually had a subject in mind, but he suffered all the agonies of his literary betters when it came to thinking up the first sentence. He frowned, licked his lips, began to bite his nails, guiltily thrust his hands in his pockets, sighed. There were always several false starts. "Now don't put this down, just let me say it so I can see how it sounds. . . ." At last, he'd decide on the lead, and still frowning nervously, look over my shoulder to make sure I included no additions or corrections of my own. When the column was complete, he read it through carefully, and even if Ed or I had been silly enough to change a word or phrase, we wouldn't have gotten away with it. Not because Hi thought what he had dictated was good, but, as he put it, "We tell everybody that I write the column myself. If you change anything, then it wouldn't be true any more." The truth, of course, is that if we had changed anything it also wouldn't have been good any more.

Occasionally The Hi-Corner has been a short feature article. There was his travelogue, for example, about our trip to the ghost town of Virginia City, Nevada. "As we were coming into it we saw different signs telling the history of it. The history is that a long time ago, in the 1860s and 1870s, gold and silver were discovered there. People got kind of greedy and it started a gold and silver rush, and before they knew what was happening there were thousands of people mining and getting to be millionaires. . . ."

Often the column has supported a civic project, and once Hi launched a project all his own: a comic-book collection for young patients at the local hospital. Most popular of all Hi-Corners have been Hi's editorials. One, which our county library board asked permission to reprint in its own publication, was on the subject of comic books:

My Mom explained to me that some parents believe that comic books are bad for kids. This is my opinion of it:

We don't have any horrible comic books in our house but I have seen some in a store. As far as I am concerned, they are just like any other comic books. Horrible things that move, like television or in movies, bother me a little, but to see them in comic books doesn't bother me in the least. You seem to be in control of it in a book. If you get nervous you can shut it up and put it away.

My Mom asked me if I think comic books help you to read better. My answer is Yes—because if you don't know what the words are you can look at the pictures and find out. Kids sometimes look at the pictures the first time they go through a new comic book, but usually the second time they read it over more carefully. After they've had a comic book for a while they read it over and learn a few words.

The third question my mother asked was if I think that comic books keep you from doing other important things, like reading books and having hobbies and various other things. My opinion of that is: If you want a hobby bad enough or want to do something real bad, the comic books won't come in your mind. Also you usually read comic books in your spare time when you have nothing else to do.

My favorite comic books are 'Classics Illustrated,' 'Hopalong Cassidy,' 'The Lone Ranger,' and 'The Marvel Family.' These are what I'd buy if I had to get them with my own money.

His column at Thanksgiving was a nine-year-old's credo:

I am thankful to live in America because it is a country that you can live in half decent. Most other countries are a lot poorer.

I am thankful to have a mother and father. In Korea kids don't have mothers and fathers very often.

I am thankful to be able to believe in whatever religion you are in. In other countries that isn't possible.

I am thankful to be able to have playmates and other activities, such as Cub Scouts.

286

I am thankful to have a brother. Kids that have brothers and sisters will always have somebody to play with. . . ."

What to write and how to write it—Hi faced that problem every Monday night and by solving it, learned a little each week about good taste and editorial judgment. And, with his little brother's assistance, he developed a news sense, as I discovered when we were going to be away for a few days and I suggested he write two columns in advance.

"If I did that, Mama," Hi explained ever so patiently, "what I wrote would seem like news now. But by the time it got in the paper, some newer news would have happened, and then it wouldn't be right to print this old news instead of it."

A year after Hiram had recovered from polio, the Snoqualmie Valley was again doing its part in the annual March of Dimes. Midway in the campaign Hiram asked, "Are they getting as many dimes as they need?"

"The drive isn't over," I said. "But they couldn't get as many as they need, because there is so much work to be done against polio, and it all costs money."

"Would it be all right if I write about it in my column this week?"

So The Hi-Corner for February 19, 1953, went as follows:

Because the March of Dimes has just been here, it reminded me a little of the people I saw at the Orthopedic Hospital who had polio. It is very important that you give money to the March of Dimes because some kids have very serious cases of polio.

For instance, a boy who had his whole body paralyzed, almost every part of his body except his head; I wasn't quite sure what his name was because I never learned all the names of the kids. In my same room there was a boy who had a paralyzed leg. There was another boy who was only about three years old, who had polio in his throat

*and neck. He couldn't hold his head up except with a
big metal brace. He couldn't talk, either, because of the
polio.*

*One of my best friends, or that is I liked him even if
he hardly knew me, was Guy. He was born with webbed
fingers but his fingers had been cut apart so there were
scars and they were different shapes. Also he was born
with bones only down to the knee in one leg; there was
skin, but no bones, so they had to cut it off at the knee.
But the other leg was a good leg—in fact as good as ten
good legs!*

*I sincerely hope that everybody will send as much as
they can possibly afford, because it still isn't too late.*

A third grader's handwriting may be good, and Hi's was
legible enough, but producing it in quantity is pretty labo-
rious; that was our reason for allowing him to dictate his
columns to us. But one week he did write his article out
himself. A friend in the third grade had had an experience
he thought Hi might like to tell about, so Hi interviewed
him during recess, writing painstakingly on sheets of lined
pencil paper: "This is some news that Paul Antone told
me for my column because I couldn't think of anything
else. . . ." The job done, Hi and Paul left their desks.
When they got back they found a playful fellow student had
snatched the written pages and thrown them away.

Hi raced to the wastebasket. It was empty. His enemy informed him delightedly that the janitor had come in and
dumped the contents into another bigger wastebasket. Hi
demanded to know which bigger wastebasket, and somehow
shook the answer out of him. The one in the hall . . . Hi
was deep in the trashbasket and had found the first two
sheets of the column when a teacher emerged from her
room and pulled him out by the seat of his jeans. His explanation that he was "looking for my column" meant nothing
to her. She sent him packing, and Hi had to stand by while

half of the hardest job he'd ever completed was wheeled out to be burned.

He didn't give up. On the school bus that afternoon, he took out his pad and rewrote the missing part of the column. When he gave it to me that evening he was apologetic. The first two pages were mangled; the boy who threw them away had taken the precaution of crumpling them up first and Hi hadn't been able to smooth them out. "And I'm sorry about my handwriting on those last two pages," he said. "See the way that word looks? Well, that's where the bus stopped real sudden at Roger's house. And that word down there—well, that's where we went over a bump."

Hi was soon experienced enough to go out on assignment. He rode with the sergeant of our state patrol unit up to the Snoqualmie Pass and back. He carried his own pad and pencil, and took all his own notes, which included statistics about snowfall, traffic control, and the types and cost of highway equipment.

That week dictating his column had a new twist. He spread his notes out on the kitchen table, written side up. They covered the entire surface of a table six feet long and three feet wide. Once he had used the material on a sheet of notepaper, he turned it over; when all the sheets were face down, he stopped dictating.

"Is that the end?" I asked wonderingly.

Hi hesitated, checked over the spread of notes, and nodded. "Yup."

"But don't you want to add some last sentence, some comment. . . ."

Hi said patiently, "Look, Mama, why keep on saying something, when there's nothing left to say?"

I nodded mutely, and allowed the author to play with his Tinker Toys unmolested.

Three years earlier, when we had owned the *Record* for only a few months, a round, blond boy named Tommy came into the shop and asked if he could "take news." Former owners had allowed several grade-school youngsters to go from door to door, offering a scratchpad to anyone who would write down an item for the paper.

"We wouldn't want you to go from door to door," Ed said, "but we would like news about the doings at your school. So if you'll be a school reporter, we'll hire you."

Tommy agreed enthusiastically. His first news consisted of a detailed report of the head colds and tonsillectomies in the fifth grade at Snoqualmie Falls. Ditto the second week. Not that he didn't like the job; the first week he brought two fifth-grade boys into the shop and announced that he wanted to show them "the place where I work." But his weekly reports got thinner—maybe he was running out of tonsils—and we finally gave him his severance pay, which came to eighteen cents.

The Hi-Corner had been running several months when Tommy, by then a big boy, stopped Hi on the sidewalk outside the post office. "You the kid writes that stuff for the *Record?*" he demanded.

Hi looked up at this awesome eighth grader, and nodded.

"Huh, *I* used to work for the paper, too. But them guys sure gave me a raw deal, boy. You'll find out," and he mounted his bicycle and rode off, whistling happily.

Hi sought us out immediately. I think it was the first time he had heard criticism of the paper, and he took it hard. "Is what he said true?" he asked Ed. "I mean, did you cheat him, or something?"

Ed told him the history of Tommy's employment. Finding the criticism unjust, Hi's concern turned to irritation. "He had no right to say that, when it wasn't true."

Ed shrugged. "A person who wants to say bad things— about you, or me, or the paper—is going to say them whether they 'have a right to' or whether they're true."

"I'd like to sock him right in the nose!"

Ed grinned. "Spoken like a true country editor. But that wouldn't stop him. Besides, he's kind of big."

Hi went outside again, his shoulders squared to resist the slings and arrows of outrageous fortune, with a quarter from his father for a treat at the soda fountain. Ed and I looked at each other. There was no need to speak our thoughts. Hi had already learned a lot about working on a country newspaper. He had been trained to spot news of general interest, to check his facts, to boost civic projects and his own community. But it would take Tommy, and all the "Tommies" yet to come, to complete his education.

iv

All summer, Ed continued the search for One Good Man. In August a printer named Don Buck telephoned from Seattle. "I saw your ad for a printer today," he said. "I've got my own shop here in town, but I could come out and work an evening shift for you until you find somebody. Just to help you out of a jam."

Don Buck turned out to be the best printer we'd ever had in the shop. His nose had been broken in two places but his disposition didn't have a crack in it. He came from Kalispell, Montana, by way of the lower echelons of the U.S. Army, and he talked like Montana and he walked like Montana, except faster, because he was a demon for work. After eight hours in his own shop, he'd put in eight hours for us. If there were bindery jobs he couldn't finish, he took them home over the week end and did them there.

"All we need now is one good man like Don," was Ed's cry as the days and weeks passed. There were applicants, ranging from mediocre to impossible. Ed interviewed some, gave others a few hours tryout, but six weeks passed and Don was still getting us out of a jam. And we were going into our heaviest production of the year.

"I've got to find someone!" Ed moaned one night in September. "There must be someone. . . ."

Don's forehead wrinkled up with friendly concern. "Well,

I'm sure getting disgusted with the printers you've been trying out. I been around here long enough for you to see my work. Would you consider me for the job?"

Ed did not faint, which proves, as far as I'm concerned, that he never will. He managed to croak, "But how about your shop in town?"

Don shrugged. "I'll sell it. I'd rather work here."

On September 10th the name of Don Buck appeared on the *Record's* masthead. He was better medicine for the weary businessman than a long vacation. For three years I had been pleading with Ed not to worry, but it was an empty plea because it didn't dissolve our debts or diminish the pile of unfinished work that caused Ed's worries in the first place. The banker had said, "Don't worry," and removed one source of pressure. Now Don was saying, "Don't worry about the backshop," and it wasn't idle talk, either, for he was soon at the bottom of that worrisome pile of work and calling for more.

In October, our fourth anniversary as country publishers, Ed was saying, "At last, we've got it whipped. By Thanksgiving, we'll have our debts down to $12,000—er, you *do* get a royalty check this month, don't you? Everything has happened to us that can possibly happen. . . ."

The royalty check came through, but so did something that couldn't possibly happen. In November, our Linotype operator's weekly head colds got so much worse that now he had pneumonia every Saturday and Sunday and had to recuperate every Monday. Finally we sent a doctor to Jim's house to prescribe proper medication and care.

The doctor was discreet when we asked him how Jim was feeling. "Pneumonia?" he said. "Possibly."

By then it was Monday night and we already had reason to wonder how we'd get the paper out. Ed and I went to Jim's house. He was sober by then, but white and shaky. Bessie, poor blind Bessie, was drunk.

Three weeks before our Christmas issue, when there was

more Linotype work in the shop than at any other time all year, Jim and Bessie disappeared. They cashed Jim's pay check Friday afternoon, bought two gallons of red wine in a nearby tavern, and drove away in the car Ed bought for them. We had lost our Linotype operator, and the only person in the world who owed us money.

Monday morning Ed telephoned headquarters of our brotherhood of weekly publishers, the Washington Newspaper Publishers' Association. "Linotype operators are scarce, Ed," the director said. "Why, we haven't had one on our list for five months. I'm sorry, but . . ." He stopped. "Say, hold the wire a minute. Fellow just walked into the office . . ."

A split second later there was another voice on the wire. "You want an operator?"

"Why, yes," said Ed, trying to keep the quiver out of his voice. "You available?"

"Sure. What's the name of your place?"

"Falls Printing, Snoqualmie. You know this area?"

"Huh! I'll get there."

"There are busses from downtown Seattle. Where are you staying?"

"No place. I just got off the Greyhound from Chicago. I'll take a taxi."

"A taxi! Look, it's thirty miles. The busses run from . . ."

"Huh! Busses! Huh! I'll be seeing you."

"Hold on a minute. What's your name?"

"Ray Darrow."

"Mr. Darrow, are you a good Linotype operator?"

"Ha! Am I a good operator! Ha!"

Forty-five minutes later a cab came around the corner on two wheels and made a neat crash-landing against the curb. The back door exploded and a dark, slender middle-aged man jumped out. He had a cigarette in the corner of his mouth, a suitcase in each hand, no coat or hat, and he all but ran through the front door. "Glad to see you," Ed got out before the man had loped past him on a dead run for the Linotype.

"This machine won't be fast enough for me," he said, dropped his suitcases, and sat down.

It wasn't. The first week we had to buy two attachments so that Mergenthaler's wonderful $20,000 machine could keep up with our man from Chicago. He pronounced it "Chicahgo" and he expressed everything—disdain, confidence, interest, and disinterest—with that wordless outburst, "Ha!"

There was never a Linotype operator like Ray. He did work in thirty-five hours which the best man we'd ever had had sweated out in forty-five. This time we were going to begin a New Year without a trouble in the world.

Just for a moment, we wondered. We gave Ray the standard form everyone in the shop had filled out, and he left two lines blank. "Who was your last employer?" and "Next of kin" were questions he ignored.

"Just a formality," Ed apologized, for courtesy is indicated when dealing with a man who is setting type at the rate of three galleys an hour. "But how come you didn't fill these lines in?"

"Huh! I don't want to let anyone know where I am," Ray said bluntly, without even looking up from the keyboard.

Ed didn't ask again. We filed the card as it was. "Why look for trouble?" Ed asked, suspicion deadened by the soothing sound of a Linotype running full speed. "After all, Ray couldn't cause any new problems. Everything's happened to us that could possibly happen. . . . Still, I wonder what his name was before he changed it to Ray Darrow? Clarence?"

I grinned absent-mindedly. I didn't care what Ray Darrow's real name was. I was trying to remember when I'd last heard Ed recite that line about everything that could possibly happen has already happened.

14

Hiram and Johnny were five and four years old when they got their first taste of country journalism by licking 2,000 postage stamps. As junior partners they gradually worked their way into the circulation department (selling subscriptions), the mailing department (wrapping papers and carrying them to the post office), the mechanical department (sorting out leads and slugs), and the editorial department (Hi's weekly column). By the spring of 1954, with four and a half years' experience behind them, our pint-sized journeymen were ready to invade a new field—commercial printing.

Ed had been teaching them the California job case, which in plain language means they were learning to sort out the individual letters of hand-set type and distribute them properly in the drawer. "All these letters," eight-year-old Johnny mused, searching for the *B* bin. "I wish I had some."

"If we did, we could be printers, too," his ten-year-old brother agreed, and thus was born the North Bend Printers, Ink.

Ed turned over to our competitors an old hand press, a proof press, and as fine a collection of damaged and obsolete type as ever graced a country print shop. The boys also received two printers' aprons, a tin of printer's ink and free access to the shelf of scrap paper.

"All we need is to get a job," they sighed. "But how can we do that, with *you* (accusingly) taking all the business?"

"You've got to advertise."

The first week of April, the North Bend Printers, Ink, placed their first ad in the *Record*. Ed drew it up for them, but he insisted they correct it. The ad, read and approved by both boys, ran as follows:

WE'RE ADVERTISING
To People Who Want
Cheep Printing

My brother John and i got
a printing Press free and we
can chisel some cards and paper
from the falls printing Company and
that way we can print cheeper.
——If you Want printing dOne cheep we're
the kids that can do it. No payroll, free materials,
no overhead, nO taxes.

WE GOT A RACKET
Hi Groshell
North Bend Printers, Ink.   Call 88-1503

Once they had worried, "Dad, did we get enough advertising in the paper this week so we can pay the workers?" Now that they were the advertisers, their concern shifted abruptly. Ed told them they had to pay for their ad; they accepted this without argument but also without any noticeable enthusiasm.

"How much?" Hi asked, eyes narrowed.

Ed calculated quickly. "Three columns wide, twelve inches deep, that's thirty-six column inches. Multiply that by seventy-seven cents an inch . . ."

The little boys responded like advertisers of all time. "I'm going to go get a ruler and measure it myself," said our canny eight-year-old, and his older brother said, "Let's make that ad a little smaller."

They received their first job the night the ad appeared. A *Record* reader, incensed by a recent series of dog poisonings, ordered a hundred handbills. Pencil in one hand, telephone receiver in the other, Hi wrote down instructions. "Picture of dog," his note said, "and underneath stuff against poisoning."

"I figured on spending one dollar," the woman said. "And I would like you boys to distribute them for me, too."

Instinct inherited from some relative other than his father took possession of our small son. "We'd have to charge more than that," Hi said solemnly, "because there is the labor of us two partners and there is materials, too. We will do it for $1.50."

This was the bid that got the job. It took the boys two hours to set the type. Then they ran the press, but since smashed fingers are one emblem of the trade we felt they were too young to acquire, we did not connect the motor. One boy turned the big wheel in place of the motor, the other slid the sheet of paper in and out of the press, and then they changed places. Presswork added two hours to their labor costs. They were grinning through a veritable blackface of printer's ink by the time they were through.

The founding of North Bend Printers, Ink., did not mean that our star columnist stopped writing. Every week Hi dictated his comments on the marble tournament, school lunches, or the opening of the baseball season, and The Hi-Corner continued as always. Due to an error of calculation by his father, Hi eventually gave up dictation and began typing his column himself.

Ed accepted an ancient portable typewriter as a trade-in on a new machine. It was truly a museum piece; Ed allowed twelve dollars for it on the new typewriter and it took twenty dollars' worth of repairs to put it in something like working order. Discouraged, he brought it home to Hi.

"I'll give you a twenty-five-dollar savings bond if you type your next four columns," he offered.

Hi had never been paid for The Hi-Corner. "Sure, Dad, sure!" he agreed, and little John breathed, "Gosh, how rich can you get?"

Hi spent an hour and a half to two hours typing each column, but he earned his defense bond. It was his first real pay check. "Just bring the bond home and let me look at it," he asked, "before you lock it up in the bank."

Hard on the heels of this big moment came recognition of another kind. The Washington State Press Club notified us that The Hi-Corner had been awarded a prize in the annual newspaper contest and that the writer should be present at the Awards Banquet in Seattle to receive it. It was the first time since the club began sponsoring such contests many years ago that a child had taken an award. It was probably the first time, also, that a child attended the Awards Banquet.

Both Hi and his partner John went with us, though neither of them knew Hi was to receive an award. They sat up stiffly at the banquet table, both tense with the responsibility of doing the right thing in this roomful of 200 confident grownups. Their clothing worried them. I had stripped them of blue jeans and sweatshirts and encased them in gabardine slacks and tweed sports jackets, the first they had ever owned, and they looked as comfortable as prize fighters who have suddenly discovered they are wearing orchid ballet costumes.

When food was served, Hi whispered, "Mama, shouldn't I take off my jacket?"

"No, leave it on, Hi."

"But Mama, are all these men going to eat supper with their coats on?"

Later, it was the dessert that worried him. For some reason I have never served cheese with apple pie. When the waitress placed this dish in front of him, Hi's face was suffused with embarrassment.

"Mama," he whispered, "there is a piece of cheese on my pie!"

"That's all right," I assured him. "Lots of people like it that way."

Hi was clearly worried about this error on the part of the Press Club. He threw hasty glances to left and right, then quickly slid the cheese off the pie, gulped it down and, obviously relieved, went about eating the pie.

No need describing the moment when the chairman of the awards committee arose and in the presence of the best newspapermen in the state read a section of one of Hi's columns and presented the award. Hi stood up, walked to the head table, shook hands, and with a look of wonder on his face I had never seen the equal of, returned to his chair. There was more of it—a lot of applause, for one thing—but I was finding it a little blurry out.

Ed said, "Remember the subscriber who criticized us for printing a news story about the award we got a few years ago?"

I nodded.

"Think we ought to run a story about Hi's award?"

"Yes!"

"That subscriber might not like it if we do. . . ."

"If you don't," I said, nearly choking as the words squeezed past the lump in my throat, "if you don't, you better look for someone else to make your paragraph marks for you."

Ed grinned. "We were so worried about what kind of a job Hi would do, and what people would think of it. Well"—he glanced around the crowded banquet room— "now we know." He reached for my hand, and squeezed it hard. "Our small partners are growing up, Mother, they're growing up."

ii

We had never held a subscription drive, except for Hiram's campaign to earn money for camp. But in the spring of our fifth year North Bend's Cub Scout committee came to me and asked, "Have you any idea how our pack could earn some money?"

There would be no more "Tommies," and other grade-school reporters, we had agreed on that. But remembering Hi's success as a door-to-door salesman, I suggested that the Cubs sell subscriptions to the *Record*. In no time the boys were engaged in one of the funniest and most successful drives a weekly newspaper ever launched.

I made our offer clear. We would pay one dollar for every new subscription and ten cents for every written news item the Cubs turned in. This money would be paid directly to the Pack Committee. There would be cash prizes, besides, for the boys themselves. The den mothers did the bookkeeping, and they understood the terms. Sometimes the Cubs didn't.

There was the little Bobcat in the brand-new blue-and-gold uniform who couldn't pronounce the word "subscription." He confided to his den mother, "But Mrs. Stapp, how can I sell them if I can't say them?" There was the energetic team made up of one third grader and one second grader, who always had a quick rebuttal for the housewife who wouldn't buy: "If you won't subscribe, then give us some cookies."

Perhaps it was because they worked in "buddy pairs," but the Cubs proved to be fearless salesmen. Weather and snarling dogs didn't stop them, nor the fact that the money they were earning was not for their own pockets but for some not easily visualized abstraction known as The Good of the Pack. Two separate sets of buddies tried to sell subscriptions to our reporter in the North Bend *Record* office. But the real highjackers were the four Cubs who misunderstood instructions about taking news items for which I had promised to pay ten cents an item.

They came back to their den mother with two or three dollars she could not account for. "This money is extra," she said. "Where did you get it?"

"That's for the news people gave us," the Cubs explained. For every news item, they had charged ten cents! They were a little puzzled, though, by the man who said he didn't have anything for the paper. "Since I can't give you any news, I suppose I have to pay double," he said, and handed the boys twenty cents.

"Was that all right?" a conscientious Cub asked the den mother, "or did we charge him too much?"

After a couple of weeks the North Bend dens had covered their own territory with terrible thoroughness. But their zeal was unabated. "All right if we turn the boys loose in Snoqualmie and Snoqualmie Falls?" the den mothers asked, and we consented. Thus still more dollars were added to the Pack's treasury, and at least one little boy got a lesson in geography.

Snoqualmie Falls is about four miles from North Bend. Driving her den of salesmen back from an afternoon of canvassing, a den mother discovered one of the boys had been selling subscriptions for $3.50 a year. "But that's the price for outside the county!" she exclaimed. "Why did you do that?"

The youngster was stunned. "Gosh," he said, "is Snoqualmie Falls in *our* county?"

Since he was a veteran campaigner, Hiram spent many a recess at the North Bend grade school giving these rookies the benefit of his experience. He and John worked for the Cubs, too. "You two are not going to get any prizes," Ed told them, "no matter how many subscriptions you sell. And your dollar commissions will go into the Cub treasury just like all the rest. But I'll make this offer. Next Saturday afternoon, the Rainiers play Portland at Sicks Stadium in Seattle. You've never been to a baseball game. I'll drive you to Snoqualmie Saturday morning when I go to the shop, and if you two can sell three new subscriptions by noon, I'll take you to the game."

Snoqualmie is the town in which twenty extra newspapers enabled the postmaster to fill every box in the post office. It was also a town which the North Bend Cubs had just swept through. Three sales in three hours!

The boys conferred in hasty whispers, then disappeared. Noon came, and they had not returned. Twelve-thirty, and Ed and I got into the car and began to patrol the streets. At last we saw them. They were working the block with the thoroughness of the man who reads the meters and the speed of the man who is convinced every dog will bite him. They progressed leap-frog fashion, John canvassing one house, Hi the one next door. John had the pad and pencil for news items, Hi carried the book of subscription receipts. When one or the other needed what his brother had, he shouted across to the next house and there was a frenzied exchange.

At last they noticed us, and ran for the car.

"We made it, we made it!" Johnny gasped, falling into the back seat. Sweat stood out on their foreheads and upper lips; their faces were a glowing red.

"Here, Dad, three new subscriptions," Hi said. "We just got the third one, in that yellow house there.

"I know we are a little late," he added matter-of-factly. "But it wasn't easy to get three subscriptions, and we decided we wouldn't come back until we did."

John nodded vigorously. It took no brains to see they meant it.

iii

That summer even I was beginning to say that everything had happened to us that could happen, and that the worst could never happen again. We had had every help problem, weathered it, and come through the storm with a staff so fine other country publishers envied us. We had seen unbreakable equipment break and foolproof machinery collapse into torpor, but by repairing and replacing we had whipped that problem, too. We still owed almost $10,000. But *Gold Mountain* was selling like hotcakes (Ed commented he wished it would sell like books), the printing business was good, and we were no longer haunted by the question, Can we make the mortgage payments this month?

Ed had forgotten to have his annual case of shingles and the day he had been carried out of the shop and to the hospital was becoming an unhappy memory, but only a memory of the past and not a fear for the future. As for the children—well, when polio season came along, sore throats and headaches and stiff necks did not throw me into the panic other mothers felt, for even if my boys were "coming down with something" I knew one terrible disease it couldn't be. So I really believed our troubles were behind us as we approached the end of our first five years of business for ourselves. In October, the magic line would be crossed, and as our friend had prophesied, "After that, they'll have to shoot you to get rid of you."

The people of our Valley will remember the summer of

1954 for two reasons. It was so cold, rainy and sunless that at least one person quipped, "Nice warm winter we're having this summer." And there was a strike.

Not a strike like the one that had panicked us two years before, when only 150 men were involved. This was the lumber strike that paralyzed the entire Pacific Northwest from June 21 until fall. In our Valley it idled 845 men. "Never buy a newspaper in a one-industry area," Ed had said sagely before we bought the *Record,* and then we saw Snoqualmie Valley and our one bit of sound good sense had deserted us utterly.

The moment we came to the Valley, we began hearing about the strike of 1935. It had lasted from May well into autumn. We heard about the brothers who owned two hardware stores but panned for gold in the Snoqualmie River to earn a living. About the grocer who extended thousands of dollars' worth of credit and then saw many of his creditors move away. Those first years in the Valley we were leaping from one crisis to the next and were not inclined to ponder whether a calamity that had fallen some fifteen years before might fall again. But we always knew that a strike at the big mill in Snoqualmie Falls was disaster for the local businessman. Not only for the grocer and the owner of the hardware store, but for us.

Monday morning, June 21st, the mill whistle did not blow. The silence, the felt but unheard echo of a sound that wasn't there, was an eloquent retort to my feeling that we'd already had every kind of trouble a couple with a small business can have. A strike—where could we find revenue to keep the newspaper going during a strike? What margin of strength had Ed built up? Or would it all come back, the desperation over money, the daily, almost hourly struggle at the shop, and finally, another telephone call from the family doctor, another race to the hospital while I tried to "keep my head"?

That afternoon Ed called our employees together. "You

people know what it's like during a lumber strike," he said, "and you know what happens to a small business like ours. So you're probably wondering what's ahead. I want to tell you. Right now we've got the best staff in the world, and the best little old newspaper in the world, and this strike isn't going to break up either one of them. I may have to go out and sell printing like I never sold it before, but we're going to put out a paper every week no matter how long the strike lasts and you're going to have jobs at no cut in hours or wages."

There was relief on many faces, but it didn't touch the relief that flooded through me. Ed was less nervous than he is about selecting a necktie. I had no reason to worry. We had weathered every crisis. We could weather just one more. I hadn't counted on the one after that.

Our Linotype operator, the ace Ray Darrow, left town. He didn't bother to notify his landlord, to whom he owed a week's rent. He didn't confide his plans to the automobile dealer, to whom he had paid all but $1,400 for the car he went away in. He didn't tell us, of course, possibly to avoid discussing the $115 typewriter he was buying from us "on time." The auto dealer had a collection problem. We had an idle Linotype, a stack of work the fastest operator couldn't finish in three days and the old question—how are we going to get the paper out?

I worked at home that Monday, and it wasn't until supper time that I telephoned the shop and the receptionist, in fearful whispers, told me what had happened. I sat down at the kitchen table and put my head in my hands. Surely, this was too much. I remembered the advice an old man had given Ed when he was a feisty teen-ager in Billings, Montana. "If you're in a fight, and the other guy knocks you down, you can figure it was because you weren't ready for him. Get up quick, and if he knocks you down again you can figure it was a lucky punch. So you get up once more. But if he knocks you down a third time, stay down, because if you don't you're going to get your fool block knocked off, and what's the sense to that?"

And what was the sense to this, if running your own business meant there was no limit to the number of times you could be knocked down? I could visualize Ed, pacing the floor, calling long distance, leafing nervously through aged and yellowing letters of application from printers, half of whom had probably gone to their reward. I remembered Ed's white face and hoarse unhappy voice the day in the hospital, when all he said, in a conversation that might well have been our last, was, "Let me know the minute the paper is out. . . ." How long to solve this problem, how long to get to his feet this time? Or was this the time that was one too many, the Sunday punch, the blow that was one more than a man can take?

I called Hi and John into the kitchen. "Boys, you have never cooked your own supper," I said, "but Hi, you're ten years old and, Johnny, you're almost nine. Do you think you could do it tonight?"

"Mama, honest, would you let us?" The eyes were bright and the voices confident.

"Here's the meat," I said, "and here's the potatoes. You'll find lettuce and tomatoes in the refrigerator so you can make a salad. John, take a box of pudding off the shelf and mix a dessert. I'm going down to the shop."

"Oh, boy, can we baby-sit ourselves, too?"

I nodded. "Be sure to turn off the stove when you're through cooking. And lock the door when you go to bed. . . ." I hurried into that blessed second car and drove to the shop.

By then I was convinced I'd find Ed in such a state of nerves that the only question would be whether to call the alienist or the family doctor. But when I entered the print shop the first sound that greeted me was not my darling's demented cries but the cheery clatter of a Linotype *in use*. Scarcely breathing, I approached the wonderful sound.

The man at the Linotype was Ed. Slowly his fingers moved on the keys, there was the click as the mats were lifted, the rapid tat tat tat as they dropped, the faint metallic clunk as the line of type dropped neatly into place. Ed's face was illuminated by the light above the keyboard, and if ever I saw a man who is neither nervous nor frightened, it was he.

"Hi, there!" he called to me. "I've been setting type all day. Look, I finished three galleys." Three galleys—our last operator's output in an hour and a half, but then, had I ever seen that last operator with such a wide and happy grin?

"I just heard," I blurted out. "What are we going to do?"

Ed shrugged. "Something will turn up. . . ."

"But the paper! Today's Monday. Now that we're printing on Wednesday, that gives us only two days."

"This week, we'll print on Thursday," Ed said cheerfully.

"But you'll be sitting in front of this machine twenty-four hours a day. You can't . . . I mean, you shouldn't . . ."

"I'm hungry," he said, unconscious of the voice of doom sounding off at his elbow. "Let's go home and have supper."

It was only six o'clock. We *never* had supper at six o'clock when we were having a Crisis.

"Supper, yes, supper," I repeated doltishly.

Ed turned off the machine, rose briskly, rubbed his hands together. "What are we having?"

"I don't know," I said weakly. "We'll have to ask the children. . . ."

We drove home together, and Ed was singing all the way.

iv

This is a success story, though it has to be a story without an ending because living happily ever after goes on and on. The strike ended. We found another Linotype operator. This afternoon the banker across the street smiled at us although at nine o'clock this morning we were in his establishment asking for an extension on a loan. We're in good health physically, and mentally have no marks or features to distinguish us from the majority. As proof that we are now perfectly adjusted to what is called "owning a nice little business all your own," we are reconciled to the fact that we still are not on our own payroll.

We're in debt, yes, and undoubtedly will be for some time to come. Borrowing money is a sound business practice if the business you sink it into is thus improved so that it can share the burden of paying the money back. We used to daydream about the unexpected inheritance arriving in time to cover the payroll, the oil well bubbling up in the back yard just as we were trying to figure out how to pay the bills. But we no longer need a miracle to make things come out all right. All we need is what we've got—a fair and even chance.

We've learned that success does not come to the man who has no problems; if nothing ever goes wrong, the chances are nothing ever goes at all, for action brings problems as surely as planting potatoes brings bugs. The man of spirit goes after the bugs, he doesn't quit planting potatoes.

One day last month we passed a landmark: Our two small partners received their social security cards. There was some delay, because first we had to secure the permission of the juvenile court, and then the boys' father couldn't remember their birthdays or their middle names and twice we had to revise their applications. But at last the cards arrived. I picked the boys up after school and drove them to the shop so that they could open the envelopes personally. We shook hands all around, and there was a good deal of kissing and congratulating, too. It was a wonderful moment, but suddenly Ed's face took on a wondering look.

"What is it?" I demanded.

"Don't you know what date it is today?"

I looked at the calendar. "October first, but there's nothing special about . . ." I stopped. October first. On that date, five years before, we had left Big Business and corporations and monthly salaries and security and made the awful plunge. "Our fifth anniversary, and we didn't even think of it!"

The small businessman and his wife fell into each others' arms, and that's where we stayed for quite some time, while a ten-year-old columnist and a nine-year-old printer kept tugging at us and asking, "Mama, Daddy, why did you yell like that, 'We made it!'?"

ABOUT THE AUTHOR

CHARLOTTE PAUL's formative years were spent in the Pacific Northwest where she was born in Seattle in 1916. After a year of musical studies in Germany and a tour throughout Europe, she returned to this country and entered Wellesley. During college she won first prize in the *Atlantic Monthly* collegiate short-story contest of 1937. She made two further trips to Europe and after graduation from Wellesley held a variety of jobs. These included office work and ballroom-dancing lessons. For two years she wrote news articles, first as assistant foreign news editor for the *Chicago Daily Times*, later as a roving correspondent for this paper in the Caribbean. Back in the United States she began a long and successful career of free-lance writing. She has sold her articles and stories to such magazines as *Esquire, Coronet, Good Housekeeping, McCall's* and many others. Her first novel, *Hear My Heart Speak,* was published in 1950, and her most recent book was *Gold Mountain,* published by Random House in 1953 and a selection of Peoples Book Club.

Now married and living in Snoqualmie, Washington, Charlotte Paul with her husband owns a weekly newspaper and commercial-printing plant. Their home stands in a meadow at the foot of a 4,100-foot mountain. At the rear of this property is a little cedar house with a big window, where the author does her writing. Intensely devoted to her valley region and its projects, she finds time to play golf, do some song-writing for a local show and cultivate her garden.

photo: Burt Glinn

The Groshell family—Ed, Johnny, Charlotte, the author, and Hi.
*"We set them up in business at the old roll-top desk. Each little
boy received one thousand envelopes, one thousand three-cent*